Building Bridges for Educational Reform

NEW APPROACHES

Building Bridges for Educational Reform

TO TEACHER EDUCATION

Edited by | Joseph L. DeVitis

Peter A. Sola

IOWA STATE UNIVERSITY PRESS / AMES

Joseph L. DeVitis is associate professor of education and human development, State University of New York at Binghamton.

Peter A. Sola is associate professor of education, Howard University.

© 1989 Iowa State University Press, Ames, Iowa 50010

Manufactured in the United States of America

First edition, 1989

Library of Congress Cataloging-in-Publication Data

Building bridges for educational reform : new approaches to teacher education / edited by Joseph L.
  DeVitis, Peter A. Sola. — 1st ed.
      p. cm.
    Includes index.
    ISBN 0–8138–0004–8
    1. Teachers — Training of — United States.   I. DeVitis, Joseph L.   II. Sola, Peter Andre,
1940–   .
LB1715.B83   1989
370′.7′1 — dc19   88–37673
                                                                                    CIP

DEDICATION

To those teachers in America
who never know where
their influence stops

Contents

3. Teacher Education:
A Tradition of Excellence and Diversity

Foreword

THERE IS A GREAT CLAMOR TODAY for reforming teacher education. The proposals from a seemingly inexhaustible number of "blue-ribbon" committees — national, regional, state, campus — seem in agreement that the reform should be rapid, should be massive, should stress both increased subject-matter expertise and professional skill in teaching, should eventuate in teacher-educational practices that are fully acceptable and accountable to all educational constituencies, and should bring teacher certification practices under some sort of centralized administrative control. The various proposals tend to be those for big, quick fixes.

To anyone familiar with a fair sampling of such proposals, the volume at hand will come as a welcome, refreshing contrast. In the introductory chapter the editors sketch for us a very coherent perspective on teacher education in America, show considerable reason for seeing teacher education as inherently innovative and sensitive to its own conditions for change, and wisely warn teacher educators and teachers to beware loss of control over their workplaces — workplaces in which they themselves have both greatest expertise and professional commitment.

I think that there is very sage counsel in all of this. Teacher education in America is too vast and complex an enterprise for us to think that one or a few big, quick fixes will suffice. Consider, for example, that there are approximately thirteen hundred institutions of higher education engaged in teacher education. These are variously private or public, free-standing teacher-education institutions or joined with art and sciences institutions, are accredited (about half) or nonaccredited by a national professional association, are closely or very loosely supervised by a state education agency. These institutions might be turning out only beginning teachers, or they might be engaged as well in graduate research in education — and, in either case, they might or might not also be engaged in in-service education. The professional staffs of these institutions and the populations from which they recruit teacher candidates vary greatly from state to state and region to region.

But, suppose we are lucky and do find one or a few valuable big, quick

fixes. The complexity that exists still indicates that teacher-education programs need sensitivity to local conditions and opportunities. Here again,
the examples presented in this volume will be valuable, for several of them
show how innovation can proceed with regard to adding richness to detail
rather than through modifying total programs.

Again, I think this is a valuable contribution to professional teacher
education, and I am sure that the reader will come to join me in wishing
that the editors will entertain the idea of periodically bringing forth vol-
umes in the future, which will add to our set of helpful examples for
innovation in teacher education.

JOE R. BURNETT

University of Illinois at Urbana-Champaign

Preface and Acknowledgments

THIS BOOK IS WRITTEN for those who wish to engage in the continuing conversation and controversy surrounding teacher education in America. It is especially timely for those who seek to renew an academic and professional arena of discourse that has profound consequences for the future of reflective citizenship and democracy. In a period of increasing trends toward pseudocredentialism, uniformity, and nationalization of school policy, this volume will be of particular interest to those teachers and teacher educators who seek to build different—and diverse—bridges for reform in their respective educational institutions. In essence, the editors have attempted to present representative samples of the richness of diversity in some current and evolving teacher-education programs across the United States. We believe that these examples of teacher-education programs should help guide curricular and structural change in schools and departments of education.

The editors gratefully acknowledge the support of colleagues who have encouraged this project and helped guide us in productive directions in the course of our inquiry: Anne E. Campbell of the College of Education, University of Florida; George M. Drew, dean of the School of Education, University of Tennessee at Martin; Earle H. West, associate dean of the School of Education, Howard University; and Faustine C. Jones-Wilson, professor of education, Howard University. Finally, we thank Joe R. Burnett, professor of education, University of Illinois at Urbana-Champaign, for his helpful editing; Joyce Bonaparte, Howard University (retired), who typed many of the draft chapters in this book; Mary Beth Sola for her assistance in organizing the final draft; and Laura E. Oldham for her art work in preparing the charts and graphs.

Both authors have equally contributed to the editing of this book. Their names are listed in alphabetical order.

Introduction

1 | Teacher Education in America: An Overview

CUSTOMARILY TEACHER EDUCATION comes under fire whenever various important interest groups decide that something is drastically wrong with education in general. In the last several years the American public has been inundated by a plethora of education reform reports, beginning with *A Nation at Risk* (National Commission on Excellence in Education 1983), through the National Commission for Excellence in Teacher Education (1985), to the more recent reports of the Holmes Group, including "Tomorrow's Teachers," a report by education deans (Jacobson 1986) and the Carnegie Commission on Education and the Economy (1986). All these reports represent powerful constituencies at national levels. At the same time a majority of state legislatures, boards, and departments of education have joined the reform movement (usually organized by the governor) trying to mandate increased credentialing and testing of teachers. Inevitably, there are clarion calls for noticeable improvement in education, which then bear directly on those institutions that are charged to prepare teachers.

This collection of essays, written by contributors from selected colleges and universities across the country, represents a cross section of teacher-education programs in terms of mission, goals, size of program, and institutional ethos. Each of these schools appears to be addressing reform issues head-on. These essays are meant to serve a dual purpose: (1) to unearth some of the little-known, hidden richness and diversity in present and future teacher-education programs; and (2) to show that teacher education in America is exercising its responsibility to be proactive and not simply defensive in its commitment to educate teachers of the citizenry in reflective, critical canons of democratic decision making. The ultimate purpose of teacher education is to help persons to grow as human beings and as professionals in training for societal service. Such objectives weigh heavily once one considers the quite unassuming background of teacher education.

3

> Teacher educators have, by and large, humble social-class origins and low status in comparison with their academic colleagues. . . . Worst of all, the knowledge base of education is considered by academicians to be largely exogenous. These personal and occupational differences compound the historical problems of status experienced by normal schools turned colleges of education. (Fuller and Bown 1975, 29)

> The status of education faculty is particularly lowly because for the most part it involves not only reproduction [as opposed to production activities], but the reproduction of the masses and not the elite. (Prakash 1986, n. 45; cf. Schwebel 1985; Lanier and Little 1986)

Whether these characterizations are totally accurate is almost beside the point. The perception is, and perhaps always has been, that teacher educators are appropriately "poor cousins" in their academic communities. This discomforting posture (at least for teacher educators) has been routinely exacerbated by shrill bombast and diatribe, as in the case of James Koerner's *The Miseducation of American Teachers* (1963) and Robert Mitchell's *The Graves of Academe* (1981). A "headline-reading" public, yesterday and today, often misses the more subtle sins of commission and omission in such critiques. For example, Koerner does acknowledge that his brief against teacher education is "filled with judgments, private evaluations, even prejudices," that is, it is built on largely circumstantial evidence and "suasive" argumentation supported by "very few [actual] data" (Koerner 1963, 4). With none too subtle irony and scorn Mitchell admits that his explicit mission is to make the presumably "pedestrian" subject matter of "pygmy educationists" less "boring" by emphasizing its "startling and horrifying attributes" (Mitchell 1981). Yet more distinguished leaders from fields *outside* professional teacher education have been known to jump on the "antieducation" bandwagon. (Arthur Bestor, James B. Conant, and Hyman Rickover stand as perhaps the most well known of these critics.)

Teacher educators meekly ask "Why?" and the response has usually awakened a similar melody in each decade since the 1950s: prospective teachers, the liberal arts faculty note, presumably need (a) more thorough subject-matter preparation and (b) more specific, intensive knowledge of teaching. The former requirement has traditionally been espoused by specialists in the liberal arts and sciences (and increasingly so by education leaders in recent years); the latter requirement is more typically made by teacher educators and researchers who search in diligence for a "science of education."

Nevertheless, some of these petitions take on a curious tone once one ponders analogues on training programs in some other professions. (The larger question as to whether teaching is a full-blown profession or a mere semiprofession only serves to magnify the implicit oddities to follow.) As an example, teacher educators have been far more receptive to general and liberal education than have their brethren in engineering—a seldom mentioned point, which is notably cited by Jencks and Riesman (1969).

> Education professors are probably more eager to expose their students to the liberal arts than are engineering professors. Educationists have never had the same self-confident contempt for the humanities and social sciences that engineers have had. . . . Education professors have often welcomed proposals that future teachers spend their first two years in general education. In the long run they hoped this would raise the competence and status of teaching (p. 235).

This has proven to be a relatively false expectation. Condescending and sanctimonious broadsides, rather than concerted collaboration, have been the more prevalent reaction. What is perhaps especially galling to teacher educators is that whenever teacher education is charged with failure, one sure thing can be counted on: their liberal arts colleagues will seldom leap into the fray to accept partial responsibility or culpability. Given the major thrust of contemporary liberal arts' criticism of teacher education, that is, the alleged necessity for more emphasis in the liberal arts, the findings of the Carnegie Commission on Higher Education (1973) appear even more startling.

> Now approximately three quarters of a prospective teacher's time is spent in arts and science courses. As the Study Commission on Undergraduate Education and the Education of Teachers has observed, however, the needs of classroom teachers are frequently not considered in the determination of course offerings or in the way subjects are taught. (p. 90)

Meanwhile, difficulties in pinpointing any indigenous context for education as a "discipline" have traditionally led to all manner of academic and practical complexities for beleaguered educationists. Yet, oddly enough, education as a field of study can be seen to require as much, if not more, subtle and divergent ways of thinking and valuing than are normally practiced in some other more generic academic areas. Education can be viewed as (a) an *academic* study, (b) an *applied* domain, and (c) an inherently *contextual* enterprise in which acute integrative inferences from many fields of knowledge and valuation become a necessity (DeVitis 1986).

> As an academic study, focus on education as an institution would seem to offer as much substance and justification for research as, for example, the dynamics of banking (in economics) or the nuances of party caucuses (in political science). As an applied domain, education necessitates action-oriented, clinical connections; for, as B. O. Smith (1969) has so ably argued,

> it cannot fruitfully function in a theoretical vacuum. Finally, as John Walton (1974) . . . sees it, educationists have to be "psychologists, sociologists, philosophers, anthropologists, and statisticians" as well as mere educationists. In a word, their context is as complex as all life "under Heaven." (p. 123)

Whether we have reached the point of a true "science of education" is another debatable (and in the editors' eyes) moot question. Instead we would hope that current and proposed programs in teacher education continue to reserve room for both the "artist" and the "scientist." This expectation is based largely on the assumption that education will remain as broad and challenging as anything on Shakespeare's stage — an arena needful of concerned, creative, disciplined actors with diverse gifts and contributions (cf. Eisner 1979).

At this point we perhaps need to discuss some of the basic realities that have influenced education as an institution since the 1840s — the primary era of "common-school" reform in America. In elaborating some assumptions regarding the educational past we may be able to clarify some of the content and context for present passions in educational reform. These historical perspectives may assist readers in placing current criticism in the broader kaleidoscope of American social and educational history.

At the outset several fundamental assumptions need to be articulated concerning the institution of schooling. The first question is: Who, indeed, actually makes educational policy at the institutional as well as the public level? Obviously, various "publics" play important roles in policy making. However, those publics tend to be either more powerful or more restricted in their practical ability to influence policy. Historically the publics that govern local and state education policy (e.g., school boards) have been mainly composed of members of professional middle-class society. If professor of education, disciple of John Dewey, and social critic George S. Counts' memorable thesis is correct, a profound change has occurred in the composition of the boards that have had the most direct control over educational policy during the past one hundred years (Counts 1927).

At the institutional level (i.e., teacher education) it is the various states that mandate certification requirements. The local boards must conform to these minimal state requirements. At present the Carnegie Forum Advisory Council has organized planning groups to devise a set of professional teaching standards to be applied nationally. Those groups are in consultation with many other groups, including representatives from the Educational Testing Service (ETS), which develops and administers the National Teacher Examination (NTE). It is perhaps noteworthy that the above publics really do not represent "you" and "me" but powerful special-interest groups.

The so-called Progressive Era was, to many historians, the period in which the public began to abdicate its role in policy making. The complex nature of society and its institutions, including education, ushered in the concept of "efficiency" and the rise of the "expert." The latter played a large part in convincing ordinary people to defer to the technocrat (Karier, Violas, and Spring 1973). The formation of policy thus became a function of expert leadership. As such, others (such as you and I) were relegated to lesser role functions in the policy-making realm. Special-interest groups (some avowedly representing you and me but more often than not attuned to their own interests, such as the business community) tended to foster narrow agendas. For example, on interest-group terms, increase in productivity became contingent on "better schools" (Cetron 1985; McNett 1982).

In light of the above discussion one might ask another basic question: What is, indeed, the purpose of public education? We believe that the appropriate response to that query must be couched in conditional terms, that is, "It depends." It depends, first of all, on which of the various publics one is addressing and more directly on which public has the *power* to define the purpose of public education.

A hundred or so years ago various publics would have been engaged in defining educational purpose. The development of private Catholic elementary and secondary schools would be one such example of a public not being fully served by the local schools and thus opting to create its own system of education (McCluskey 1964). Another example would be the growth of the noncommon high school curricula during the Progressive Era (Sola 1972, 1976, 1978). Teachers once looked with suspicion when the business community of the 1890s began to argue for a "better fit" between school curricula and job specifications (Violas 1978). Disagreements between various publics such as teacher unions and business organizations in the early twentieth century spawned renewed interest in redefining the purpose of education (i.e., its curricula, methods, and underlying philosophies). Today these groups (business, labor, state and local boards of education, and corporate foundations) are largely coming together as one on the overall purposes of education.

The composition of many of the commissions and institutional groups that have summoned calls for reform in teacher education reflects such a shift in public policy making. These diverse and, at one time, ideologically competing groups now seem to be cooperating (cf. Southern Regional Education Board and Northeast Regional Exchange). The cooperation among these constituencies may or may not be harmful. However, it does seem that any ill-conceived, precipitous rush for "reform," without careful consideration of potential and likely consequences, may be fraught with unintended mistakes and adverse outcomes.

The next important consideration, how society wants to educate its public schoolteachers, depends largely upon the issue raised earlier: Which public defines the purpose(s) of education? The latter would generate the type of curricula to be taught to teachers in terms of explicit formulation of public policy and implementation of that policy through the mandates of certification requirements. At a recent meeting with representatives from ETS regarding the content of the National Teacher Examination, one editor of this anthology was informed that the current emphasis is to train future teachers by testing their ability to manage the classroom. This example serves to illustrate the essential problem in understanding how to define the purpose of education. It also demonstrates how specific areas of teacher education curricula are shifting — and not necessarily for clear, philosophical, rational, and educationally sound reasons but because of often inchoate pronouncements from various and sundry commissions, state and regional advisory boards, or foundation reports. Some of these recommendations may, indeed, constitute well-intentioned suggestions for change; however, given the limited number of years one prepares to be a teacher, which current requirements will be deleted in order to accommodate new developments in teacher education?

The development of public schooling from the 1790s to the present offers a complex and oftentimes perplexing picture of American social reality. Any analysis of this development reveals conflicting interpretations regarding the purposes of education (Spring 1986). In this volume we are presenting one possible interpretation of the purposes of education; and, as the essays in this volume attest, a diversity of approaches to the education of teachers exists and will hopefully multiply. We firmly believe that this diversity has an inherently positive effect on the issue of the improvement of teacher education. Perhaps an eventual synthesis might evolve from this analysis that will benefit teacher education.

From the beginning the founding fathers held certain ideas about which publics ought not be involved in deciding public educational policy. They especially excluded the federal government. Except for enforcing the Constitution, educational policy was thought to be the primary responsibility of the states and, to a lesser extent, that of local governments. In reviewing the historical search for educational purpose, the era from 1780 to 1840 illustrates that the states developed most of the institutional structures for educational policy. These structures actually tended to centralize the context and control of education (Karier 1986; Katz 1975). Local school boards were losing their power to set educational policy including curricula, selection of textbooks, funding, and teacher requirements. (Here we are, of course, discussing the issue of local versus state control and not what the particular policies may have been.) The founding fathers correctly feared that a centralized national government would create a counterpurpose to the various state and local purposes of education in a free society. A centralized national purpose for public education in the preindustrial era would doubtlessly have had little effect on the power of local or state educational policy. However, that situation was to change dramatically by the end of the nineteenth century.

The purpose of education in colonial America may be perceived as largely religious in nature. From the postrevolutionary era to 1840 it tended to reflect more explicitly political purposes; and by the 1850s economic and social purposes were more visibly part of the mosaic (Cren:in 1970; Curti 1959; Katz 1968; Kaestle 1973). One of the cardinal issues in analyzing current purposes of public schooling is: Which of the above purposes underlies various interpretations of what is, indeed, accurate in understanding how present disparate publics characterize the role of the public school (Spring 1986)? Education has been portrayed as capable of fulfilling many roles. We want to raise another issue of purpose, that of educating the individual to be able to seek his or her own way in life—perhaps an idiosyncratic idea in this age of conformity.

This conformity may be traced to the Progressive Era, especially as regards an emerging "national purpose" in education. The rise of industrialism and the "corporate liberal state" created still another set of purposes for public education (Karier, Violas, and Spring 1973; Karier 1975; Spring 1976; Violas 1978).

In addition to these myriad developments is another significant question, that of professionalism. Education may or may not be a profession; indeed, it does not appear to meet all the criteria necessary for professional status (Rich 1984). Furthermore, education can legitimately be viewed as an arm of the state, as it were, and teachers are, in that sense, agents of the society. Yet the purposes and control of primary and secondary public education is not, on the whole, under the aegis of teachers. It thus is not meeting a primary criteria for a profession—control over curriculum. This inherent internal liability leaves educators especially open to special-interest groups. For example, the latter may perceive weaknesses in the economic sector as a direct result of the "impoverished" quality of American education—a presumed cause-and-effect relationship that is not fully substantiated in fact (Cuban 1985).

While this text does not directly develop the purposes of education (the reader, however, will doubtless discover various underlying purposes in the teacher-education programs presented), we hope to show how some of those purposes are mirrored in the current reform literature. Recommendations for the improvement of teacher education are definitely reflected in these essays. However, the historical analysis of who makes educational policy and what is the purpose of public education are not openly addressed in this volume at each point of discussion. Nevertheless, we urge the reader to consider carefully how these examples of teacher-education programs form an interpretive lens for educational policy in general. These are crucial issues that must be addressed because we believe that differences in educational philosophy provide perhaps the key element in defining (1) the public that defines educational policy and (2) the purpose of public education. At bottom the issue may well be in deciphering which publics possess the effective power to define educational purpose.

Each of these essays offers descriptive and interpretive analyses written by representatives from a cross section of teacher-education programs in the United States. Readers may not always agree with their respective philosophical approaches, but we can respect their individual commitments to excellence. We also believe that there might be some agreement on how we can educate teachers effectively through diverse methods that have been developed over the past several decades. For example, Donald R. Cruickshank's *Models for the Preparation of America's Teachers* (1985) presents a set of instructional strategies that demonstrate effective methods for teacher-education programs: microteaching, simulation, reflective teaching, and protocols. We believe that these and other methods represent some proven bases for educating technically sound, highly capable teachers. Perhaps sufficient quantitative data has been collected to demonstrate how we can educate the preservice teacher. On the other hand, agreement on sound philosophical underpinnings of teacher education seems to have yet to be attained. As noted earlier, the diversity of philosophies at our fingertips might well be considered a great strength in maintaining continued dialogue and vitality in our schools and society.

An irony in this study is that, surprising as it may seem to some critics, there has been ample evidence of attempts to alter teacher-education programs in the last twenty years. As mentioned above, a cursory perusal of Cruickshank's latest monograph shows that there have been some twenty-two separate reform proposals since the early 1960s. The variety of the recommendations is extensive enough to belie the popular belief that teacher education has been almost as dry and stagnant in its ideas for change as have academic units in the arts and sciences. Cruickshank's litany of reform proposals includes the following: the AACTE TEAM Project (LaGrone 1964); Teacher Corps interventions; Smith et al.'s AACTE-supported *Teachers for the Real World* (1969); Charles Silberman's *Crisis in the Classroom* (1970); the teacher-effectiveness movement; teacher-education mandates in Ohio in the early 1970s; "community building" and multicultural programs, which reflected both political and social realities since the 1960s; artistic models such as those begun by Arthur Combs at the University of Florida (and since modified by PROTEACH at the same institution, as is detailed in this volume); Travers and Dillon's "teacher as actor" and "role acquisition" models (1975); performance/competency-based education, once hailed as a pedagogical savior and now in less healthful stages of decay; PTE (Personalized Teacher Education), a relatively small program at the University of Texas' Research and Development Center; Robert Howsam and colleagues' *Educating a Profession* (1976), AACTE's Bicentennial Commission project; B. O. Smith's *A Design for a School of Pedagogy* (1980); Mortimer J. Adler's *Paideia Proposal* (1982); Dale Scannell's AACTE-sponsored *Educating a Profession: Profile of a Beginning Teacher* (1983); sample proposals from leading education deans (Gideonse 1982), which led to the 1986 Holmes Group report; and national surveys by prominent corporate spokespersons such as Ernest Boyer's *High School: A Report on Secondary Education in America* (1983).

Many of the above reform proposals have already been cast by the wayside, a circumstance that provides some critics uneasy pause for consideration: which educational reform will be in vogue next year? Willy-nilly, other proposals have been built upon some of these past ones while other new curricula are quickly ushered into place. The latter is especially the case when political climes seem ready for refreshment. However, an important missing element appears to underlie any meaningful opportunity for significant change: joint efforts at the national, state, and local levels may be necessary. Systemic restructuring would seem to be crucial before any lasting change is to occur. In a provocative essay, "Reforming the Teaching of Teachers," Madhu Prakash (1986) poses this case forcefully.

> Reformers realize that to improve the quality of America's public school teachers, we cannot limit reform efforts to programs of teacher education. It is essential to make other, more far-reaching societal changes. These include improving the conditions of work as well as the social and economic status of teachers.

Harry Passow (1984, 683) makes a similar plea: "All of us have a role to play in reforming our schools and our society. Reforming schools, however, is very different from reforming society. . . . Both must occur simultaneously if real reform is to take place."

Likewise, the 1986 Carnegie Task Force on Teaching as a Profession proposes that about forty billion dollars be spent to harness structural redesigns throughout educational and societal institutions. Such a recommendation will pose a painful test of commitment to a citizenry and political leadership still in the throes of an ever-lengthening "Me-Decade" characterized by a kind of "meanness mania" toward larger social programs and social consciousness in general (Gill 1976). However, before such proposals as extended teacher education (i.e., five- and fifth-year as well as prospective sixth-year curricula) can rightfully gain full acceptance, it seems legitimate to ask whether preservice teachers should obligate themselves to further training and personal financial hardship in a society that pays its entry-level teachers less than its urban firefighters and sanitary engineers.

Indeed, the new Carnegie report (1986) addresses this issue by calling for both higher teacher status and vastly increased salaries that will allow teachers to compete with other professionals at both the entry level and advanced career stages. As a practical matter, to do otherwise might create another teacher shortage similar to those of the 1950s and 1960s in the very near future (Hawley 1986). With stop-gap recruits called into the profession, oftentimes people not able to find another livelihood, real matters of quality and excellence would seem to be further shortchanged. (This quandary should pose some serious doubts for governors — as in New Jersey and Virginia and the Southern Regional Education Board — who have been encouraging "alternative routes" to teacher certification for those candidates without fully articulated, professional degree programs in education.)

More directly as regards colleges and universities that prepare teachers, they will have to devote themselves to teaching as a pre- and in-service enterprise. Particularly in major research campuses, especially those belonging to the Holmes Group, renewed dedication to instructional activities has been long overdue both in liberal arts units and schools and departments of teacher education. In 1969 an astute student of higher education characterized college teaching as a "neglected art" — one in which many of its practitioners equate university instruction with the quantitative ingestion of food particles (Sanford 1969). Still today Ernest Boyer (1986) refers regretfully in his public addresses to the "endless sea of passivity" engendered by that same enterprise. This plight manifests itself as a general university-wide syndrome not limited to teacher education.

> Of course, the schools of education produce chiefly elementary and secondary teachers. The average college teacher is even more poorly prepared. Graduate schools, from which college teachers come, pay almost no attention to teaching; they fill the student's time with specialized courses and assume that if he can earn his Ph.D., he can teach, or else that he will not have to teach. And it is next to impossible to persuade a graduate student in history or sociology or psychology to take a course in the school of education. . . . Students seem afraid that education courses might corrupt them or lower their status. (Sanford 1969, 170)

Implicit in these remarks is a forceful challenge to the present status and reward structures of colleges and universities, especially the leading research institutions. Are they willing to modify their systemic priorities so that *teaching* and other *instructional* purposes and processes become more completely actualized? Or will the current quest for "prestige" and "visibility" (usually evidenced by productivity in publications and grants) continue to reign supreme (Green 1980)? In the end a "genuine commitment to teaching [would require] a fundamental change in fashions in academic policies. It means being 'born again' to value the unglamorous challenge of rearing another generation of learners" (Prakash 1986).

Unless and until college and university administrators and faculty, teacher educators and liberal-arts colleagues alike, commit themselves and their institutions in critical and practicable ways to "what it is like to be in a classroom, what one is there to do, or how one deals with this or that situation" (Sanford 1969, 170), their part in addressing solutions to problems in teacher education will likely remain part of the problem itself. Teachers in the trenches should not be expected to be too patient with educationists who, acting in bad faith, play parlor games with one of the most precious of human activities. If teachers and teacher educators cannot fully control their wider social, political, and economic destinies (and they *cannot*), they still possess substantial responsibility for participating in tough and tender dialogue on the important questions facing their own profession today. For policy makers, politicians, government officials, and academic administrators, this means that teachers and teacher educators want to be accountable for those policies and practices that they themselves have a hand in creating. Teachers should not be counted on to countenance a top-down approach to reform, as has been the case too often in the recent past, and still be expected to be ready, willing, and eager to perform as told. They are not hired hands; and education will never become a true or fully humane profession so long as they are treated in that fashion. All the participants, in and out of academe, will have to join hands as critical and interpretive analysts in the best tradition of what it means to be genuinely liberally educated if teacher education is to make a difference.

If this occurs, we will have started on the road to *reeducation* toward tolerance of diversity in ideas and the pure wonderment—and potential wonders—that journey could entail.

The essays that follow are thus not intended to proffer any quick-fix solutions or ultimate panaceas. Indeed, the search for such solutions might itself lie at the root of many social ills in the life of American culture. More specifically, it surely would be presumptuous to advocate "a singular model of teacher preparation . . . at a time when those who teach teachers are debating numerous ways to improve professional training" (Futrell 1986, 3). Instead, this sharing of diverse programs and viewpoints represents a sincere but humble groping toward renewed understanding of a very difficult domain of discourse, values, policies, and practices, that is, that peculiar institutionalized entity known as teacher education. If some of the essays appear to speak with some pride and others perhaps too modestly, let their authors be forgiven; for they communicate some of their excitement that hopefully might enable readers to rekindle and quicken the learning process. The contributors to this volume already have begun the adventure that we are referring to as reeducation. For those who teach teachers, theirs is no mean contribution. It also speaks to a solitary young voice in *Those Who Can, Teach* (Ryan and Cooper 1972, 237) who was sagacious beyond his years: "Everyone cares about teacher education—but not very much." If the reformers of the 1980s have helped to change public consciousness to the contrary and if these essays can further contribute to that development, we will rest a little more comfortably (but not complacently) in knowing that this project, too, has made a difference.

The main body of this text presents detailed descriptions and interpretive analyses written by contributors from each of thirteen fairly representative programs in contemporary American teacher education. To assist readers who may wish to use this collection as a source book for possible ways to think about institutional change, the editors have ordered the contents as follows:

Part One introduces the reader to *extended* teacher-education designs for initial certification drawn from programs that especially aim to strengthen and refine linkages between liberal and professional education.

Part Two contains a representative sampling of both fifth-year and five-year initial certification programs. These models reflect a possible growing trend toward the professionalization of teaching, that is, efforts to solidify the public as well as academic status of the profession. (They hold much in common with some of the programs outlined in Part One.) Such programs recognize that reflective teaching demands additional time for a teacher to be fully prepared in general studies, subject matter, and pedagogical skills.

Part Three focuses on some distinctive theoretical and methodological approaches from a variety of programs across the country. Each is dissimilar in philosophical underpinning, curriculum design, and implementation. Each also represents what we consider to be the rich diversity seldom talked about in contemporary American teacher education. The following programs are detailed in these essays:

- LaSalle University's "developmental" education model, which articulates a developmental scheme integrating psychological, social, physiological, and moral growth patterns throughout its teacher-education curriculum
- The University of Colorado's PROBE (problem-based education) program, which represents an inquiry/tutorial approach to teacher educa-

tion founded on the "case study" and "problem-situational" models utilized in such programs as the McMaster University Medical School and the Harvard Business School

- The University of Houston at Clear Lake City program, which encourages understanding of general trends and issues through its future-studies design for teacher education. Like the Colorado plan, the Houston-Clear Lake model is predicated upon individually tailored programs and small class size
- Hunter College's Training Tomorrow's Teachers Program (TTT), which demonstrates how a teacher-education program can fully utilize the urban environment, working closely with local schools in the community in implementing field-based experiences in the preparation of teachers for inner-city schools
- Berea College's humanistic, cognitive, and experiential approach, which shows how its nationally recognized work/study concept and other life experiences become integrated into the total framework of a teacher-education program
- Wittenberg University's international teacher-education design, which permits global, multicultural dimensions to provide focus and direction for faculty, students, and curricula throughout its campus environment

Finally, where do we go from here? We invite both critics and supporters of American teacher education to retrace the beginnings—the sociohistorical roots that have generated the contents, processes, and basic structures of educational institutions in this country. They will doubtless rediscover a common and profound theme of diversity (particularly in higher education) and indigenous suspicions about nationalization and homogenization of policy and practice. (This historical reality may be shifting as a result of reform movements of the past several years. Ironically, state-level reforms in education have tended to increase the possibility of nationalization and homogenization.) In the past America's admittedly imperfect system of decentralized education has at least managed to permit a relative degree of freedom in the perception and interpretation of educational problems and their attendant possible solutions.

In this regard it is important to reiterate that the founding fathers made no explicit mention of education in their early documents. Education was primarily an overt function of religious and familial institutions in the Puritan and colonial eras. Between 1790 and 1840, presumably the national period in our nation's formative growth, debate on educational policy grew more intense with state control dominating local control. In each epoch education was inextricably linked to overriding social, political, and economic forces usually beyond its control. The 1980s are not a different time and place in that significant respect. Such linkages continue to plague intellectual and practical efforts to define, clarify, and assess educational aims and outcomes. Indeed, education serves so many different and varied publics that its policy makers and practitioners often spend more time trying to meet the expressed demands of opposing interest groups than developing clear, defensible, and sound educational programs. By this we mean programs based on reliable empirical evidence, reasoned argumentation, and creative canons of unfettered intellectual discourse.

In terms of some recent national commission reports on education, most notably *A Nation at Risk,* Lawrence Stedman and Marshall Smith (1983) identify underlying political intentions and effects in the reports themselves.

> These reports are political documents; the case they make takes the form of a polemic, not a reasoned treatise. Rather than carefully marshaling facts to prove their case, they present a litany of charges without examining the veracity of their evidence or its sources. By presenting material starkly and eloquently, the commissions hoped to jar the public into action, and to a great extent they have been successful. Caveats and detailed analysis of evidence might have lessened the reports' impact.

Or, in the words of Paul Peterson (1983, 4): "[National commissions] do have their function in American politics, but fact-finding, rigorous analysis, and policy development are usually not among them. Commissions are appropriate for dramatizing an issue, resolving political differences, and reassuring the public that questions are being thoughtfully considered."

Though the present text does not develop directly the overall aims of education, significant threads of that issue inevitably emerge. It is our hope and belief that this collection of essays provides more ample evidence of reasoned analysis and argumentation than do the national commission reports. It has already been argued that *any* analysis of education in general, and teacher education in particular, must address assumptions surrounding the explicit and implicit intentions of educational "purpose." That is to ask: who is it to serve, who defines the parameters and limits of the enterprise, who pulls the purse strings, who certifies the participants, and who polices the established members of the guild? Perhaps most importantly, how do we legitimately go about changing educational purposes that need obvious modification or even drastic overhaul? More specifically, how do these purposes become transmitted—and, if need be, transformed—by teachers and teacher educators in our schools and colleges?

These questions have been partially broached in the relatively brief history of American teacher education starting with its mid-nineteenth century roots, its childhood development in the late nineteenth century (when education was typically a lesser sibling of psychology or philosophy departments, if taught at all), through its adolescent growth period in early twentieth-century normal schools, to its present separate, but unequal status in most comprehensive college and university environments. A number of the papers in this compendium trace these past patterns of development and propose new models by which to augment the academization and professionalization of teaching. Some of the models resemble fairly long-standing designs that had been implemented well before calls for educational change became currently popular. Others of the reform proposals in this volume have been generated as a direct result of the present excellence reform movement.

We believe that the major threads of theory, practice, policy, and the actual implementation of teacher-education programs have been, in a general sense, explored herein. The chapters to follow emphasize the common integrating theme of "strength through diversity" in recognition of that historical tradition in American higher education as well as the reality and promise it still holds today.

The editors conclude with one final important caveat. None of the exemplars presented in this text should be arbitrarily selected as a model for change without one's first analyzing very carefully and critically many philosophical and practical concerns. Significant factors in those peculiar internal and external structures and substructures of one's own institution will have much to say about any realistic and viable plans for either short-term or long-lasting reform. These factors include considerations of campus climate and ethos, geographic locale, constituent base, academic traditions and vagaries, and the labyrinthine (and sometimes serpentine) paths of politics both on and off campus. These potential obstacles may be cause for concern and reflection but not necessarily inaction.

BIBLIOGRAPHY

AACTE Committee on Performance-Based Teacher Education. *Achieving the Potential of Performance-Based Teacher Education: Recommendations.* Washington, D.C.: American Association of Colleges for Teacher Education, 1974.

Adler, M. J. *The Paideia Proposal: An Educational Manifesto.* New York: Macmillan, 1982.

Bestor, A. *Educational Wastelands.* Urbana, Ill.: University of Illinois Press, 1953.

Boyer, E. L. *High School: A Report on Secondary Education in America.* New York: Harper & Row, 1983.

_____. *College.* New York: Harper & Row, 1986.

Broudy, H. S. *The Real World of the Public Schools.* New York: Harcourt Brace Jovanovich, 1972.

Broudy, H. S., B. O. Smith, and J. R. Burnett. *Democracy and Excellence in American Secondary Education.* Chicago: Rand McNally, 1964.

Bruner, J. S. *The Process of Education.* Cambridge, Mass.: Harvard University Press, 1962.

Carnegie Commission on Education and the Economy. *Report of the Task Force on Teaching as a Profession.* Princeton, N.J.: Carnegie Foundation for the Advancement of Teaching, 1986.

Carnegie Commission on Higher Education. *Continuity and Discontinuity: Higher Education and the Schools.* New York: McGraw-Hill, 1973.

Cetron, M. *Schools of the Future.* New York: McGraw-Hill, 1985.

Combs, A., R. Blume, R. Newman, and H. Wass. *The Professional Education of Teachers.* Boston: Allyn & Bacon, 1974.

Commission on Multicultural Education. *Directory: Multicultural Education Programs in Teacher Education Institutions in the United States.* Washington, D.C.: American Association of Colleges for Teacher Education, 1978.

Commission on Public School Personnel Policies in Ohio. *Realities and Revolution in Teacher Education, Report No. 6.* Cleveland: Greater Cleveland Associated Foundation, 1972.

Conant, J. B. *The Education of American Teachers.* New York: McGraw-Hill, 1963.

Counts, G. S. *Social Composition of Boards of Education: A Study in the Social Control of Education.* Chicago: University of Chicago Press, 1927.

Cremin, L. A. *American Education: The Colonial Experience.* New York: Harper & Row, 1970.

Cruickshank, D. R. *Blueprints for Teacher Education: A Review of Phase II Proposals for the USOE Comprehensive Elementary Teacher Education (CETEM) Program.* Washington, D.C.: U.S. Department of Health, Education and Welfare, 1970.

————. *Models for the Preparation of America's Teachers.* Bloomington, Ind.: Phi Delta Kappa Educational Foundation, 1985.

Cruickshank, D. R., J. Holton, D. Fay, J. Williams, J. Kennedy, B. Myers, and B. Hough. *Reflective Teaching.* Bloomington, Ind.: Phi Delta Kappa, 1981.

Cuban, L. "Corporate Involvement in Public Schools: A Practitioner-Academic's Point of View." In *The Private Sector in the Public Schools: Can It Improve Education?* edited by M. Levine. Washington, D.C.: American Enterprise Institute, 1985.

Curti, M. *The Social Ideals of American Educators.* Paterson, N.J.: Littlefield, Adams, 1959.

DeVitis, J. L. "Teacher Education in Academe: A Failure of Consideration." *Contemporary Education* 57, no. 3(1986):122–25.

Dewey, J. "The Relation of Theory to Practice in Education." In *Teacher Education in America: A Documentary History,* edited by M. L. Borrowman. New York: Teachers College Press, 1965.

Eisner, E. W. *The Educational Imagination: On the Design and Evaluation of School Programs*. New York: Macmillan, 1979.

Evertson, C., W. D. Hawley, and M. Zlotnick. "Making a Difference in Educational Quality through Teacher Education." *Journal of Teacher Education* 36, no. 3(1985):2–12.

Fuller, F. F., and O. H. Bown. "Becoming a Teacher." In *Teacher Education: The Seventy-fourth Yearbook of the National Society for the Study of Education*, edited by K. Ryan. Chicago: University of Chicago Press, 1975.

Futrell, M. H. "National News Notes." *NEA Higher Education Advocate*, June 16, 1986, 3.

Gideonse, H. D. "The Necessary Revolution in Teacher Education." *Phi Delta Kappan* 64(1982):15–18.

Gill, E. *Meanness Mania*. Washington, D.C.: Howard University Press, 1976.

Goodlad, J. I. *A Place Called School: Prospects for the Future*. New York: McGraw-Hill, 1983.

Green, T. F. *Predicting the Behavior of the Educational System*. Syracuse: Syracuse University Press, 1980.

Hawley, W. D. "Toward a Comprehensive Strategy for Addressing the Teacher Shortage." *Phi Delta Kappan* 67, no. 10(1986):712–18.

Hawley, W. D. "Breaking Away: The Risks and Inadequacy of Extended Teacher Preparation Programs." *American Journal of Education*, in press.

Howsam, R. B., D. Corrigan, G. Denemark, and R. Nash. *Educating a Profession*. Washington, D.C.: American Association of Colleges for Teacher Education, 1976.

Jacobson, R. L. Tomorrow's Teachers: A Report of the Holmes Group. *The Chronicle of Higher Education* 32, no. 6(1986):27.

Jencks, C., and D. Riesman. *The Academic Revolution*. Garden City, N.Y.: Doubleday, 1969.

Kaestle, C. *The Evolution of an Urban School System*. Cambridge: Cambridge University Press, 1973.

Karier, C. J. *The Individual, Society and Education*. Urbana, Ill.: University of Illinois Press, 1986.

————. *Shaping the American Educational State*. New York: Free Press, 1975.

Karier, C. J., P. C. Violas, and J. Spring. *Roots of Crisis: American Education in the Twentieth Century*. Chicago: Rand McNally, 1973.

Katz, M. *Class, Bureaucracy and Schools*. New York: Praeger, 1975.

————. *The Irony of Early School Reform*. Cambridge: Harvard University Press, 1968.

Koerner, J. D. *The Miseducation of American Teachers*. Boston: Houghton Mifflin, 1963.

La Grone, H. *A Proposal for the Revision of the Preservice Professional Component of Teacher Education*. Washington, D.C.: American Association of Colleges for Teacher Education, 1964.

Lanier, J. E., and J. W. Little. "Research on Teacher Education." In *Handbook of Research on Teaching*, edited by M. C. Wittrock. New York: Macmillan, 1986.

Levine, M., ed. *The Private Sector in the Public School: Can It Improve Education?* Washington, D.C.: American Enterprise Institute, 1985.

McCluskey, N., ed. *Catholic Education in America.* New York: Teachers College Press, 1964.

McNett, I., ed. *Let's Not Reinvent the Wheel: Profiles of School/business Collaboration.* Washington, D.C.: Institute for Educational Leadership, 1982.

Martin, D. S. "Substance, Not Form, in Renewing Teacher Education." *Contemporary Education* 56, no. 2(1986):80–84.

Mitchell, R. *The Graves of Academe.* Boston: Little, Brown, 1981.

National Advisory Council on Education Professions Development. *Teacher Corps: Past or Prologue.* Washington, D.C.: U.S. Government Printing Office, 1975.

National Commission for Excellence in Teacher Education. *A Call for Change in Teacher Education.* Washington, D.C.: American Association of Colleges for Teacher Education, 1985.

National Commission on Excellence in Education. *A Nation at Risk.* Washington, D.C.: U.S. Government Printing Office, 1983.

National Education Association. *Excellence in Our Schools: Teacher Education, an Action Plan.* Washington, D.C.: National Education Association, 1982.

Northeast Regional Exchange, Inc. *Education under Study.* Chelmsford, Mass.: Northeast Regional Exchange, 1983.

Olson, P., L. Freeman, and J. Bowman, eds. *Education for 1984 and After.* Lincoln: University of Nebraska Press, 1972.

Olson, P., L. Freeman, J. Bowman, and J. Pieper. *The University Can't Train Teachers.* Lincoln: University of Nebraska Curriculum Development Center, 1972.

Passow, A. H. "Tackling the Reform Reports of the 1980s." *Phi Delta Kappan* 65, no. 10(1984):674–83.

Peterson, P. E. "Did the Education Commissions Say Anything?" *Brookings Review* 2(1983):4.

Prakash, M. S. "Reforming the Teaching of Teachers: Trends, Contradictions and Challenges." *Teachers College Record* 88(Winter 1986):217–40.

Rich, J. M. *Professional Ethics in Education.* Springfield, Ill.: Charles C. Thomas, 1984.

Rickover, H. G. *Swiss Schools and Ours: Why Theirs Are Better.* Boston: Atlantic-Little, Brown, 1962.

Ryan, K., and J. M. Cooper. *Those Who Can, Teach.* Boston: Houghton Mifflin, 1972.

Sanford, N. *Where Colleges Fail: A Study of the Student as a Person.* San Francisco: Jossey-Bass, 1969.

Scannell, Dale. *Educating a Profession: Profile of a Beginning Teacher.* Washington, D.C.: American Association of Colleges for Teacher Education, 1983.

Schwebel, M. "The Clash of Cultures in Academe: The University and the Education Faculty." *Journal of Teacher Education* 36, no. 4(1985):2–7.

Silberman, C. E. *Crisis in the Classroom: The Remaking of American Education.* New York: Random House, 1970.

Sizer, T. R. *Horace's Compromise: The Dilemma of the American High School.* Boston: Houghton Mifflin, 1984.

Smith, B. O. *A Design for a School of Pedagogy.* Washington, D.C.: U.S. Government Printing Office, 1980.

Smith, B. O., S. Cohen, and A. Pearl. *Teachers for the Real World.* Washington, D.C.: American Association of Colleges for Teacher Education, 1969.

Sola, P. A. "The Chicago Association of Commerce and the Organization of Extracurricular Activities in the Chicago High Schools, 1914–1925." *Vocational Aspect of Education* 30, no. 77(1978):119–27.

_____. *Plutocrats, Pedagogues and Plebes: Business Influences on Vocational Education and Extracurricular Activities in the Chicago High Schools, 1899–1925.* Doctoral diss., University of Illinois, 1972.

_____. "Vocational Guidance: Integrating School and Society in Chicago, 1912–1916." *Vocational Aspect of Education* 28, no. 71(1976):117–23.

Spring, J. *The American School, 1642–1985.* New York: Longman, 1986.

_____. *The Sorting Machine: National Educational Policy since 1945.* New York: David McKay, 1976.

Stedman, L., and M. S. Smith. "Recent Reform Proposals for American Education." *Contemporary Education Review* 2, no. 2(Fall 1983):85–104.

Study Commission on Undergraduate Education and the Education of Teachers. *Teacher Education in the United States: The Responsibility Gap.* Lincoln: University of Nebraska Press, 1976.

Travers, R., and J. Dillon. *The Making of a Teacher.* New York: Macmillan, 1975.

Verduin, J. R. *Conceptual Models in Teacher Education.* Washington, D.C.: American Association of Colleges for Teacher Education, 1967.

Violas, P. C. *The Training of the Urban Working Class.* Chicago: Rand McNally, 1978.

Walton, J. "A Confusion of Contexts: The Interdisciplinary Study of Education." *Educational Theory* 24, no. 3(1974):219–29.

1 | Extended Teacher-education Programs

2 | Exploring New Frontiers in Teacher Education: The Austin Teacher Program

WILLIAM FREEMAN

INTRODUCTION

Austin College is a private, liberal arts college located in Sherman, Texas. The college enrolls about 1200 students annually and grants only one graduate degree—the M.A. plus Texas Teacher Certification— for the elementary and secondary schools to about thirty students a year who complete the five-year, nontraditional Austin Teacher Program.

The current Austin Teacher Program is the result of years of creative planning and experimentation. Initiated in 1968 and fully implemented in 1972, the program is designed to prepare sensitive, perceptive teachers who are well qualified to provide leadership toward excellence in teaching. Because the traditional undergraduate course approach to a major in education has been abandoned, the teacher-education student is free to pursue a bachelor's degree in one of the regular liberal arts disciplines. This unusual freedom is the result of a firm conviction on the part of the education faculty that a liberal arts education is an essential element in the preparation of outstanding teachers. Basic requirements constitute approximately one-third of the courses needed for graduation. There is thus ample opportunity for in-depth study in particular areas of special interest.

When the teacher program was planned, it was appropriately decided that an overhaul of the entire sequence of teacher requirements was necessary, encompassing all parts of the certification process in the analysis for improvement. Such an approach seemed essential if an institution was seri-

William Freeman is a professor and chairperson of the Education Department at Austin College, Sherman, Texas.

ous about seeking a better solution to the teacher-preparation dilemma. If Austin College had not taken such an involved leap, the results would have been far less satisfactory, because efforts to improve would have been only a tinkering exercise. As it was, the Austin program did not become another casualty among the many failures of teacher-education programs that were attempting to be innovative during the late sixties and early seventies.

Considering the number of rare and uncommon components included in the Austin program, it has withstood the tests of time remarkably well. With only a few deletions and amendments over more than a decade, the program is still functioning with most of the original design and a few innovations added through the years. Such an accomplishment is, indeed, noteworthy because most of the exemplary programs in teacher education in the United States that were federally or foundation-funded during the sixties and early seventies are no longer in operation. Austin College had the commitment, dedication, creativity, and foresight of its administration and teacher-education faculty to continue the improvements after funds from other sources were no longer available. Since 1972 when the first few students accelerated their teacher program by attending summer sessions during their undergraduate years, Austin College has been graduating students for the teaching profession in a program that substantially goes beyond the demands of critics who complain about the preparation of teachers in colleges and universities.

Philosophical Positions

The following statements and rationales constitute the key factors that undergird the Austin program.

1. It is committed to meeting the changing needs of a changing social context. Therefore, it is developmental and flexible in structure, able to make changes as needs arise, basing such change on planned, periodic, qualitative evaluation of the program's effectiveness and of the social and professional contexts in which the program operates. It is a teacher-education program that is structurally developmental and flexible and commits itself to regular, carefully planned change. The program recognizes the importance of the present and the future and seeks to prepare its students to teach effectively in the present and to be capable of dealing constructively and creatively with the rapid changes that will continue to characterize twentieth and twenty-first century society.

2. It is based on a liberal arts education. The liberal arts education involves the prospective teacher in the study of the collective wisdom of humankind's most important learnings, accomplishments, and modes of

thought across a broad spectrum described by the arts and sciences. In addition, intensive study in one or two areas of the liberal arts provides the students with a comprehensive fund of knowledge and methodology in the discipline(s) they intend to teach.

3. It is a five-year program designed to include a professional graduate year that terminates in a master of arts degree. It is based on the assumption that the quality program desired could not be completed in the traditional four academic years. In order to provide the students with more opportunity to become liberally educated and to acquire competence in their discipline or disciplines, an additional professional year has been added.

4. The curriculum is designed to assist the students in the development of the knowledge, attitudes, and skills that will enable them to teach effectively. The objective of the curriculum is that the students become effective teachers through their participation in the activities provided within that curriculum. The program insists that subject-matter knowledge, by itself, is not enough to ensure effective teaching, nor is development of a set of teaching skills based upon understanding of pedagogical literature, nor is a positive attitude. Thus, the curriculum provides opportunities for the students to develop in all three of these areas through both theoretical and practical learning environments. Furthermore, by taking this position, the program demonstrates the belief that effective teaching — the appropriate, individualistic blending of knowledge, attitudes, and skills put into practice — can be perceived by its faculty, its students, and other partners in the process of teacher preparation.

5. It assists the student in designing and implementing an individualized, personalized program of preparation for effective teaching. Just as there is no such thing as the teacher who conforms to one mold or model of effective teaching, so also there is no such thing as the typical student. Rather, they enter the program with personality, prior experiences, abilities, and needs different in kind and degree from those of their peers. From the very first involvement in the program, the students are assisted in assessing those experiences, abilities, and needs that are then used as a base upon which to build a personalized teacher-preparation program from freshman through graduate year. Every student is helped to find his or her own best way to become an effective teacher.

6. The students must assume an active role in their program of preparation to graduate. By its nature, the program requires that the students be actively involved in analyzing their own instructional needs and in planning for those learning experiences that will promote their growth toward the goal of becoming effective teachers. The faculty expects each prospective graduate to make steady progress toward becoming a self-directed learner,

assertively seeking assistance from faculty members and other resources as needed.

7. Just as the Austin program is developmental and flexible in nature (designed for planned, periodic change), so, too, are the roles assumed by its faculty. Because it is designed to respond constructively and creatively to change, the faculty is responsible for assessing need as well as making changes in the program's structure and, consequently, in its roles as a faculty. Because the program is individualized for each student, the faculty does not merely instruct; it also guides and directs the individual toward the goal of effective teaching, and creates, coordinates, and facilitates activities that promote the individual's attainment of that goal.

8. Evaluation of the prospective graduate for the purpose of determining teaching effectiveness is continuous, pluralistic, and subjective. A review of professional literature reveals no one set of criteria that can be used to identify the effective teacher. Nevertheless, the Austin faculty believes that effective teaching can be perceived. Thus, a faculty utilizes practicing classroom teachers, school principals, and even peers to evaluate strengths and weaknesses of a student's teaching performance. While any one such observation is subjective in nature, the collective professional judgments of those named above tend to yield an accurate measure of teaching effectiveness.

9. It is based on a cooperative alliance of Austin College, its education department, and the public schools. Though the program faculty and staff assume primary responsibility for the operation of the program, all three parties to this alliance recognize clearly the values and benefits of well-trained classroom teachers both for themselves and for society as a whole. Active collaboration on the preparation of effective teachers is, thus, a primary concern of the alliance. A secondary function of the alliance is the development and implementation of programs that, though not directly related to the preparation of preservice teachers, improve or enhance the operation of the three members of the alliance.

10. It assists the student in identifying and responding constructively to the rigorous, sometimes conflicting, standards of performance and behavior expected of teachers by society and by all partners to the teacher-education process. Society expects its teacher-education faculty and schoolteachers to be professional people. It places major responsibilities for leadership upon these positions. Students preparing to enter and participate in the Austin program are developing a professional role model that includes working with others fairly and humanely, resolutely protecting confidential information, demonstrating dependability, and being wholeheartedly committed to the task of teaching their assigned pupils.

PROGRAM CHANGES

In formulating the Austin Teacher Program, the numerous planning sessions with college administrators, faculty, staff, students, alumni, public school personnel, consultants, and authors of many books and articles that were read resulted in the partial list of unique features presented below.

It was decided to change the program from a four-year B.A. degree program with traditional education courses to a five-year M.A. degree program with nontraditional courses giving greater emphasis to the liberal arts. (Although an additional twelve months and thirty-six semester hours would be added to the curriculum for teacher-education students, no additional education courses or credits in education were required.) Formerly, educational psychology, sociology, and philosophy courses were taught in the Education Department. They are now taught in the separate disciplines of psychology, sociology, and philosophy. Elementary education students concentrated or majored in elementary education; now they concentrate in one of the various academic disciplines. (Secondary education students continued to have two concentrations or majors in academic fields.) Education credits were offered at the undergraduate level. Now all credit courses in education (with one exception for secondary students and two for elementary students) are offered at the graduate level and, at the same time, permit three of the nine graduate courses (four semester hours per course) required to be in disciplines outside of education.

The program was also changed from a campus-based, theory-oriented course structure to a public school classroom base with practice integrated with theory, including noncredit, partial credit, and full credit experiences. It went from a late and limited involvement in the teaching process to an early and extensive interaction with teachers, students, and learning activities in the public school. Noncredit and partial credit labs were required at the freshman, sophomore, and junior levels in order to give prospective teachers exposure to the teaching profession early enough to make career choices based upon actual experiences.

The program was constantly evaluated and continuously developed according to assessment reports each term and each year. Program assessment changed from a quantitative, objective evaluation to qualitative, subjective analysis of the ongoing procedures. It changed from a program that was generally assessed every five years to a program that would be continually evaluated with regular feedback that gives faculty frequent information about the program without being pressured by outside accreditation agencies.

A difficult change was from a faculty that was segregated according to secondary or elementary school levels teaching certain desired courses to a faculty that gave less importance to their own personal interests and specialties while giving primary attention to helping all students achieve professional competency. (It mattered not whether the student planned to teach first or tenth grade, reading or mathematics, middle or high school—all faculty were concerned first with students becoming effective teachers.) The program changed from a faculty that prided itself on being "good talkers" to a faculty that sought to acquire the skills of being good listeners; from always giving the answers to constantly seeking the solutions; from encouraging students to be passive to involving students actively in the learning process; from being the one and only resource to being a facilitator and coordinator of learning activities utilizing a multitude of resources.

A critical change was from a restricted amount of time and involvement in the public school classroom during the senior year (known as student teaching) to at least eighty hours of teaching at the undergraduate level. In addition the program required at least one full term (semester) of internship-type teaching at the graduate level, which culminated a series of previous teaching experiences in the classroom during prior years. (Most of the intern assignments result in paid positions with full teaching responsibilities without supervising teachers in the classroom.) It changed from a limited use of public school personnel in the teacher-preparation process to extensive use of public school teachers, principals, and central administration personnel.

Additional changes included use of the Materials Learning Center because the program became centered both physically and educationally around a wide variety of resources for use in the preparation of lessons for the school classroom. (Students are encouraged not only through verbal reminders to utilize all available resources but are taught to do so by demonstration and examples of faculty and supervising teachers.) It changed from conceiving of students as groups to relating to them as individuals in need of a variety of teaching tools. It changed from assuming that students all need the same teaching to recognizing that students have different needs that must be met with different kinds of resources just as students in the public schools must have their needs met in a variety of ways, varying the structure according to student readiness, strengths, and weaknesses.

It changed from faculty dictating what to do and ways to do it to students directing their own learning, developing skills in discovering the best approach for themselves as they prepare to teach, striving to utilize fully their own personalities and unique strengths (as opposed to everyone doing the same thing at the same time regardless of individual needs). The program was also modified from having a standard set of skills to be acquired to relying upon an individualized list of behavior patterns designed by and for each student separate from the group. It changed from a predetermined list of what it took to be a competent teacher to a subjective list of behavior patterns that was likely to be different for each student.

Finally, a file system that only had minimum certification information for each person was developed into a portfolio containing maximum data concerning teaching competencies, including records of teaching experiences, subjective evaluations by faculty, peers, teachers, and principals related to the acquisition of teaching skills and attitudes.

CONCERNS, FEARS, AND FRUSTRATIONS CAUSED BY CHANGE

One of the major aspects of launching the Austin Teacher Program was participating in a conference arranged by the department and supported by the Stone Foundation at Estes Park, Colorado, during the summer of 1969.

The purpose of the Estes Park Conference was to bring outstanding educators, public school people, department faculty and staff, students, and other Austin College personnel together to react to the recommendations of the Austin College Education Department faculty and students for the new teacher program. The conferees were divided into subgroups to critique ten positions that formed the basis for the new program. After two days of intensive work, the subgroups shared their reactions with the total group. From these reports came the final revision for the program that was launched the following fall.

While the new program was being established, the old one was being phased out. Offerings at the master's degree level not related to the program were eliminated. This transitional period gave the faculty time to properly focus on its primary task: preparation of teachers at the elementary and secondary levels.

As the launching took place, faculty members constantly faced problems and concerns brought about by taking risks. Seven of these issues are discussed below.

1. How do you expect students to enroll in a new program that requires a master of arts degree along with teacher certification when no other institution in Texas does likewise (not in 1968 or in 1986 as this is being written)? Why would students put another year and another large sum of money into a program at Austin College when they could go elsewhere and get a teacher's certificate at the B.A. degree level and not be out that additional time and expense?

Students would not put another year of time, study, and money into a teacher-education program that was the same as any other program. Students would not enter it if it meant just another year added to the traditional four-year program. This program had been overhauled and was different from the others. They were attracted by the improved quality, uniqueness, relevancy, and practicality that the additional year offered. (One reason the state legislature has not required a master's degree for teacher certification in Texas is because of the fear that colleges and universities will only add more of the same mediocrity without improving the quality of the teacher-education programs.)

2. What assurance is there that the new program will be any better or even as good as the old program? Will it eventually become just another program with boring course work except it will be five instead of four years of boredom?

Without a commitment to rework, revise, restructure, tear up, and rebuild the entire program, there is almost no likelihood that a new program will be an improvement over what has gone on before. Also, without careful and continuous monitoring, evaluating, and making appropriate changes as a result of ongoing assessment data, there is little assurance of the continuation of a better program. No matter how much time passes it is necessary to go through the revamping process periodically in order to prevent the tendency to hang on to a program that may be outdated, irrelevant, boring, and mediocre.

3. Will the increased involvement in the public school classroom lead to a watered-down curriculum with all practice and no theory? How can you have quality control when the new approach calls for public school teachers to be directly responsible for teaching students many of the basic pedagogical skills?

Once an intensive involvement with the public school is in operation utilizing teachers more fully in the preparation of students for the teaching profession, there is always the danger of college faculty members becoming less active in supervisory roles, retreating to the ivy-covered towers. In such situations there is certainly the possibility of colleges losing their quality control as well as failing to maintain a proper balance between theory and practice. Austin College avoids these pitfalls by having a faculty who stays involved with the public schools and cooperates closely with them, working side by side rather than relinquishing important responsibilities.

4. How can you get students to take the noncredit and partial credit labs that are such a vital part of the new program when their schedules are already heavy and the demands are great in the liberal arts curriculum? Besides, how do you fairly equate teaching loads if noncredit and partial credit courses are taught?

If the noncredit and partial credit labs are profitable, worthy, and meaningful, giving students something concrete for the time invested, then students will participate willingly, and they will find the time to do so. However, if the labs are not beneficial, then students will refuse to participate in them. Students must perceive the noncredit and partial credit experiences as being worthwhile, giving them definite skills needed for the career they have either chosen or are investigating as a possibility. Noncredit and partial credit courses are considered a part of the faculty teaching load because the administration is progressive in its approach to meeting student and faculty needs. Austin College is fortunate to have such an administration.

5. How can you keep a faculty working together enthusiastically when so much time is expected of them and when everyone is treading in new territory? How can you get even a small group of six or eight faculty members cooperating on innovative pursuits over an extended period of time—at least long enough to establish cohesiveness? Is it possible for faculty to maintain an exemplary posture after the newness wears off and after federal and foundation money expires?

Faculty will go far beyond the usual, put forth much more effort than normal, cooperatively devote extraordinary amounts of time if they have support, praise, encouragement, a sense of accomplishment, and the belief that they are a part of something challenging, creative, innovative, and exciting. Otherwise, if faculty begin to think they are doing it alone, that nobody really cares, that what they are doing is neither appreciated nor seems to make a difference in quality or excellence, then low morale will ensue with the eventual downgrading of the program. The Austin program faculty spent much time during the first five years building a unified perception among its members concerning the goal of excellence. This does not mean that all faculty members should be of the same mind, but it does mean that they need to work very hard not to let their differences interfere with the goal of improvement.

6. How can you trust students to direct their own learning? Are stu-

dents really interested in quality, involvement, independent work, and a program that is striving to be truly professional?

One of the greatest risks taken in the Austin Teacher Program was for the faculty to agree to trust students. The faculty had to take the first step. Mutual trust had to occur for the program to succeed, because the program is built on the assumption that students will trust faculty if faculty trust them. There are always a few cases in which neither faculty nor students are trustworthy; but these instances are few, and they do not spoil the large majority who function with unexpected reliability. When students are given responsibility, they usually assume responsible tasks. When students are included in the operation of a program, they feel more obligated to succeed in that program. When students are considered equally important as human beings on par with faculty members, they respond by increasing their respect and caring for the faculty. Faculty then begin to see students in a different light. They establish relationships that communicate understanding, appreciation, confidence, and warmth. These positive attitudes and feelings are made possible in the teacher program because faculty and students learn to trust one another.

7. How can there possibly be enough paid intern positions for all students who are qualified for such a position during one of their fifth-year graduate terms?

When the intern possibility became a reality, there were no school districts employing interns as part of their teaching faculty. Teacher aides were the closest thing they had to an intern position. Therefore, it was the job of the teacher-education faculty to sell the schools on the paid internship idea. In the early years it was a slow process, but this was not a problem because there were only a few students who were qualified to be interns. As the number of intern possibilities increased, the number of requests from schools for interns increased. (Presently there are usually more intern positions to be filled than there are interns to fill them.) The pay for the intern positions also increased. The number of intern positions available and the amount of money paid to these interns have far exceeded the expectations of the faculty who included this important component in the design program.

Needless to say, the changes during the launching period for the program resulted in courage, anxiety, trepidation, and, at times, confusion. However, amazingly, out of it developed a program that evolved to be a bright spot in the drabness (we felt) of teacher-education programs throughout the country. The leap into the dark was, indeed, risky. But, at the time, there did not seem to be any other choice—that is, if the department wanted to be in the business of preparing master teachers.

AN UNUSUAL PROGRAM REVIEWED

For over a decade Austin College has been producing an unusual product in teacher education. The development, implementation, and continuation of the Austin Teacher Program are significant features because the program has consistently held to those improvements in teacher education that are being advocated today by critics as necessary in order to have a quality program. Some of these unusual features are stated below.

The Austin program is based on a developmental design for teacher preparation, including four undergraduate education labs, the first three of which carry no or partial course credit, and a fifth or professional year, which terminates with the earning of the M.A. degree with a specialization in elementary or secondary education and Texas teacher certification. Only students who complete all requirements for the M.A. may be recommended for teacher certification. Generally, the prospective teacher participates in one education lab during each of the four undergraduate years.

Education 11

Teacher education lab experience is designed to acquaint the student with teaching as a profession and the formal program. The entry-level lab, Education 11, may be taken as early as the second semester of the freshman year. It is designed to (1) orient students to the five-year program, (2) introduce students to an investigation of teaching as a profession, and (3) assist students in examining their unique personal backgrounds for experiences that bear on effective teaching-learning behaviors.

To accomplish these ends, Education 11 students attend seminar meetings with their coordinator (a program faculty member) in which they discuss aspects of the program as presented in *The Latest Word,* an in-house publication that is the program handbook, and discuss all facets of the teaching profession (e.g., the impact of public education laws, minimum competency testing as a requirement for certification, availability of jobs, salaries, unionization, etc.). During this lab the students also observe teachers and students in a variety of public school classrooms and engage in microteaching to get a feel for the teaching act.

The students begin to assess their development of behavior patterns characteristic of effective teaching by writing an autobiography highlighting those experiences they feel are useful as starting points for the development of effective teaching. The autobiography is placed in the student's competency portfolio, which becomes the repository for the material generated by the student, faculty, and public school personnel as evidence of the student's development toward a professional career and teacher certification.

Education 12

Teacher education lab experience is also designed to provide the student with classroom experiences in a variety of capacities including teaching. Prospective teachers who successfully complete Education 11 take Education 12, a partial credit lab in the undergraduate sequence. Its major activities include (1) furthering the acquisition of a conceptual, theoretical base for effective teaching; (2) developing systems for observing and analyzing the teaching process; (3) applying skills learned in classrooms including the preparation and teaching of lessons; and (4) using the evaluation of the results of this lab to establish further goals.

During the first third of the term the students meet on campus in seminar sessions with a teacher program faculty member. The purpose of these meetings is to further the student's development of a conceptual/theoretical base for effective teaching through reading assignments, preparation of lesson plans, analysis of goals/objectives and learning activities.

The middle third of the term provides an opportunity for the students to engage in systematic observation in a variety of classrooms and schools. From their field notes the students prepare a written report analyzing the salient features.

In the final phase of the lab the students participate daily in an assigned class. In addition to continuing with some systematic observations, the students begin to enter more thoroughly into the teaching-learning process. The amount of actual teaching time depends to a great extent on the classroom teacher's perception of the student's confidence, competence, interest in children, and demonstration of initiative. Before completing Education 12 students are expected to prepare, present, and evaluate a teaching unit that is of two or more weeks' duration. While engaged in the field experience, Education 12 students meet in weekly, small-group seminars to discuss both positive experiences and problems encountered. In individual conferences the coordinators also share what they see going on as the result of on-site observations they have made of each student's teaching. The ongoing evaluation of each student by classroom supervising teachers also provides important information for these conferences.

As a concluding act, the Education 12 students finish the semester by evaluating their teaching performance in terms of those effective teaching behaviors successfully demonstrated and those that have yet to be developed.

Education 51

Advanced teacher education lab experience, with partial credit, is designed to permit the students to develop a personal philosophical and methodological foundation for their teaching. The prospective teacher who decides to continue in the program following Education 12 enrolls in Education 51, usually in the junior year. Education 51 is a campus-based activity that provides the students with the opportunity to (1) explore the commitment to teaching, (2) examine the purpose of education, and (3) articulate their philosophy of education.

Activities in Education 51 allow the students to examine and refine their system of beliefs about education. In addition, students critically examine a chosen area or areas of the public school curriculum and the variety of methodologies that may be used in teaching that portion of the curriculum. The faculty of the program believes that effective teachers must be able to articulate and defend their beliefs. Beliefs about teaching, however, must be tested in order to be authentic—tested not only through reading, discussion, and observation, but through actual practice. To accommodate this testing of beliefs students from the public schools are brought on campus to participate in a lab situation. Education 51 students are afforded freedom to experience and evaluate a variety of methodologies.

During Education 51 the prospective teacher is asked to complete the formal process of application for admission to the Austin Teacher Program and to begin the process of formal admission to the graduate year. A student's application for admission includes (1) official transcripts of all college work, (2) written recommendations from three Austin College faculty members, at least two of whom must be outside the education department, (3) evidence of satisfactory completion of the Pre-Professional Skills Test, and (4) a five-year degree plan on which are listed the courses the student intends to take to complete the master's degree. All of these materials are placed in the student's competency portfolio, which is then made available to the Teacher Education and Graduate Admissions Committee for consideration of admission to the Austin Teacher Program.

Education 52

Advanced teacher education lab experience is designed to provide the student with additional teaching competencies and information necessary for planning the graduate year. The final undergraduate lab, Education 52, usually taken in the senior year, is a term-long activity combining at least fifty hours of classroom teaching with a weekly on-campus seminar conducted by the lab coordinator. In Education 52 the student engages in a classroom teaching experience of greater depth than in the previous labs. This usually means that the student teaches one hour or one period per day for approximately ten weeks. Upon successful completion of Education 52 the student is awarded one academic credit (equal to four semester hours).

During the orientation to Education 52 in the first few weeks of the term, students and the coordinator read the contents of portfolios to determine specific areas of teaching behavior that need to be strengthened or further developed. Students may be in charge of instruction for an entire class early in their field experience but, once again, they must show their classroom supervising teacher that they are ready and willing to assume this responsibility and to discharge it effectively. During their teaching experience students are observed by the Education 52 coordinator and other faculty members and are also evaluated, in writing, by their classroom supervising teacher.

During Education 52 the student applies for admission to the graduate program. Requirements for application include (1) an updated transcript of all college work, (2) official score report on the Graduate Record Examination, and (3) data indicating that conditions placed on admission to the teacher program have been met.

In concluding the description of the undergraduate curriculum of the Austin Teacher Program, a few additional remarks are in order. First, members of the education faculty are well aware that the program demands a great deal of time and effort on the student's part for relatively little academic credit. They believe, though, that the undergraduate curriculum selects and cultivates students fully committed to excellence in teaching for entry into the graduate year. Second, Austin College shows its commitment to the teacher program by counting the coordination of an education lab as a teaching assignment equal to that of a full credit-bearing course.

Graduate Year

The graduate year of the program provides students with opportunities to acquire knowledge that undergirds the teaching profession and to build and refine teaching skills. In the graduate phase of the program, students must earn nine course credits for the M.A. and certification. Four course credits are earned through the completion of Education 598, Research and Synthesis in Education; Education 557 or 558, Elementary or Secondary School Curriculum; Education 556, Topics in Education; and an elective. Graduate students may take a maximum of two independent studies as part of the master's degree program. An independent study gives the students an opportunity to develop, with a faculty member's guidance, an individualized course unique to their needs. All graduate students are strongly encouraged to earn additional credits in subjects they will teach. Three course credits are earned with successful completion of the graduate teaching experience, a one-term, full-day assignment. Two graduate course credits are required outside of the Education Department. It is possible for some students to take more than two courses outside the department, depending upon their undergraduate program and special needs.

After careful review and discussion of supervising teachers' evaluations, lab coordinators' summaries, observation reports, academic performance, and other germane data contained in each portfolio, the education faculty recommends students for either an internship or graduate student teaching. For various reasons, those recommended for graduate student teaching need somewhat more guidance in the classroom during the early part of the graduate field experience, though the faculty considers them capable of completing the program in a satisfactory manner and becoming competent teachers. Graduate student teachers are placed in a supervising teacher's classroom but are given increasing responsibility until they are in charge of all planning, instruction, management, and evaluation. Interns are assigned a room and classes much as a first year teacher, though an assigned supervising teacher helps orient the interns and observes and advises them throughout the field experience. All interns and graduate student teachers, assigned to schools for 12–16 weeks, all day, meet weekly with faculty members on campus for seminars that focus on strategies for teaching.

The Students

Students are stimulated and encouraged to be assertive. They are discouraged from being passive people who are dependent on the faculty to tell them how to teach and are more concerned about grades and credits than becoming effective teachers.

Many students entering Lab 11 these days take the faculty seriously about becoming assertive learners almost immediately and proceed confidently and independently through to the M.A. Others enter Lab 11 expecting faculty to tell them how to be effective teachers. Faculty expect the latter, given time to grow in the undergraduate labs, gradually to shed that cloak of dependency and passivity and to emerge as self-starting, independent learners who have demonstrated effectiveness as classroom teachers by the end of the graduate year. Faculty treat students as partners in the learning process and, consequently, learn a great deal from them. Faculty expect graduates to be educational leaders of the future in their classrooms. Faculty remain in contact with every graduate of the program through the publication of a department newsletter, *Action,* which is published two times a year and through which assistance is asked in improving the program. A large number of the graduates are devoted respondents to these requests. Thus, years after completing the teacher program, many students remain partners with Austin College in the enterprise of preparing teachers for the twenty-first century.

The Faculty

Today, rather than being isolated from one another and interacting with students only in limited, formal ways, the faculty spend a great deal of the time communicating with one another and the students. In the place of a curriculum that in 1966 was "stale, routine, and subject-centered," the curriculum now is by its design in a constant state of upgrading. This continuously emerging curriculum endeavors to exploit the best that is being thought and said and done in teacher education and to spread this current wisdom throughout the program's every level.

AN EXAMINATION OF THE RESULTS

After a two-year period of experimentation the College in early 1970 institutionalized the Austin Teacher Program as a fully approved five-year program. The College's governing bodies gave wholehearted support to the concept that the program had earmarks of improving the quality of teacher education; thus, it was evident that the faculty outside the Education Department became enthusiastic, too, about offering a different approach to prepare teachers, one that strongly emphasized the liberal arts curriculum. The Texas Education Agency also recognized the Austin Teacher Program as a valid, effective, and acceptable alternative for the preparation of teachers in the state of Texas. Therefore, the new teacher-education program moved from an experimental program to a fully approved one for certifying teachers.

Listed below are some of the results of instituting a new and different program in teacher education.

1. One of the biggest achievements during the early institutionalization period was the ability of the faculty to become comfortable in a some-

what routine way with a program that required flexibility, individualization, ongoing evaluation, and change when evidence pointed to such a need. The program was not designed to be fixed or set in concrete but to be evolving. It was necessary, therefore, for the faculty to devote much time to in-service activities, utilizing assistance from a variety of resources including numerous consultants. As the institutionalization of the program became a reality, the establishment of unity among the faculty and staff in the department was essential for the new program to succeed. It was through the many conferences, retreats, consultations, and meetings that the faculty sustained each other during the initial risk-taking activities. Although most of the faculty members were able to adjust and cope quite well, there were a few who had great difficulty, and some faculty turnover each year was not unusual.

2. Students in college, especially those planning to become teachers, welcome a strong liberal arts background and the opportunity that is provided in their undergraduate as well as graduate years to include many liberal arts selections. Unfortunately, too many teacher certification programs today limit students in this regard due to the large number of education courses that are required. The fact that Austin College initiated noncredit and partial credit laboratories and a graduate year as requirements for teacher certification gave impetus to a strong liberal arts curriculum.

3. In order for students to know if they want to enter the teaching profession, they must have exposure early in their college life to the classroom teaching and learning environment. It is important that admission procedures to the teaching profession include ample opportunities for involvement in the day-to-day business of teaching so that students and their professors can intelligently decide if they are appropriately suited for the profession. Austin College's extensive laboratory programs in the public schools beginning at the freshman level are invaluable means of achieving such a goal.

4. It is essential that there be extensive cooperation and collaboration between colleges and public schools for the preparation of teachers. Austin College excelled in establishing ties and involvements with public school personnel in initiating and evaluating the teacher program as well as in the ongoing processes. Classroom teachers have assumed wider responsibility and leadership roles in the preparation of teachers at Austin College than would be true at most any other institution in the nation. Such cooperation and involvement have been highly praised by students as one of the highlights of their experiences in the program.

5. Regardless of some national trends and situations, teacher education has to be thought of as a profession. Consequently, the program to prepare teachers must be a professional one—not just a certification proce-

dure that is tacked on to other college requirements. Austin College moved to a graduate year, requiring a master's degree with the teaching certificate, thereby emphasizing the professionalism of a teaching career. Students had to be committed if they wanted a career in teaching. Students had to give more than the usual time and money, if they wanted an education leading to a teaching certificate. In order to build a legitimate profession, such expectations of dedication and commitment are vital. Students do respond positively to these kinds of expectations, as the Austin College experience shows.

6. There is a better way to prepare teachers than merely offering education courses in the traditional mold with much repetition of information, irrelevant data, and boring methodology. It is necessary to "practice what you teach" and to engage in a trusting relationship with students. Student respect for the profession increased immeasurably as relationships between faculty and students were enhanced.

7. There are faculty members who will work together as a team and demonstrate the importance of cooperation, sharing, and caring to prospective teachers. Faculty members *will* take opportunities to be student-centered, and they *will* spend the time needed in public schools working at all levels.

8. Students do want quality in their teacher education program, and they will spend extra time and money to get it. When Austin College went to the additional year and included a master's degree along with certification, students did not go elsewhere for their teacher certification programs. In fact, better students were attracted to the program. When noncredit and partial credit labs were required on top of the usual heavy load, and when a foreign language requirement for graduation was kept for teacher-education students but dropped for other students, there were no decreases in the number of students entering the program. There were, however, decreases in the number of incompetent students seeking teaching certificates as insurance policies for obtaining a teaching position. Thus it was discovered at Austin College that a quality program does not discourage quality students from entering the teaching profession. In fact, it has the opposite effect. There is evidence that students who enter the teacher program are above the national average concerning their SAT scores. Also these students score considerably higher in all areas of the State Pre-Professional Skills Test than the state average.

9. Faculty members *will* return to the public school classroom by either participating in exchange agreements, teaching part-time, substitute teaching, or engaging in demonstration teaching. One of the education faculty's older members exchanged for a semester with a third grade teacher in an open elementary school in a Dallas suburban school district; another faculty member spent one fall semester teaching part-time in a kindergarten

program; and another faculty member taught an English course in the local high school for one semester.

A SUMMARY

What has gone on before and what is taking place now in teacher education at Austin College must be carefully analyzed in light of the needs for the next five to ten years. An institution that does not continue to develop and constantly evaluate its program for teacher preparation, regardless of the pressures exerted by an accrediting agency, will soon find itself stagnant and ineffective. The problem today with too many teacher-education programs is that they fail to change when different approaches are mandated. Therefore, critics bring forth justified reports for the public to read labeling teacher-education programs as ineffective.

The Austin Teacher Program was developed and implemented in the late 1960s and 1970s when the critics were not as loud as they are today, yet their concerns were just as appropriate then as now. Why has it taken educators in most institutions so long to even talk about change? There is always the reluctance to pioneer. (See Baker 1984.)

Although Austin College was ahead of other institutions in the changes that took place over a decade ago and remains in that position even today, it must continue to forge ahead. Because Austin College is currently doing most if not all of the things critics say should be done in teacher education, it can not rest on its laurels. New advances must be made. New frontiers in teacher education must continue to be explored.

BIBLIOGRAPHY

Baker, T. "Extended Teacher Education Programs: A Survey of Attitudes in Texas." *The Journal of the Texas Association of Colleges for Teacher Education: Teacher Education & Practice* 1, no. 2(1984):43–50.

Benderson, A. "Teacher Competence." *Focus: Education Testing Service* 10(1982):6–21.

Combs, A. W. *The Professional Education of Teachers*. Boston: Allyn and Bacon, 1965.

Freeman, B. *Exploring New Frontiers in Teacher Education: The Austin Teacher Program*. Department of Education, Austin College, 1986.

Freeman, B., ed. *The Decade: A Review of the Austin Teacher Program*. Department of Education, Austin College, 1981.

Love, V., and B. Freeman. *The Austin Teacher Program: A Concept of Teacher Education*. Department of Education, Austin College, 1971.

Staff. *The Latest Word*. Department of Education, Austin College, 1985.

Steinacher, R. *The Five Year Non-traditional Austin Teacher Program: Preparing Teachers for the 21st Century*. Department of Education, Austin College, 1981.

3 | Subject-field Depth and Professional Preparation: New Hampshire's Teacher-education Program

MICHAEL D. ANDREW

SIGNIFICANT RESTRUCTURING OF TEACHER EDUCATION should take into consideration two guideposts. First, restructuring should be guided by a vision of what constitutes an outstanding teacher for tomorrow's schools. A vision of outstanding teachers for tomorrow's schools establishes the philosophical underpinning for program development. The second guidepost requires attention to the persistent criticisms of the procedures of traditional teacher preparation. A clear understanding of the criticisms of conventional teacher preparation suggests new procedures to try and old procedures to discard.

The Five-year Teacher-education Program at the University of New Hampshire in Durham began in 1974 with both a vision of the outstanding teacher and a somewhat radical array of procedures for preparing the desired teacher. Although the vision has undergone some transformation, it has guided teacher preparation efforts for twelve years. The procedures, while subject to continual modification, have proven themselves generally successful. They have been positively evaluated by students and faculty and have survived a rigorous process of continual appraisal.

THE VISION

The teacher we hoped to prepare for tomorrow's schools was described in the early 1970s as a "teacher-leader" (Andrew 1974), a person who was first

Michael D. Andrew is director of teacher education at the University of New Hampshire. Dr. Andrew was the initiator of the University's Five-year Teacher-education Program.

44

an expert in classroom instruction but who was also to grow into leadership roles in curriculum development, curriculum decision making, and improvement of instruction of peers and beginning teachers. The primary goal of the preservice preparation program was to prepare the potentially outstanding classroom teacher. To achieve this end certain assumptions were agreed upon about the nature of the ideal teacher. These assumptions can be divided into the necessary conditions for good teaching and the contributory conditions for good teaching.

Necessary Conditions

The necessary conditions are considered to be characteristics, knowledge, skills, and attitudes that are basic requirements for most good teachers. Many of these conditions are well established or the potential is evident in the candidate prior to professional training.

1. The ideal beginning teacher should have better than average academic skills.

2. The ideal beginning teacher should have a strong general education.

3. The ideal beginning teacher should have sufficient depth in a special subject field to give confidence, credibility, and the background for further graduate work or other career options if desired.

4. The ideal beginning teacher should provide evidence of teaching potential, commitment, and appropriate interpersonal skills for successful teaching. These skills have been defined to include the ability to communicate effectively with children and adults, good listening skills, sensitivity to the needs of others, and the ability to deal positively with children and adults.

We look upon these attributes as necessary although they are not sufficient conditions for the ideal teacher we hope to prepare. We have been guided in structuring our program to provide means for assessing these characteristics. First, we have set academic standards for admission that insure that we draw our students from the top half of the university's academic population. Second, we require a broad general education in line with that required for all other university graduates. Third, we require a subject-field major; and fourth, we include a clinical experience at the beginning of the program to determine adequate evidence of teaching potential, commitment, and appropriate interpersonal skills. Further, we defer admission to the final phase of the program until the student's senior year. This allows ample time to gather feedback on the necessary conditions of teaching from a variety of sources. Continued development of the necessary conditions is not excluded from the design of the professional sequence; indeed, we have developed elements of that sequence to refine and further develop the necessary conditions.

Contributory Conditions

The contributory conditions are those factors that will enhance teaching. They are the areas of knowledge, skills, and attitudes that are the central concerns of the professional program in teacher education.

1. The ideal beginning teacher should work from an understanding of children that emphasizes a knowledge of development and the best of our knowledge of ways of learning and related theories of teaching.

2. The ideal beginning teacher should have available a variety of proven teaching models and be assisted in the development of an educational philosophy and effective personal style of teaching. This condition is supported by our knowledge of the wide range of effective teaching methods, the documented value of flexibility in teaching style, and our vision of a teacher as one who has a clear sense of professional identity as well as effective teaching practices.

3. The ideal beginning teacher should have knowledge of the structure of public education and procedures for effecting change in that structure.

4. The ideal beginning teacher should have knowledge of the significant assumptions and philosophical points of view that underlie teaching and schooling and should have defined a personal philosophy of education.

Basic instructional components to achieve these goals have been developed as the major professional core of the five-year program.

THE PROCEDURAL GOALS

The means that were developed to prepare the ideal beginning teacher were designed to first match the vision described above while at the same time being mindful of feedback about traditional procedures in teacher preparation. This feedback has remained remarkably persistent. We have paid special attention to the following points:

1. The large number of required education courses in the typical undergraduate preparation program takes students away from gaining depth in the academic disciplines and from gaining a strong general education.

2. Many education courses appear to be irrelevant and/or trivial and are often viewed by students as redundant.

3. The best way to learn about teaching is from actual classroom experience plus examination of that experience with the help of skilled analysts and practitioners. There is usually too little of this experience in teacher-education programs.

4. Teacher educators and teacher-education programs remain too aloof from schools. There needs to be more of a partnership providing better programs and greater acceptance of the programs and their graduates.

From this framework of feedback about the traditional preparation of teachers and our vision of the ideal beginning teacher, the Five-year Teacher-education Program at the University of New Hampshire was developed.

MAJOR PROGRAM THEMES
Three major themes provide a framework that gives a unique identity to the University of New Hampshire's Five-year Teacher-education Program. These themes are as follows:

1. The centrality of philosophy of education for producing the ideal beginning teacher
2. The importance of a personalized and humanistic framework for preparing the ideal beginning teacher
3. The reliance on guided clinical experience as the vehicle to produce acceptable beginning teaching skills

Theme One: The Primacy of Philosophy
The teacher we envision is an instructional leader who will develop into a leader in school decision making. The essential decisions of the classroom teacher as well as the curriculum leader are value judgments that arise from a personal philosophy of education. Critical decisions in education reflect one's views on the nature of knowledge, the nature of the learners, the nature of effective teachers, and the proper goals of education.

While scientific inquiry may provide information to inform our choices in these areas, it provides neither singular nor conclusive guidance. To illustrate: in testing, should we favor the norm-referenced or the criterion-referenced approach? In viewing our students should we side with the behaviorists and assume that the student can be shaped in any desired direction, or should we take the side of the humanists who see the student as an autonomous, innately positive force with unique tendencies that influence what can be taught or learned? In a similar manner decisions on major educational issues outside the classroom must be reasoned from a philosophy of education or they will be dictated only by the weight of politics, expediency, or tradition. What balance should be struck in the curriculum among knowledge, skills, and processes? What is the proper place of values in the curriculum? What moral and behavioral standards should the school uphold? What should be the boundaries of religion in public education?

We seek to enable the beginning teacher to make reasoned, principled, moral judgments in the best interests of our children. To make such judgments requires analysis of competing positions and analysis of assumptions underlying these positions. These are the procedures and content that are critical in an active study of the philosophy of education.

To meet these goals a teacher-preparation program must have a strong philosophical dimension, one that involves both faculty and students in continuing moral discourse over the nature of education. We have sought to achieve this end by the way in which core professional courses are taught, by the direct requirement of work in philosophy of education, and by a persistent challenge for our students to develop their own style of teaching and a related personal philosophy of education. The continuing moral-philosophical discourse begins in the first course (Exploring Teaching) and continues through to the final requirement for a master's degree—the thesis statement and oral exam. This final experience, one of two available options, asks each student to develop, support, and defend a personal philosophy of education.

Theme Two: A Humanistic Framework

A humanistic framework involves the individualization and personalization of learning about teaching. A humanistic framework follows logically and necessarily from a belief in nurturing individual teaching style and personal philosophy and from a view of teachers as autonomous classroom decision makers and instructional leaders.

A humanistic framework requires the following:

1. Forthright and intensive individual counseling concerning the appropriateness of a career choice to teach

2. The opportunity for each student to engage in open dialogue with peers and instructors both during the intensity of clinical experience and in the more reflective climate of classroom discussions of education

3. The individualization of program content and sequence to best meet each student's developmental and practical priorities

4. Individualized placements in clinical settings to maximize the possibilities of obtaining a good fit between the student's personal style and philosophy and the clinical environment

The program has sought to provide for these humanistic needs through small classes, a preference for a seminar/discussion format in most course work, an early career decision-making course combining classroom experience with individual counseling, professional feedback, peer group discussions, journals and a formal self-assessment paper, education program advisors, frequent clinical supervision, and weekly small group (five to seven persons each) discussion sessions during clinical experience.

Theme Three:
Extended Clinical Experience to Develop Teaching Skill

We have heeded those researchers and commentators who have concluded that the best way to teach methods is in the context of real experience. Theory removed from personal practice is just that: theory unconnected to practice. While unexamined or unstructured experience may do little to direct growth to an effective teaching style, we remain convinced that extended, structured, and guided experience in real classrooms provides the best avenue to an effective teaching style. The process of growth to acceptable levels of confidence and performance is often slow. It is filled with predictable obstacles, growth phases, plateaus, and depressions. After twelve years of experience we are more committed than ever to the need for a semester of part-time introductory classroom experience for effective career decision making and a full year of supervised internship for the development of effective beginning teaching skills. The use of this extensive period of experience must be carefully planned and monitored. Weekly contact of university supervisors through seminars and individual conferences seems most beneficial. Even more critical is the role of the classroom teacher. This person must be committed to helping the novice develop an effective personal teaching style. This person must also have considerable skill in structuring learning experiences and in clinical supervision.

PROGRAM STRUCTURE

The General Education Requirement

Students enrolled in the five-year teacher-preparation program must complete a four-year baccalaureate program in one of the several schools or colleges of the university. Each school or college has its own degree requirements; however, all candidates for the bachelor's degree must obtain a passing grade in a minimum of 128 credits, must maintain a cumulative grade point average of 2.00 on a 4.00 scale and must successfully complete the following general education requirements:

1. One course in writing skills (must be taken during the student's first year)

2. One course in quantitative reasoning (must be taken during the student's first year)

3. Three courses in biological science, physical science, or technology, with no more than two courses in one area

4. One course in historical perspectives

5. One course in foreign culture

6. One course in fine arts

7. Two courses in social science or philosophical perspectives

8. One course in works of literature and ideas

Major Field Preparation

All candidates in the five-year program must complete a major outside of education. For secondary candidates this major must be in the area in which teaching certification is sought. For candidates seeking certification for elementary teaching, any subject-field major may be acceptable although students are advised to pursue majors in the academic areas of the elementary school curriculum or in areas dealing with human learning and development.

The requirement of an academic major for elementary teaching candidates was a radical departure from conventional teacher preparation. This change came about for several reasons. First, the elementary education major was filled with many curriculum and methods courses that were often criticized by students and graduates as irrelevant to the realities of classroom experience. Furthermore, these courses were often redundant, the subject matter was criticized as being trivial, and teaching methods were sometimes contradictory to methods suggested for students. Since the courses were university-based, they were generally taught by college professors who had long been absent from public school classrooms.

The assumption was made and substantiated by much of the literature on methods instruction that learning the techniques of teaching was best done in the reality of classrooms. Thus by extending the practicum to a full year of internship with more intensive supervision, the job could be better done. This approach left fewer curriculum and methods courses at the undergraduate level and opened the possibility of a subject-field major.

Many advantages of the subject-field major for elementary teachers have become apparent. The first is that this approach seems to have been partly responsible for attracting more academically able students into elementary teaching. Research evidence shows that love of a subject area is a major reason for attracting students to teaching. Our own research shows that while love of subject is a less important factor for elementary teachers than for secondary teachers, subject-matter content is still a major reason drawing academically able students toward elementary teaching (Andrew 1983). The necessity of pursuing a professionally oriented major in education seems to have dissuaded many good students from preparing to teach.

Perhaps, too, the absence of an education major dissuaded some candidates from pursuing teacher preparation. Nonetheless, the long-term result has been that elementary candidates in the five-year program are more academically able.

Second, the major in education carries a nationwide stereotype—whether warranted or not—of being an easy major. This image in itself dissuades many good students from preparing to teach.

Third, the education major provided students with limited career options. A major in English, science, math, or history is appropriate for many career paths or advanced graduate work. A major in education seems to limit one's options to teaching. The possibility of a variety of career options has remained very appealing to potential teachers.

Finally, the subject-matter major gives students depth in an area of personal interest. This directly or indirectly enhances teaching and gives the student a strong academic self-concept.

The Professional Preparation Program

PHASE ONE: EXPLORING TEACHING. During the student's undergraduate work the initial phase of the teacher-preparation program begins with early experience in the schools where students work as aides or teaching assistants (Exploring Teaching). Generally students take this course as sophomores. This initial phase provides students with an opportunity to explore various kinds of teaching tasks, participating in at least sixty-five hours of instructional activities with experienced teachers in the schools. The students also attend a weekly seminar that helps them make more realistic decisions about teaching as a career.

The fieldwork emphasis is on participation rather than observation. Students are encouraged to take on teaching tasks immediately. Seminars, which are limited to enrollments of fifteen students and taught by full-time faculty, focus on topics such as the authority and modeling roles of teachers, community expectations placed on teachers, living on a teacher's salary, and the classroom teacher's role in helping children with special needs. Classroom teachers, school administrators, and other school personnel provide important input in field-based seminars. Student performance in Phase One weighs heavily in later selection procedures.

PHASE TWO: PROFESSIONAL COURSE WORK. The second phase of the program normally begins in the junior year and requires a minimum of four credits to be completed in each of four areas of study: educational structure and change, human development and learning, alternative teaching models, and alternative perspectives on the nature of education. A detailed rationale for the four major areas of preservice professional courses is developed in *Teacher Leadership: A Model for Change* (Andrew 1974). A variety of minicourses, some including experiences in local schools, are available in these required areas.

Working with their advisors, students develop highly individualized programs. Credits in these four areas may be taken at either the undergraduate or graduate level. This allows students to have greater flexibility in fulfilling the requirements of their major department.

Candidates for elementary teaching must complete two additional courses in mathematics, one of which focuses on the teaching of mathematics to children and another that is a clinically oriented course in fundamentals of reading instruction. These may also be taken at the undergraduate or graduate level.

Allowing a wide range of student choice in professional courses causes some concern that students will miss some essential content. The justification for individual programming rests on four assumptions. First, students preparing to teach have different perceived needs and interests at different stages of development. Giving choices within important areas increases the chance that students will see their education course work as relevant.

Second, one cannot expect preservice teachers to have dealt with everything they will need to know to be competent professionals. There are many areas of knowledge pertinent to becoming a good teacher. There is not time to do it all nor is there agreement on which knowledge is most critical. Much of the specialized preparation of teachers should be *expected* to take place during internship and in later years as in-service learning.

There is a tendency to expect beginning teachers to have every bit of specialized preparation that is peculiar to each specific job environment or that is a favorite of a particular administrator, education official, or professor. This unreasonable demand on preservice preparation is central to the dilemma facing teacher education today: the inability to balance strong academic preparation, subject-field depth, and general education with adequate initial professional preparation.

We cannot do it all. Even in a five-year framework that usually includes two summers of course work beyond five academic years, we are increasingly constrained by a continuing proliferation of specific professional requirements forced on us by national and state agencies. We are also continually faced with professors who want the number of credits of their courses to increase or their course to be required.

Third, in-depth study of a limited topic is often the best way to teach general skills, attitudes, and concepts. Most of our options within the four professional areas are in-depth studies of particular topics instead of broad, introductory coverage courses. In general, we believe this approach to education is more effective in three ways: it gains student involvement; provides substantive, in-depth learning; and thereby teaches the general skills and attitudes we feel are of primary importance. For example, students electing a two-credit course in alternative perspectives on the nature of education entitled "Controversial Issues in Education" select current educational issues of concern to them, such as the exclusion of sex education in a local school, creationism and evolution in the curriculum, or school prayer. Students are required to do extensive library research on their topics (in groups) and to prepare arguments on all major points of view on the issue while being certain that the interests of all relevant parties are considered. The professor oversees and critiques the process and provides instruction on how to construct and assess arguments for various positions. Care is taken that students make connections between social and legal contexts and the educational issue at hand. Surely there are many other important controversial educational issues emerging today. Surely there will be many new ones in the future. Our concern is not which specific content students cover but rather that they learn the skills and attitudes of thorough analysis, investigation of all relevant points of view, and synthesis of a well-formed, personal position on educational issues.

Fourth, the use of a variety of subject-matter options under each professional area allows the best use of faculty interests and strengths. Most teacher-education faculty are able to identify subtopics within the four general professional areas that represent their current research interests and scholarly backgrounds. This keeps faculty enthusiasm for teaching in these basic areas high and helps to provide better teaching. It is also clear that this model produces a strong correlation between official course descriptions and actual course content. This situation seldom applies with broad survey courses.

The success of the multioption approach to professional course work is perhaps reflected in the consistently high student evaluations of these courses. A study in 1982–83 revealed that professional course instructors in teacher education at the University of New Hampshire received an average rating from students of 4.55 on a 5-point scale (5 being the highest rating). This course evaluation is done for all instructors at the university. The professional course instruction in education as a whole ranked on a par with the best teaching at the university as perceived by students.

Nonetheless, the issue of individualized programs in teacher education is challenged by a persistent orthodoxy that holds that college educators (or state agencies) can and must determine what knowledge, skills, and attitudes all beginning teachers need and demand that all students study and master these requirements. Many feel that these requirements must also be learned in a fixed sequence. While educators are often quick to champion personalization and individualization of instruction for children in schools or attention to developmental needs, many still are reluctant to put such practices into effect in teacher education. To some college professors and administrators the belief in requiring a standard body of knowledge is augmented by the fact that required courses insure predictable class enrollments. A variety of options leads to student selection, and certain courses or certain professors may be avoided.

There is also an enduring unwillingness to consider or admit the tentativeness and superficiality that exists in many areas of educational knowledge. Likewise, there is a tendency to ignore evidence supporting both the diversity of effective teaching styles, the appropriateness of different styles for differing learners, and the pluralistic nature of American public and private education, which offers varied school environments with varied educational objectives. It is equally difficult for some to believe that desirable skills and critical knowledge may best be learned through in-service education as a teacher develops and is ready and willing to tackle new challenges.

PHASE THREE: INTERNSHIP AND GRADUATE STUDIES. The final phase of the preservice teacher-education program consists of a year-long, postbaccalaureate internship as well as graduate study related to one's chosen area or level of teaching. Students usually spend one full academic year plus one or two summers completing Phase Three.

Internship. The year-long internship is the centerpiece of the five-year program. The internship provides the principal instruction in teaching methods. A full year of closely supervised internship offers the opportunity to integrate methods instruction with actual classroom experiences. This format for instruction in methodology represents a firm and central commitment to the five-year program. During the internship, methods instruction is the focus of the regular review of interns' lessons and their curricular plans by cooperating teachers and university supervisors. Methodology is the usual emphasis of biweekly supervisory conferences following observation of one or more class periods of teaching. At least one of these conferences is combined with analysis of a videotape of the intern's teaching.

Methodology is also the focus of some of the weekly intern seminars. In these seminars a university supervisor and five or six interns discuss common concerns, share successes, and suggest procedures for dealing with individual problems. Seminars are occasionally brought together for large-group meetings. An initial large-group meeting includes cooperating teachers. A later group meeting focuses on development of resumes and on other matters relative to job seeking.

The success of the internship experience is closely tied to site selection. Placement is the result of a personalized process that begins in semester one of the senior year. The director of field experiences meets with each prospective intern and discusses placement possibilities, taking into account the intern's strengths, weaknesses, needs, and preferences. Several students will usually visit a particular intern site and placement decisions are much like hiring decisions. A successful placement requires mutual acceptance and concludes with a meeting of intern and cooperating teacher. A preliminary working agreement is then discussed. The school principal and university director of field experiences often attend this meeting.

Second in importance to an appropriate intern site is the intense nature of university support and instruction provided to interns. Supervision in the University of New Hampshire five-year program has evolved to a point that far exceeds the conventional model of autonomous university supervisors who make one to three visits during student teaching. Five-year program supervisors have relatively small teaching loads. Supervision of five or six interns is the equivalent of a one-course teaching assignment. Supervisors are required to visit each intern a minimum of twelve times. The norm is a biweekly visit.

Supervisors meet weekly as a faculty subgroup. During these meetings, individual intern and common supervisory problems are discussed. Plans are coordinated for the weekly intern seminars, and large-group meetings or group activities are developed. These meetings are chaired by the director of field experiences.

The Graduate Concentration. The graduate program requires a twelve-credit concentration and electives from a variety of university programs. Concentrations are offered in many areas of study. Preservice secondary teachers often choose concentrations in their major field. A number of university departments are giving attention to selection of specific graduate courses most appropriate for each prospective teacher. Students pursuing concentrations in their subject area usually elect the master of arts in teaching degree, although a few work toward a master's degree in the subject field of study.

Several concentrations are available in the seven graduate programs of the Department of Education. The most popular concentrations are in reading/writing, special education, and early childhood education. Students choosing these concentrations work toward a master's degree in education.

A minimum of thirty credit hours of graduate work plus a final project or thesis are required for the master's degree. A typical program includes the twelve-credit internship, a twelve-credit graduate specialization, six credits of electives, and development of a set of thesis statements defended in an oral exam. Students may obtain teacher certification before completing all requirements for the master's degree. About half complete the master's degree and certification requirements before entering teaching.

Standards and Admissions Procedures

There is open admission to Phase One, "Exploring Teaching." Initial screening is done at the end of Phase One with school personnel, university instructors, and students each having a vote on the student's continuation to Phase Two. Students doing poorly in "Exploring Teaching," based on the judgment of instructors and cooperating teachers, are counseled to seek alternative career plans. This counseling is usually persuasive. If it is not and the student wishes to go on, he or she may be granted a second "Exploring Teaching" opportunity or may be dismissed from the program. The attrition rate after Phase One is approximately 30 percent.

Once in Phase Two juniors, seniors, or graduate students may choose from the four professional course areas. In consultation with an advisor students may choose the course sequence and timetable that best fits their needs and interests. The typical student completes half of the required professional course work as an undergraduate and half at the graduate level.

The second screening process takes place in the year prior to internship (early in the senior year). Considerable evidence is taken into account. The student must apply to the Graduate School and take the Graduate Record Examination. A teacher-education committee then examines transcripts, grade point average, GRE scores, recommendations, and evidence from education department instructors plus the folder of papers and recommendations from "Exploring Teaching."

The minimum for a regular graduate school admission recommendation consists of the following:

1. GPA - 2.75 (on a 4.0 scale)
2. GRE - Sum of raw scores on the verbal and quantitative measures to be 900 or above
3. Three strongly supportive letters of recommendation
4. An undergraduate preparation appropriate for the intended area of certification
5. A positive recommendation from the "Exploring Teaching" experience

The importance of direct evidence of teaching potential is clear from the following excerpt of the Teacher Education Admissions Policy:

> The Teacher Education faculty at the University of New Hampshire believes that direct evidence of teaching potential and evidence of appropriate interpersonal skills for successful teaching are essential criteria for admission to the final stages of the UNH Teacher Education Program. Teaching potential is normally apparent by performance in Education 500. Thus, the Education 500 recommendations by the cooperating teachers in the school and by University faculty are considered seriously in all admissions decisions. We also believe that successful teachers must be able to communicate effectively with children and adults, have good listening skills, be sensitive to the needs of others, and be able to deal positively with children and adults. This collection of interpersonal skills is taken into account in admissions decisions. Evidence of this is gathered from Education 500, from contacts of University faculty with students, and from letters of recommendation required for admission to the five year program.

The average academic record of admitted students has been quite consistent over the past ten years. This information is repeatedly made known to students and most who are not close to this average do not apply.

CHARACTERISTICS OF STUDENTS

Enrollments

Switching from a four-year teacher-education program to a five-year teacher-education program requiring admission to graduate school undoubtedly affects enrollment. In 1973 we predicted a 50 percent drop in enrollment. Our initial enrollment drop was nearly 40 percent. Of course, many unanticipated factors have influenced the number of students seeking careers in teaching over the past twelve years, so it is difficult to ascertain the impact of the move to the five-year program.

One interesting comparison is to look at the change in numbers of five-year graduates compared to the number of four-year teacher-education graduates at the University of New Hampshire. Four-year options have existed in the following areas: music, home economics, math, physical education, and occupational education. Enrollment trends are seen in Figure 3.1.

A clear and surprising trend is the steady increase in numbers of five-

Fig. 3.1. Enrollment trends

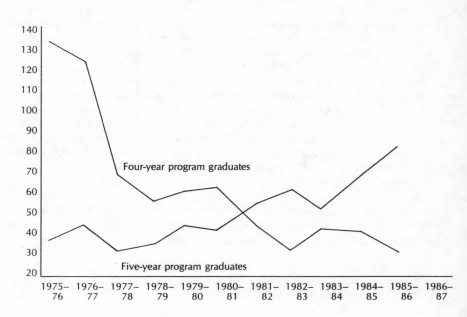

year graduates during a period of national decline in teacher-education program enrollments generally. Until 1983 this trend proceeded without benefit of any direct recruitment efforts. The trend seems to be attributable in part to the strong appeal of a program with unusually high standards and a reputation for high-quality instruction.

Evaluating the Five-year Program

ACADEMIC CHARACTERISTICS. The academic characteristics of students in the five-year program is one of the strongest indications of program success. Students admitted to the final phase of the program over the past twelve years have maintained an undergraduate grade point average of about 3.1 on a 4.0 scale. There has been little year-to-year variation. (See Table 3.1.) This compares to a university grade point average of approximately 2.8 for graduating seniors (a 2.0 is required for graduation), and a graduate school admissions grade point average of 3.1 for all graduate programs of the university.

Table 3.1.　Academic characteristics of five-year students, UNH Teacher-education program

Year	Number	GPA	GRE score verbal	GRE score quanti- tative	Combined GRE
1978	69	2.99	511	523	1034
1979	55	3.01	518	515	1033
1980	45	3.02	531	509	1040
1981	57	3.01	493	513	1006
1982	37	3.05	501	530	1031
1983	57	3.01	530	551	1081
1984	65	3.05	527	522	1049
1985	83	3.30	524	542	1066
Average		3.07	517	526	1043

During the past eight-year period the Graduate Record Examination scores of all students admitted to Phase Three of the five-year program have averaged 517 on the verbal aptitude test and 526 on the quantitative aptitude test. Combined verbal and quantitative scores averaged 1043. Scores on the GRE are higher for the past two years than ever before (Table 3.1). Approximately 40 percent of those admitted to the five-year programs have been honors students as undergraduates.

The academic quality of students attracted to the five-year program is illustrated by examining the profile of the top 40 percent of the students admitted during 1983 and 1984. Forty-seven students in this sample had an average grade point average of 3.38. The average verbal score on the Graduate Record Examination was 591. The average quantitative score was 598. The combined average was 1189. Twenty-four members of this group graduated *cum laude*. Eleven graduated *magna cum laude*. Four graduated *summa cum laude*. Seven were elected to Phi Beta Kappa. Eleven were selected to other national societies honoring academic achievement.

Clearly the academic characteristics of students in the UNH Five-year Teacher-education Program are outstanding. Not only do they represent a group academically far superior to prospective teachers described in national summaries, they also represent significantly better than average senior students at the University of New Hampshire and are comparable to all graduate students at that institution.

Students in the program at UNH are significantly different academically from those described as representative of the national teacher talent pool. Do they differ in other ways as well? The evidence is less clear but there are some unusual facts that seem to indicate significant differences.

THE NUMBER WHO TAKE TEACHING JOBS. One characteristic distinguishing UNH program graduates is their high job-securing rate. Over 90 percent of five-year program graduates have obtained jobs in their first year after program completion. This figure has remained consistent (85–93 percent) over the twelve-year history of the program. The record has held during a period of great oversupply of teachers. Two factors seem to explain this high job success rate. The first is superior qualifications for competition in the marketplace (a strong subject-matter background and general education, outstanding academic credentials, extended internship experience).

The second is great commitment to a career in teaching. Students who select the Five-year Teacher-education Program at UNH have a strong desire to teach. They persist in spite of high academic standards, an additional year (or more) of higher education, ever-escalating costs, plus the sometimes gloomy reports of job prospects, job status, and poor pay.

SUMMARY

Current Status of the Program

The guiding vision of the ideal teacher seems to have been reasonably achieved as a result of twelve years of evolution of the University of New

Hampshire's Five-year Teacher-education Program. The necessary conditions for the ideal teacher have been largely guaranteed by admissions standards. Where these necessary conditions have not been achieved has most often been in cases where we have failed to hold to our own standards. Teachers who have better than average academic skills do perform better. Those we admit who are below average are most often the students who have difficulty in the classroom with effective communication with both students and adults. Likewise, those students we admit with weak recommendations regarding teaching potential, as evidenced in the first clinical experience, are most often the students who have difficulty mastering teaching skills during internship.

The contributory conditions for the ideal teacher, those aspects of the ideal teacher which we have intended to develop in our program, are being achieved at a satisfactory level. We continue to make modifications to improve our program. At the present time we have identified several areas of concern that offer significant challenges for program improvement. The most pressing concerns are as follows:

1. Financial Support for Students in the Fifth Year. Until the salary for teachers reaches levels competitive with other professions requiring similar education, there is a need to help promising and needy students with the financial burden of an extra year of college preparation. We continue to work to increase paid internships and scholarship support.

2. Specialized Training and Subsequent Rewards for Cooperating Teachers Who Work with Interns. The significance of the cooperating teacher in a year-long internship cannot be overemphasized. We find that committed cooperating teachers gain greatly from courses, workshops, and ongoing seminars dealing with the mentoring/coaching role, the integration of methods instruction into the intern's experience, and the techniques of clinical supervision. It is clear that teachers who gain this extra preparation should be adequately compensated for their significant role. We are working to expand both the preparation and rewarding of cooperating teachers.

Applicability to Other Institutions

We can predict with confidence that experienced teachers and school administrators will support changes similar to those instituted at the University of New Hampshire. It is equally clear that many leaders in teacher education and in education in general are moving to support changes very similar to those made at UNH (Boyer 1983; Goodlad 1984; National Commission for Excellence in Teacher Education 1985; The Holmes Group 1986; Carnegie Commission 1986). Moreover, it is certain from our experience that teacher educators, once involved in an extended program such as that described above, will be enthusiastic in their support of it.

While institutions with large teacher-education programs can expect a possible initial decline in enrollments with changes similar to those described herein, our experience shows that an increase in admissions standards will gradually have very positive effects. Outstanding students who once turned away from teacher education will be attracted to more rigorous programs. They will also be attracted to programs that offer subject-field majors, individualized programs, and extended clinical experience.

The time seems optimal for change. A resurgence of student interest in teaching and a national improvement in teacher salaries foretells a period of better supply and demand for prospective teachers. Public leaders are encouraging radical reform of teacher education. The leadership for such change should come from within the profession. There may be no better time than now to make significant improvements in teacher education.

BIBLIOGRAPHY

Andrew, M. D. "The Characteristics of Students in a Five Year Teacher Education Program." *Journal of Teacher Education* 34, no. 1(1983):20–23.

———. *Teacher Leadership: A Model for Change.* Washington, D.C.: Association of Teacher Educators, 1974.

Boyer, E. L. *High School: A Report on Secondary Education in America.* New York: Harper and Row, 1983.

Carnegie Commission on Education and the Economy. *Report of the Task Force on Teaching as a Profession.* New York: The Carnegie Foundation, 1986.

Goodlad, J. I. *A Place Called School: Prospects for the Future.* New York: McGraw Hill Book Company, 1984.

The Holmes Group. *Tomorrow's Teachers.* East Lansing, Mich.: The Holmes Group, Inc., 1986.

National Commission for Excellence in Teacher Education. *A Call for Change in Teacher Education.* Washington, D.C.: American Association of Colleges for Teacher Education, 1985.

4

Improving Mentor Teacher Seminars: Feminist Theory and Practice at Lewis and Clark College

MARY KAY TETREAULT

JANE BRAUNGER

NOVEMBER 19, 1987: A select group of experienced high school teachers has gathered at Lewis and Clark College, Portland, Oregon. They are mentor teachers in a new master of arts in teaching program, here to discuss a draft of this essay about the program. Since September their interns, students in the program, have been working with them in the schools. Since the previous June the mentors have been meeting monthly with us to discuss readings chosen to spark reflection on important current issues in education.[1]

The paper proved to be a catalyst for releasing a torrent of ideas and feelings about the seminars. In fact the section about the seminars provoked the most discussion. We had a sense of unease about how the seminars were going; this session threw into sharp relief the difference between mentors' expectations for the seminars and the reality. They had expected the interns to be involved in at least some of the seminars. "We wanted," said one, "to share our journey as teachers with them." Without the interns in attendance and with agenda and readings chosen by us, most of the mentors said the seminars had become "too theoretical."

One purpose of the seminars was to help the mentors view their teaching experience as a source of instruction for the interns. Ironically, the seminars seemed to have separated the mentors from their own best source of knowledge—their experience. We were puzzled. Why should this conflict

Mary Kay Tetreault is dean of the School of Human Development and Community Service at California State University, Fullerton. Jane Braunger is a language arts specialist in the Department of Curriculum, Portland, Oregon, Public Schools.

between theory and practice have arisen? One mentor teacher offered a stunningly simple explanation, "We're not used to honestly being asked what we know, what we think. We're used to being told what to do." To the extent that assigned readings "told them what to do," the mentors seemed to lose trust that we valued their thoughts and experience.

Had our setting the agenda for the seminars created a problem? The answer was a resounding yes! Other mentors spoke of feeling as if they were in training sessions in the seminars. One noted that it was like being in a class, so graduate credit seemed more appropriate than a stipend. (A small grant from the Templeton Foundation supported program planning and mentor teacher seminars.) Additional comments reflected the mentors' general response to an all too familiar situation for them as teachers, their lack of power in a group. They spoke of feeling some competition, of monitoring their seminar contributions, especially in the summer months before interns were matched with mentors. Not knowing exactly what we wanted from the seminars, a number assumed we were using the discussions to assess them as potential mentors.

How were we to make sense of the rich but troubling perceptions we had just heard? In the aftermath of that seminar our feelings ranged from confusion and puzzlement to disappointment and anger.

In this chapter, we will demonstrate how this seminar provided the occasion for reexamining certain components of our innovative program of teacher preparation. Lewis and Clark's Master of Arts in Teaching Program prepares prospective high school social studies and language arts teachers through a fifteen-month campus- and field-based course of study. From the beginning the program planners saw the importance of a community of educators for the preparation as well as the support of preservice teachers through their induction into the schools. Seminars were designed to enlist mentors in our common enterprise of educating teachers.

This paper focuses on the mentor teacher seminars. Admittedly, the seminars are but one slice of the program. However, it took the wrenching experience of the seminar described above to initiate this critique of the program. The ensuing analysis of the seminars led us to see that the lens of feminist theory was even more illuminating in reflecting on the program than it had been in its planning. Once involved in this process we came to see the need for a reconceptualization of programs in teacher education in light of feminist theory.

The scholarship on women has the potential for a major rethinking of teacher education because it treats gender as a problematic area for study rather than as part of the natural order of things. This recognition, in turn, forces us to rethink our educational purposes, the profession of education, students, the curricula, and pedagogy. But as many scholars have documented, the process is slow-going and it is common initially to add women and gender without a fundamental rethinking of the field or discipline (Tetreault 1985; DuBois et al. 1985).

A couple of examples will illustrate our point. When feminist educators became aware of the need for changes in females' education, we called for an end to sexist policies and practices in education. We were not yet conscious of the extent to which we defined our educational purposes as the education of males for political, economic, legal, social, and cultural activities in the public sphere. This limitation of educational purposes to the public or productive processes of society went unchallenged until Jane Roland Martin called for a fundamental redefinition. She pointed out that this traditional definition worked to the detriment of education for the private or reproductive processes of society—the bearing and rearing of children to maturity; the related activities of keeping house, managing a household, and serving the needs and purposes of family members and engaging in the emotional work that is necessary to human relationships. Martin called for more than educational equity for our daughters; she challenged us to redefine our educational purposes for all students by integrating the productive and reproductive processes of society, liberal and vocational education, rationality and connection, and self and others (Martin 1981, 1982).

When feminist teachers and administrators first began thinking about gender issues in their profession, they noted that teaching is a profession where 85 percent of the teachers are women but an even greater number of the administrators are male. The emphasis was on gaining access for women into careers in administration rather than exploring the extent to which the profession is gendered. Later, scholars began to probe gender as a relevant category in the profession and to call for a feminist deconstruction and reconstruction of the profession that would develop a more critical stance (Lather 1986).

Our analysis of this program from the perspective of feminist theory proved to be a way of making sense of our initial confusion and disappointment about the seminars. But more importantly, it helped us to see that we, like others engaged in early efforts in a field or discipline, added gender to our program and did not engage in a fundamental rethinking of teacher education from the perspective of gender. Nonetheless, this reflection on the mentor teacher seminars and the larger program of which they are a part is offered in the spirit of enabling others to build on our insights to plan and implement teacher-education programs congruent with feminist theory.

THE MENTOR TEACHER SEMINARS

Within the context of collaborative teacher preparation, we designed a twenty-hour series of seminars to give us and the mentors a fuller understanding of issues in education: the purposes of education; the complexities of teaching and learning processes; the importance of incorporating a gender-balanced, multicultural perspective in courses; and the richness of seeing similarities and differences among adolescents. We had a practical, short-range agenda as well. We wanted the mentors' reactions to our professional education curriculum. Did they think our curriculum was on track? We hoped they would point out concepts we had overlooked, and content and methodologies missing from both the field-based and on-campus components of the program.

At the same time we wanted to provide mentor teachers with a community of their own, a place where they could grow as reflective practitioners. The seminars were not only to support their work with the interns, but also to meet their expressed need for intellectual stimulation. We were part of this community, too, and looked to seminar discussions on teaching, learning, and growing as professionals to expand our vision of excellence in teaching.

We organized three mentor-teacher seminars that first summer around the professional education curriculum the student interns were studying: purposes of schooling, ethnographic research methods, adolescent development, curriculum theory, instructional models, and research and instruction in the content areas. We sent the mentors appropriate readings and course proposals in advance. (Readings included Martin 1985, Lipsitz 1981, Tetreault 1985, Rudduck and Hopkins 1985, Hyman 1976, Langer 1984, and Eisner 1982.) Their response to the readings in the seminars was halting, and to the proposals, nonexistent. Although we all wrote to focus our thoughts at the beginning of each session, a number of the teachers chose to remain silent. Those who did participate in discussion tended to use a point from the reading as a channel into talking about their own teaching. But the comments seemed restricted to examples of good or bad practices. There was little discussion of the "whys" behind these "hows": the theoretical positions that were sources of the teachers' educational philosophy. Without exploration of influential experiences and insights, the group discussion remained pragmatic.

The idea that as a group we could come to a fuller understanding of issues in education than we could as individuals did not emerge in these sessions. Rather, the teachers seemed to stay in place, somewhat isolated from each other. While individuals responded to each other's comments, they seldom elaborated on others' thoughts through articulating their own. In a way the discussions were like taking roll: all present and accounted for as shown by individual comments. Everyone seemed comfortable enough, but the group lacked a sense of cohesiveness.

The first two fall term seminars focused on collaboration in teaching and supervising. In September we asked mentors to reflect in writing and share their experience of work with student teachers, then to brainstorm about working in this program with an intern for a full year. The teachers described the opportunities they saw. Interns could collaborate in observation, planning, and evaluation of instruction; they could become members of the class community by participating in discussions and facilitating small-group work. Mentors could take more time introducing interns to issues in classroom organization and management, supporting interns' learning through analysis of their own classroom experience. Mentors could also share professional resources with interns, introducing them to the school and district support network. One teacher saw the extended classroom time as an opportunity to help interns make the transition from liberal arts major to high school teacher. He noted ruefully that many new teachers expect to teach only what they have studied in their discipline. The full year's internship offered support for important risk taking in learning and teaching new material. Another mentor suggested a dialogue journal between mentor and teacher as a way of chronicling and analyzing this experiential learning. Behind this range of ideas for collaborative teaching we could see the flexibility of expert teachers. They planned to provide for the interns' needs, for autonomy as well as for support in the classroom. Still, the majority of comments seemed directed at us; group members seldom expanded on others' ideas. We wondered if the mentors felt like students in a required class.

Then during an October session, after a guest presentation on supervision, we were given a clue. One teacher, silent for the first hour of the session, expressed annoyance with what he perceived as our intent in the session. Were we suggesting that excellent teachers needed instruction in supervisory format, that is, the value of holistic responses to teaching over checklists? Quite an animated discussion ensued. One mentor recounted how he invited the intern to observe and critique his teaching. Taking that risk, opening himself to scrutiny is important, he felt, to prepare the intern for receiving similar evaluation from him. Another mentor suggested analyzing the dialogue journals as part of interns' coursework in curriculum and instruction.

Still, the initiating remark pointed at unresolved conflict about these seminars. Were we convening the mentors for instruction in working with interns? Were we suggesting that, in fact, they weren't excellent teachers? This teacher's remark seemed to pose the question.

The ideal climate for the seminars would invite participation. We wanted the group members to encourage each other, planning and reflecting on creative working and learning relationships with the interns. Instead, at this point, we seemed to have some cooperative students responding to discussion topics but not feeling much ownership for the group or its process. And we had some nonparticipants, either by their silence or their absence. As a model for collaborative learning, our seminars fell short.

To the relief of the mentors the draft of this essay named the problem of the stuck seminars. Before the November meeting we'd had a general sense of the seminars' shortcomings. In analyzing that session we were struck by a fundamental omission on our part: we had never asked these teachers what they needed to know to be mentors. We had never asked ourselves how the knowledge of mentors differs from that of teachers. Instead, we concentrated on mentors' response to program components and their ideas for meeting the interns' needs. In consequence, our seminars failed to address the basic need of the mentors themselves. The mentors helped us to see related faults of the seminars: a lack of attention to community building in the seminar design; little consensus building on the purpose of the seminars; and failure to validate mentors' experience and ideas within the seminars, and by extension, within the program.

This question of what knowledge is valuable and who decides became our wedge into a wider feminist critique of teacher preparation. We now saw the importance of acknowledging issues of power and domination, exposing the profession as gendered, and reconceptualizing pedagogy. Ultimately, we believe, such analysis will transform teacher education.

ISSUES OF POWER AND DOMINATION

Critics have pointed out how the profession of teaching has been dominated by administrators and academics (Lortie 1977). Feminist theorists are contributing to our understanding of relations of domination and subordination, particularly the tradition of allowing some perspectives to dominate while others are ruled out, of creating the world from one point of view (Miller 1976; MacKinnon 1982). It was only after reflecting on one of the mentors' frank insights about their situation ("We're not used to honestly being asked what we know, what we think") that we understood how we had been insensitive to issues of power and domination as we conceptualized the seminars. We'd presented ourselves as authorities in choosing readings for the seminar and designing courses for the interns. We'd not attended adequately to the mentors' sense of authority—what they knew and how they knew it. Thus, the seminars put them in a more passive, less powerful role.

In future seminars we would want to raise the issue of power and domination and model its analysis through feminist theory. We began by thinking about issues of power and domination for the mentor teachers in relation to the college. How did they view their own higher education experience, particularly their teacher education? How did they feel about being engaged in a collaborative teacher-preparation program at Lewis and Clark College?

These questions, however, soon led to others about sharing our authority as teacher educators with the mentors and how they perceive their authority in general. Do teachers feel trapped between two power centers — the schools in which they work and the universities in which they received their education? Do they see themselves as authorities in the schools, and if so, in what contexts? What do they perceive as the sources of their authority? To what extent is their status as a teacher in the community, their knowledge of curriculum, of teaching methodology, of classroom management a source of their authority?

THE PROFESSION AS GENDERED

The mentor teachers' feelings of powerlessness led us to ask, What impression does viewing our profession from a socially sanctioned male perspective make on us as teachers? Teaching is a woman's occupation, so defined because of the number of teachers who are women, but in reality male dominated because it is controlled by men and stereotypic male values permeate it. These anomalies can be uncovered only by an awareness of the extent to which issues of gender place the profession in a double bind. On the one hand, teaching is judged according to criteria drawn from the traditional male professions like law and medicine. When these male-defined criteria are applied to entry into the profession, the knowledge base in the profession, socialization into the profession, the concept of career, the career ladder in the profession, and the traits deemed necessary for successful teaching, education does not measure up and is indeed labeled a "semi-profession" (Acker 1983; Mitrano 1978).

On the other hand, teaching, like work in the other helping professions, is formulated as an extension of women's traditional role in the family. It has been pointed out that the teacher's role in socializing children to conform to a society that is patriarchal is not all that dissimilar from the mother's role (Lather 1986; Lightfoot 1978; Grumet 1981). By linking an analysis of teaching to larger societal issues — labor supply and demand, cultural values, organizational changes, and changes in the family — and women's subordinate position in the society, we can enable teachers to see the extent to which teaching is genderized (Apple 1983, 1985 cited in Lather 1986; Strober and Tyack 1980). Lather has observed that women teachers, oversocialized to be "good girls," have "focused on responsive concern for students and worries about job performance at the cost of developing a more critical stance toward their cultural task of passing on a received heritage" (Lather 1986, 13). She proposes that we construct a profession that combines self-development with service to others.

We are now struck by how we asked the mentors to serve programmatic needs and the interns and overlooked their self-development, particularly as mentors. Self-development necessitates looking at how their profession is gendered and the consequences for themselves as teachers and curriculum designers. We did provide two readings relevant to issues of gender (Martin 1985; Tetreault 1985). However, we didn't nest these readings in an explicit program goal: a feminist perspective on teacher education. With such a goal these readings could have been a focal point for a critique of the profession as gendered. In the absence of a conscious goal of feminist teacher education, the readings remained tangential to a discussion of the profession perceived as genderless.

RECONCEPTUALIZING PEDAGOGY

We have learned valuable lessons from feminist pedagogy that could have been employed more effectively in the seminars. One important lesson is that the mentor teachers' voices need to be sought and heard. They need to have a say in seminar processes, for instance, how writing is used there; and in content, what topics and sources guide discussions. No less than their students' questions and experiences in the classroom, the mentors' questions and experiences should have guided the learning in the seminars. The aim of the seminars could be to help mentors recognize, use, and enlarge their own perspectives in relation to the themes of the seminars such as stages of teacher development and concepts of curriculum. One of our goals thus becomes building common understandings inductively from the particularity of mentors' experiences combined with and informed by the reading. This enables us to build a more complex conceptualization of a given issue, one that legitimizes mentors' voices but puts them in a larger explanatory context (see Maher 1985).

We have learned from those researchers who, committed to empowering teachers, are starting with teachers' own situation to learn how women and men who are teachers look upon their work, what they value and criticize about their occupation, and how they negotiate their work interests with sex role and family expectations (Biklin 1984; Freedman et al. 1983; Zaret 1975).

A BROADER LOOK AT THE LEWIS AND CLARK TEACHER-EDUCATION MODEL

Inception

The foregoing critique of the mentor teacher seminars indicates the value of feminist theory in analyzing this one component of our program. The following section details the planning of the model itself, including a discussion of the role feminist theory played in the early stages. Our subsequent investigation will demonstrate that we did not go far enough with conscious application of feminist theory.

One of the most important lessons from feminist theory is the importance of personal experience in building theory and understanding phenomena. With this in mind we organized the meetings to draw upon the planning committee members' personal perspectives on teaching, particularly those related to our own experiences and our internalized beliefs about teacher education. Our committee included public school and college teachers and administrators in education, history, literature, and science.[2] When we all shared how we learned to teach, one idea jumped out at us. Most of us learned to teach through an exemplifying model—by observing an excellent teacher in college or during student teaching, by observing a coteacher or a family member who was a teacher, or in a cooperative teaching experience. From this moment on we had a shared belief in the planning group: we would work to develop a field-based model of exemplifying education that utilizes excellent public schoolteachers as clinical teachers and mentors. (See Hyman 1976.)

Lewis and Clark College provides a context in which concern for issues of gender can flourish. In Spring 1984 the college completed a two-year planning process that had as its primary goal the writing of a new mission statement. One of the distinctive features of the college's mission is the incorporation of the history, traditions, and contributions of women and men, and international and intercultural perspectives. Thus the mission statement provided institutional support for the incorporation of gender from a multicultural perspective from the beginning of our planning process.

Despite this favorable climate, concerns for issues of gender were only implicit in the planning stage. We understood the value of grounding our thinking in our personal experience and the planning committee members enthusiastically drew upon and shared their own experience. But we were not explicit about the program's theoretical roots in feminism. Although on the original planning committee there were several members familiar with feminist theory, it was never a consideration for invitation to participate in the planning. The relationship between gender and education was considered in a limited way as the knowledge that an individual teacher needed about her or his students. We were afraid, frankly, that it was politically too dangerous to test the committee's willingness to support a feminist model of teacher education. We trusted the wisdom of our decision when we heard the strong opposition of one administrator to bringing about change in the schools as a valid program goal.

Description of the Model

Before launching into an analysis of our model from a feminist perspective, we will briefly describe its content and structure. This fifteen-month, sixty-quarter-hour program blends liberal arts and professional education. Further, the program's course of study is coherent, integrating knowledge about the purposes of schooling, student development and learning, classroom pedagogy, curriculum and subject matter, and teacher development and learning. Courses in the program incorporate the college's commitment to intercultural and international understanding; to balanced exploration of the perspectives, traditions, and contributions of women and men; and to reflection upon the ethical and moral dimensions of diverse communities in an interdependent world.

A full year's mentor relationship with a single teacher or a team of teachers immerses the interns in the life of the school to a greater degree than usual. Interns begin as observers in the classroom, spending a minimum of six hours a week with their mentors during fall term. Winter term they take a more active role, spending at least twelve hours a week in the classroom. Spring term, interns are in the schools teaching full-time, thirty hours per week. With such sustained involvement interns become interested not only in life in the classroom but in the entire school. Furthermore, they are exposed to a wide variety of models of teaching and gain a broad spectrum of education through observation and collaboration with their mentors.

The program begins mid-June with on-campus courses in the liberal arts; a seminar exploring purposes of education in historical, cultural, and personal contexts; and a course in educational ethnography (Table 4.1). Field experience at this time includes ethnographic observation and tutoring in varied school settings.

During the academic year, the professional education component centers on critical areas in secondary education. In the fall term interns focus on developmental issues for their students and for themselves. Studying adolescent development, they integrate field experience, empirical psychological research, and perspectives from other disciplines. They examine the influence on adolescent development of such factors as institutions, race,

Table 4.1.　Course of study, master of arts in teaching secondary programs, language arts and social studies

Summer I	Fall	Winter	Spring	Summer II
ED 500 Education: Personal & Public Issues 3 quarter hours CB: 30 hours 1,4	ED 552 Adolescent Development & Learning 6 quarter hours CB: 30 hours FB: 60 hours 1,4	ED 553 Classroom Instruction & Learning 6 quarter hours CB: 30 hours FB: 60 hours 1,4	ED 554 Classroom Instruction & Learning 12 quarter hours CB: 20 hours FB: 200 hours 1,4	ED 555 Education: Experience & Meaning 3 quarter hours CB: 30 hours 1,4
ED 551 Ethnography & Field Experience 2 quarter hours CB: 12 hours FB: 24 hours 3	LA 508/SS 508 Researching and Teaching the Liberal Arts 3 quarter hours CB: 30 hours 1,2	LA 509/SS 509 Researching and Teaching the Content Areas 3 quarter hours CB: 30 hours FB: 60 hours 1,4	Critical Issues Seminar ½ quarter hours 1	COREG 502 Organizational Cultures and Professional Life 3 quarter hours 3
COREG 501 Individual and Societal Perspectives on Adulthood 3 quarter hours 1	Liberal Arts Course 3 quarter hours 2	Liberal Arts Course 3 quarter hours 2		Liberal Arts Course 6 quarter hours 2
Liberal Arts Course 3–5 quarter hours 2		Critical Issues Seminar ½ quarter hour 1		

Note: Each course follows this sequence: Course title, number of credit hours, breakdown of campus-based and field-based experiences (CB and FB), and category of faculty teaching (1 = Lewis & Clark education faculty, 2 = Lewis & Clark liberal arts faculty, 3 = Lewis & Clark adjunct faculty, 4 = school district faculty).

class, gender, and culture. And building on extensive field observation and analysis, they design and practice instructional strategies conducive to healthy adolescent development and learning. The interns also attend to their own development in this term, specifically as researchers in their teaching field. With a liberal arts faculty member who teaches and models the research process, interns undertake intensive research in an interest area relevant to their teaching. In thus extending their own subject-matter knowledge, interns experience the value of research to their teaching.

Winter term offers increased attention to curriculum and pedagogy as interns take on more instructional responsibility in the schools. On campus they study curriculum theory and content in their disciplines while developing a knowledge of the goals, assumptions, and related skills of various instructional methodologies. Campus and school efforts blend as interns work with subject area specialists and their mentor to design, teach, and evaluate curriculum from their research project of fall term. The combination of teaching and learning allows interns to develop a student-centered philosophy of teaching and to select methodologies and materials compatible with that philosophy and appropriate to particular groups of students.

In the spring term interns are teaching full-time, returning to campus only for a seminar on classroom instruction and learning. Here they consciously relate learning from previous courses to their emerging ideas of themselves as teachers. They reflect on their teaching goals and methodologies through focused analysis of particular lessons and units. The mentors have involved the interns in collaborative planning, teaching, observation, and assessment. The interns now apply these skills to their own practice of teaching, still in conjunction with their mentor but with greater independence and responsibility.

During the final summer of the program students take liberal arts courses and a culminating seminar that integrates their learning in the program. At this time they focus on their vision of themselves as teachers growing toward excellence.

A unique feature of the program is the core curriculum that brings all students in the Graduate School—prospective and practicing teachers, public and educational administrators, and counseling psychologists—together in courses and shorter seminars. (The development of the core curriculum was supported in part by a grant from the Fund for the Improvement of Post Secondary Education.) The purpose of the core is to enable faculty and students to communicate around substantive issues in the professions. Consistent with our liberal arts orientation, we use sources in the humanities, the social sciences, and the professional literature to engage faculty and students in exploring questions of purpose and meaning in professional life. Central to our investigation are questions about the place of gender, class, and race. Thus interns apply their developing perspective as educators in a course on organizational cultures and professional life and in a second course on life span development. Interns are also required to complete two issue-oriented seminars. One weekend per term, a speaker of national reputation is invited to give a public address on a designated topic to the college, law, and graduate communities. One topic the first year was the basic tension in American professional life—between individualism and a desire for the public good. A second seminar explored issues of comparable worth, analyzing the sexual division of labor and the low value placed on both paid and unpaid "women's work."

We decided to infuse issues on women and gender throughout the curriculum rather than to offer specific courses.[3] Feminist scholars have made us conscious of the ways in which human experience is dichotomized—male and female, theory and practice, public and private, to name a few. Our rationale for a cohesive program came in part from a consciousness of the distortions a dichotomized education promotes. We chose not to design courses according to the traditional linear divisions in the teacher-education curriculum—foundations of education, educational philosophy and psychology, and teaching strategies—but to cluster learning closer to the ways teachers experience their craft. We dispute the notion that teachers learn incrementally about educational psychology and teaching methodology, for instance. They are always engaged in an interactive process involving students, curriculum materials, teaching methodology, the school, and themselves. It is simply not possible to learn one in isolation.

The women's scholarship also made us conscious of the extent to which the prevailing concept of humans is male defined and how it needs to be broadened to include women. Our goal was a multifocal, relational perspective on the human experience and so we asked throughout where issues of gender were relevant and how issues of gender interacted with race, class, and linguistic experience. For example, in one of the courses that investigates public and private issues in education, interns read Jane Roland Martin's article calling for a broadening of our educational purposes to include education for both the public (productive) and private (reproductive) processes of society (Martin 1985). In one of the Graduate School's core courses, Organizational Cultures and Professional Life, questions of gender are infused through articles tracing the evolution of our thinking about women and gender (Tetreault 1985), comparing feminist theory and organizational theory (Kanter 1979), arguing for the articulation of a theory of reproduction as well as a theory of production (O'Brien 1982), and presenting a case study of elementary teachers in Boston who struggled to understand and then deal with the structural constraints imposed on them in their schools (Freedman et al. 1983).

The course on adolescent development incorporates issues of race, class, gender, and exceptionality throughout by pairing autobiographies by women and men, who are also minorities (Hong-Kingston 1976; Wright 1945), by drawing upon the psychology of women (Gilligan 1982), and presenting a case study discussing how adolescents resolved issues of love and work in a women's history course (Tetreault 1986). Although the course on research in the content areas did not include specific feminist topics or materials, students in the course were supported in researching topics from a feminist perspective. What is of importance here is the resulting curriculum development by the interns on women and gender in social studies and language arts. In the course on teaching and learning interns read literature assessing teacher expectations based on a student's race, class, and gender (Rist 1970; Sadker and Sadker 1982) and learn about a relational model of good teaching versus a management model (Eisner 1982; Lazerson et al. 1985; Lightfoot 1978).

Selecting the Mentors

Nearly two years of preparation preceded the arrival of the mentor teachers at the first seminar. Exploratory visits with school administrators confirmed widespread interest in our program. Next we observed social studies, language arts, and science classes in some of the high schools to get a feel for the quality and tone of education in the district.

The following year negotiations with interested districts began in earnest. Numerous meetings raised questions central to establishing this partnership. Was the district interested? How could teachers be identified? What could we realistically expect the mentor-intern relationship to be? What kind of support would mentor teachers need to make this attractive to them?

These meetings confirmed our view that school district personnel had much to contribute to collaborative teacher education. Administrators saw such a program as recognizing teachers' good work and giving them an important stake in the training of teachers. It had the potential to improve education in the public schools and provide professional development for the faculties involved. Administrators also saw benefits to their students. As one observed, "You can't have too many good teachers in a classroom."

In determining criteria for selection of mentor teachers we drew upon work we had done while evaluating and planning for our in-service Master of Arts in Teaching Program. We also drew some of our thinking from conversations with Andra Makler. As part of an NCATE and Oregon Teachers Standards and Practices Commission (TSPC) evaluation of our education programs, we developed a five-year plan that had as its central and defining feature the identification of the characteristics of successful teachers. We envisioned excellent teachers as we recommended the following criteria to school districts for nomination of mentor teachers:

A. recognition of excellence in teaching from their peers, parents, and students
B. a commitment to quality education which includes:
1. an understanding of the teacher's role as central to the learning process and critical in the shaping of excellence

2. a mature understanding of themselves as teachers with a sense of their own autonomy, efficacy, and uniqueness
3. a philosophy of teaching and learning that places the student and the teacher at the center and that integrates education for the public processes of society — for work and citizenship — with the private, generative processes of society
4. knowledge about and respect for the intellectual and social development of their students including differences and similarities among students because of gender, race, ethnicity, social class, exceptionality, religion, and linguistic experience
5. valuing liberal education, multidisciplinary approaches to learning, and an openness to new ideas in their field
6. the ability to incorporate these ideas into a coherent education for their students
7. an openness to integrating women and intercultural and international perspectives into the curriculum

We expected, of course, that nominees would have an interest in participating and committing time to this program and currently be assigned as either a language arts or social studies teacher at the secondary level. We also indicated our preference for teachers who held a master's degree and had more than five years teaching experience.

Interested teachers wrote essays of application. Their essays revealed a lot about the applicants. Central to their self-definition was pride in being an excellent teacher and a strong commitment to teaching. Their resumes revealed numerous ways they had found to grow and to improve their teaching — through publication of curricula, through districtwide curriculum work, by assuming leadership roles in their unions, associations, departments, and schools. Some were the recipients of grants to do independent study, to travel, to produce video documentaries, or to participate in writing projects.

An idea universally conveyed by the mentor applicants was their excitement at "being instrumental in helping shape prospective teachers" and of having the opportunity to "share the knowledge they have acquired over the years about teaching." They understood that a full year's commitment opened up ways they could support a beginning teacher's development that wouldn't be possible in ten weeks. Mentor teachers saw this as part of their own natural growth as teachers. As one of them wrote,

> I come also as a learner. Teaching can be isolating work. Generally, we conceptualize a lesson alone, teach it alone and evaluate it alone. A lack of reflection on the meaning of teaching can easily result. I would look forward

to being involved with a group of thoughtful teachers who want to share ideas on teaching and learning.

Another wrote in her application, "If you're looking for a 'finished' teacher, I'm not one. I am a teacher who would love the opportunity to grow with your program."

The theme of teaching as a solitary activity and the desire for a community larger than their school's community was expressed by others. One applicant likened teaching to "being trapped in a box for 180 school days with few channels to colleagues other than the discourse of the lunchroom table." She noted that although her school community was comprised of many colleagues who believed they could and would improve and who shared ideas and strategies with one another, there was a need for more opportunities to learn from a dynamic community of teachers who were committed to sharing and facilitating the growth of colleagues. Another summed it up by writing, "I would like to have the chance to work with a community of high school and college teachers who are committed to making education work."

They had a vision, too, of what they could do for the interns. A social studies teacher wanted to help new teachers see teaching as an "art form." Another saw this model fostering interns' involvement in their own education, a goal he had for his high school students as well. He noted that he could set an important tone by encouraging interns' creativity and responsibility at the outset of their careers. A language arts teacher looked forward to introducing her intern to the benefits of collaboration with teachers in other disciplines. Too often, she noted, isolated classrooms can "cement differences instead of encouraging exchanges." Modeling practical applications of educational theory appealed to another mentor who spoke of helping interns develop a rationale for employing different classroom methodologies. Finally, a number of mentors wrote of the importance of demonstrating their own beliefs about teaching. One stated her conviction that teachers at all stages can and will improve.

The next step was interviews with the teachers, which took place in their schools. We wanted to know more details about their experiences as classroom teachers, what they taught, and for how long. We were very interested, too, in learning more about how they thought about teaching. Did they think of it collaboratively? How did they think they might work with student teachers? What did they think might be some "new and innovative" ways to use interns in their classrooms? Were they able to make the time commitment? We did not ask, nor were we invited, to observe in any of the teachers' classrooms. By June of 1986 a core group of mentors was in place.

Reflecting back on the selection of mentors with gender in mind, we see several things. Embedded in our criteria for mentor teachers is a feminist agenda — the integration of education for the public and private processes of society, respect for similarities and differences among individuals because of gender, race, ethnicity, and other characteristics, and an openness to integrating women and intercultural and international perspectives into knowledge. But we did not explicitly address gender issues as part of the application process for mentors. Although the mentors received our criteria for the selection of mentors before they wrote their letter of application, none mentioned gender issues in their application. Further, we reproduced one aspect of the gender stereotyping in the profession. All of our mentor language arts teachers are female and all but one of our social studies teachers, male. Although one of our criteria for mentor teachers was a sensitivity to incorporating gender-balanced and multicultural perspectives, we'd not attended to balancing the number of female and male teachers in the two content areas.

Although our program brochure identifies incorporation of the institution's commitment to a "balanced exploration of the perspectives, traditions, and contributions of women and men" as one of its unique features, the specific inclusion of topics and materials on women and gender is left up to the individual instructor. A review of individual courses reveals that most paid some attention to women and gender; we believe that more is needed if we are to honor our claim.

CONCLUSION

It was not difficult to alter the "conveyer belt model" of teacher education through clustering learning in a field-based program. Why, then, was it more formidable to challenge the male model of thinking about education? In part, it is because we have been oversocialized to be "good girls"; we were primarily concerned about doing a good job as program developers and not pushing people too far. It also has to do with the politics of education. Knowing that people in education are traditionally conservative, we worried we would alienate prospective partners if we explicitly espoused a feminist agenda. Thus we did not explicitly address gender issues as we sought to build partnerships with school districts and recruit mentor teachers. As we developed course proposals, we treated gender as one of many topics in education.

Our experience in designing the program, writing about it, and sharing our writing with the mentor teachers has allowed us to be researchers in the practice context. Stepping back, focusing on what we were doing has both encouraged and alerted us. Through reflection we see how much we have learned by developing our model of teacher education. We also see how much we have yet to learn.

Reflection on these seminars has started us thinking about challenging the problem-solving, authority orientation of the schools. We see the conflict inherent in preparing teachers who value divergent thinking and their own experience as knowledge, and then sending them into schools devoted to pursuit of "the right answer" organized around decision making that excludes teachers. We've learned from our mentor teacher seminars the importance of developing a critical stance toward educational institutions within which teachers' beliefs about teaching are explored and their formative influences analyzed. By fostering a climate of inquiry and collaborative learning in the mentor teacher seminars, we can model this regard for the validity of varying experiences among our intern teachers.

We've also reflected on the static definition of excellence in teaching. In inviting excellent teachers to be mentors in our program, can we suggest that they—and we—continue to develop, learning new ways of being and doing in the classroom, in a seminar with peers, with an intern teacher? As we continue to build a cadre of mentor teachers, we will address the ways in which mentoring differs from teaching. We will model for the teachers and ask them to share among themselves ways of observing a classroom, of rationalizing and designing curriculum, of talking with an intern teacher about her or his teaching, of collaboratively teaching. We will, in short, acknowledge that excellent teachers need to learn how to be mentors; that they can do so in a supportive community committed to their learning as well as their interns.

The mentor teacher seminars pointed out the importance to genuine community building of shared ownership in the enterprise. We cannot assume that a common interest, in this case collaborative teacher education, is sufficient to team building. We have seen how community building presents various and sometimes conflicting demands: acknowledging the complexity of individuals, mediating between their needs and those of the group, and attending to democratic processes as the group defines and coheres around its shared purpose. Mentors come to this group from existing communities, their schools. It is important to allay teachers' concerns about the time and the unfamiliar, more autonomous role this new community asks of them. One teacher noted that the presence of several mentors from one school may have introduced issues from that community into ours, for example, setting a tone of competition and fear of evaluation in our seminar. To set our own collaborative tone for this community means involving the mentors at the outset. Grounding their preparation as mentors in their own experience will allow the mentors to go on to analyze that experience and the beliefs about teaching it generated.

Our own "journey" as participants in this model has shown us the time and energy it takes to reconceptualize a teacher-education program according to a feminist perspective. But we think it is worth the struggle. A generation of teachers educated to internalize the values of feminism hold out the potential for transforming education in a meaningful way.

NOTES

1. We wish to thank the following mentor teachers and their school districts: William Bigelow, Gail Black, Michael Bontemps, Linda Christensen, William Cromley, Kris Demien, Herbert Grose, Pam Hooten, Jan Martin, Thomas McKenna, and Gary Noble (Portland Public Schools); Marilyn Duistermore, Jack Felmet (Beaverton Public Schools); Joan Montague and Josephine Wollen (Lake Oswego Public Schools); and Prudence Twohy (Catlin-Gabel School).
2. We wish to thank the public school teachers and administrators from the Portland Public Schools: William Bigelow, social studies teacher; Jill Kanter, language arts teacher; Jack Ubik, middle school principal; and Harriet Adair, elementary school principal. Those from other school districts were Jim Carlisle, secondary school principal, Beaverton Public Schools; Mike Goodrich, science teacher, Lake Oswego Public Schools. Lewis and Clark faculty included Mike Amspoker, biology; Nancy Grey Osterud, history; Jean Ward, communications; and Susan Dunn, Mary Kay Tetreault, Carole Urzua, and Jim Wallace, education.
3. The Lewis and Clark education faculty also involved in course development were Andra Makler, Jim Wallace, and Vern Jones. Their assistance was greatly appreciated.

BIBLIOGRAPHY

Acker, S. "Women and Teaching: A Semi-detached Sociology of a Semi-detached Profession." In *Gender, Class and Education,* edited by S. Walker and L. Barton, 123–39. New York: Falmer Press, 1983.

Apple, M. "Work, Gender and Teaching." *Teachers College Record,* 84(1983):611–28.

Biklin, S. K. "Can Elementary School Teaching Be a Career? A Search for New Ways of Understanding Women's Work." *Issues in Education* 3(1985):215–31.

DuBois, E. K., E. P. Kennedy, C. Korsmeyer, and S. Robinson. *Feminist Scholarship: Kindling in the Groves of Academe.* Urbana, Ill.: University of Illinois Press, 1985.

Eisner, E. "An Artistic Approach to Supervision." In *Supervision of Teaching,* edited by Thomas J. Sergiovanni, 53–66. Alexandria, Va.: ASCD, 1982.

Freedman, S., J. Jackson, and K. Boles. "Teaching: An Imperiled Profession." In *Handbook on Teaching Policy,* edited by L. Shulman and G. Sykes, 261–99. New York: Longman, 1983.

Gilligan, C. *In a Different Voice.* Cambridge, Mass.: Harvard University Press, 1982.

Grumet, M. "Pedagogy for Patriarchy: The Feminization of Teaching." *Interchange on Educational Policy* 12, nos. 2 and 3(1981):165–84.

Hong-Kingston, M. *The Woman Warrior.* New York: Alfred Knopf, 1976.

Hyman, R. "Teaching Strategies for Pluralistic Teaching." In *75th Yearbook of the National Society for the Study of Education, Part II.* Chicago: University of Chicago Press, 1976.

Kanter, R. M. *Men and Women of the Corporation.* New York: Basic Books, 1979.

Langer, J. "Literacy Instruction in American Schools: Problems and Perspectives." *American Journal of Education* 93(1984):107–32.

Lather, P. "The Absent Presence: Patriarchy, Capitalism and the Nature of Teachers' Work." Paper presented at the American Educational Research Association annual meeting, San Francisco, Calif., April 1986.

Lazerson, M., J. Block-McLaughlin, B. McPheerson, and S. K. Bailey. *An Education of Value: The Purposes and Practices of Schools.* Cambridge: Cambridge University Press, 1985.

Lightfoot, S. L. *Worlds Apart.* New York: Basic Books, 1978.

Lipsitz, C. "Early Adolescence — Social Psychological Issues." Paper presented at the Association for Supervision and Curriculum Development annual conference, St. Louis, Mo., 1981.

Lortie, D. *Schoolteacher.* Chicago: University of Chicago Press, 1977.

MacKinnon, C. "Feminism, Marxism, Method, and the State: An Agenda for Theory." *Signs: Journal of Women in Culture and Society* 7(1982):514–45.

Maher, F. "Pedagogies for the Gender Balanced Classroom." *Journal of Thought* 20, no. 3(1985):48–64.

Makler, A. "Cooperative Teachers: Mediators of Change, Mediators of Culture." Unpublished Qualifying Paper, Harvard Graduate School of Education, Cambridge, Mass., 1986.

Martin, J. "Becoming educated: A Journey of Alienation or Integration?" *Journal of Education* 167(1985):71–84.

_____. "Excluding Women from the Educational Realm." *Harvard Educational Review* 52(1982):133–48.

_____. "Sophie and Emile: A Case Study of Sex Bias in the History of Educational Thought." *Harvard Educational Review* 51(1981):357–72.

Miller, J. B. *Toward a New Psychology of Women.* Boston: Beacon Press, 1976.

Mitrano, B. "Teaching as a Woman's Occupation: A Feminist Critique." *Journal of Education* 160, no. 4(1978):50–63.

O'Brien, M. "Feminist Theory and Dialectical Logic." *Signs: Journal of Women in Culture and Society* 7(1982):144–57.

Rist, R. C. "Student Social Class and Teacher Expectations: The Self-fulfilling Prophecy in Ghetto Education." *Harvard Educational Review* 40, no. 3(1970):411–51.

Rubin, L. *Worlds of Pain: Life in the Working-class Family.* New York: Basic Books, 1976.

Rudduck, J., and D. Hopkins. *Research as a Basis for Teaching: Readings from the Work of Lawrence Stenhouse.* London: Heinemann Educational Books, 1985.

Sadker, M. P., and D. Sadker. *Sex Equity Handbook for Schools.* New York: Longman, 1982.

Strober, M. H., and D. Tyack. "Why Do Women Teach and Men Manage? A Report on Research on Schools." *Signs: Journal of Women in Culture and Society* 5, no. 3(1980):494–503.

Tetreault, M. K. "Feminist Phase Theory: An Experience-derived Evaluation Model." *Journal of Higher Education* 56(1985):363–84.

————. "It's So Opinioney." *Journal of Education* 168, no. 2(1986):78–95.

Wright, R. *Black Boy.* New York: Harper and Brothers, 1945.

Zaret, E. "Women/School/Society." In *Schools in Search of Meaning,* edited by J. McDonald and E. Zaret. Washington, D.C.: ASCD, 1975.

2 | Fifth-year and Five-year Certification Programs

5 | Memphis State's Extended Teacher-education Program

ROBERT L. SAUNDERS

INTRODUCTION

Expectations of Americans for their schools have always been high, periodically elevating so quickly and so dramatically that schools experience serious credibility problems. In such periods schools are often branded as failures.

Such a condition was developing in April 1983 when the National Commission on Excellence in Education submitted its report entitled *A Nation at Risk* (1983). Quickly following were about two dozen other reports having similar thrusts and producing similar findings and recommendations. Within a relatively short period of time, just a year or so, the groundwork was laid for many governmental and regulatory agencies demanding major changes in American schools.

Many of the dissatisfactions voiced about education during the past three years relate ultimately to two inseparable needs: (1) to achieve the desired levels of quality in teaching and (2) to prepare teachers to reach the level of teaching effectiveness being desired.

Little is to be gained from arguing that teacher education has done the best job it could, given its limited resources through the years and the serious constraints under which it has operated. Of more value is to acknowledge that teaching and teacher education clearly do not meet the expectations held for them by the public and to then do all that is possible to bring performance up to expectations.

To do this a three-dimensional action plan would seem to be essential.

Robert L. Saunders is dean emeritus of the College of Education, Memphis State University.

Like a three-legged stool, if any one of the three dimensions is weak or missing the entire effort will fail. First, teacher-education programs must attract students with strong academic credentials and the personal qualities needed for effective teaching. Second, these students must be prepared through programs that are of high quality, rigorous, demanding, effective, and credible. Third, the best of the graduates of these programs must be enticed into entering the teaching profession and remaining in it.

Each of these three assertions is elaborated upon below to help establish a rationale for the new programs being developed throughout the country including the one at Memphis State University, where the author is located and was heavily involved in conceptualization and development of the program.

1. *Attracting highly qualified students into teacher education.* It is well documented and highly lamented that in recent years teacher-education programs have attracted a disproportionately small share of entering college freshmen who hold strong academic credentials. The converse is also true, that is, teacher-education programs have attracted a disproportionately large share of students with weak academic credentials. The recent surge of increased requirements for admission, retention, and graduation have helped, but only by causing the most highly qualified students from the applicant pool to actually complete preparation programs and become eligible for licensure as teachers. The elevated requirements have done little to attract larger numbers of highly qualified students into teacher education.

There are several reasons for the overall decline in academic ability of teacher-education students, the more obvious being (a) the decreased attractiveness of the teaching profession—low salaries, poor working conditions in schools, reduced status accorded teachers by the general public, (b) the increased attractiveness of other professions, and (c) the access by women and minority students to more attractive and more lucrative careers (business, medicine, engineering, computer sciences, etc.), which formerly were essentially closed to them.

Desperately needed are some magnetic forces that will quickly pull greater numbers of high-ability students into education. The new, extended programs being established could become one such magnetic force.

2. *Preparing highly qualified students in teacher-education programs that are of high quality, rigorous, and credible.* The extended programs being initiated in several institutions across the country address this point by incorporating changes designed to remove several constraints and shortcomings now found in traditional teacher-education programs.

3. *Enticing the most highly qualified graduates of significantly im-*

proved teacher-education programs to actually enter the teaching profession and to remain in it. This is a critical dimension of the overall problem in education today and is one often overlooked by political leaders and the general public. The declining applicant pool alluded to above is greatly exacerbated by this closely related problem — and both problems are caused primarily by the same set of circumstances.

Studies have shown that only about one teacher-education graduate in three elects a career other than teaching, often because the reward system in education is not competitive. Half of the teachers who enter the profession leave within five years. Some return later but less often today than in years past. It is not unusual for those teachers leaving their classrooms to accept jobs that pay more even though the jobs require less skill, expertise, and energy.

Much more could be said about each of these three needs, but the purpose of this chapter puts a primary focus on the second need: preparing highly qualified students in teacher-education programs that are of high quality, rigorous, and credible. It should be noted, however, that the other two needs are addressed secondarily. Extended programs clearly purport to help recruit highly capable students and the heavier reliance on longer and more effective internships should enable graduates of extended programs to be inducted into teaching in a more satisfying and effective manner, thereby increasing the likelihood that they will remain in teaching.

In the next section the role of teacher education in the overall reform movement is addressed. Included are descriptions of how preparation programs evolved into their present state and a recently emerging rationale for a new model. A case is made later that some form of an extended program for the initial preparation of teachers is the new model needed.

IMPROVED TEACHER EDUCATION — A VITAL PART OF SCHOOL REFORM

It is both fair and appropriate for the school reform movement to eventually center around teacher education as has been the case for the past twelve to eighteen months. For it to have been otherwise would be to deny the importance of this facet of education, to deny the widespread belief that good schools are dependent upon effective, well-prepared teachers.

This section is based on the above premise. It includes six main themes: (1) a brief historical perspective, (2) an emerging rationale for extending preparation programs beyond the current, four-year model, (3) various models that can be used to extend programs, (4) extended programs currently in operation, (5) some of the problems, issues, and risks involved in extending preparation programs, and (6) several advantages that can be expected to accrue from extending teacher-education programs beyond the four-year model.

Historical Context

Teacher preparation, like preparation programs for other professionals in this country, has evolved through the years, taking giant steps forward at critical points in time. Sometimes the giant steps were taken amidst and in reaction to severe criticism of the profession from within and without, not unlike circumstances today in regard to education. Such was the case in medical education, for example, when, as a result of the Flexner Report of 1910, Johns Hopkins University initiated a revolutionary and forward-looking program that rather quickly and thoroughly transformed medical education in this country.

Teacher education has evolved more slowly than most other professions; however, at several points preparation programs were significantly extended. Although a few normal schools were in existence by the mid-1880s and a university chair of pedagogy was established as early as 1879 at the University of Michigan, teacher training attained postsecondary status in a universal sense only at the turn of this century when two-year normal schools became commonplace. The secondary school-level normal schools had replaced "teacher institutes," an earlier model, which ranged in length across the country from several days to several months.

About a fourth of the curricula of the normal schools, once they were postsecondary, was devoted to pedagogy. By the mid-1920s most normal schools had been extended into teachers colleges, which had four-year curricula. Although the proportion of the curriculum devoted to pedagogy remained about the same, overall a doubling effect actually occurred due to the change from a two-year to a four-year curriculum.

This significant extension of programs took only about two decades to occur. It is important to note that during this period teachers prepared and certificated through the normal schools worked side by side with teachers certificated through the four-year teachers colleges in the same way that graduates of teacher institutes remained active in the profession long after the entry of normal-school graduates. Many state teachers colleges ultimately became departments (and later schools or colleges) of education in multipurpose colleges and universities. Some departments of education within colleges and universities originated as such, but their origin and development paralleled the evolutionary development of normal schools and teachers colleges.

This historical perspective is intended to help make the point that during its relatively short existence teacher preparation has experienced two major extensions. Both extensions occurred within periods of great societal concerns about education. It is logical to believe that the current debates about school quality and the push for excellence provides teacher educators an opportunity to take another giant step forward in the preparation of teachers.

Extended Programs: A Logical Next Step

One of the earliest cases made for extending the traditional four-year program occurred in 1976 in the American Association of Colleges for Teacher Education (AACTE) publication *Educating a Profession* (1976). The report made a strong case for adding badly needed "life space" to the curriculum. In 1979 the AACTE assembly of delegates passed a resolution (and reaffirmed it a year later) supporting "the exploration of major structural changes in preparation programs, including the extension of programs beyond four years."

AACTE expanded upon this thrust by developing a series of position papers with their genesis being the earlier cited report, *Educating a Profession*. The three papers emphasized programmatic issues: *Profile of a Beginning Teacher* (1983c), *Competency Assessment* (1983a), and *Extended Programs for Teacher Education* (1983b).

The report on extended programs is the most pertinent to this paper. It described the limitations inherent in the four-year model and set forth reasons why it would be inadequate for the future. A case was made for schools, colleges, and departments of education (SCDEs) to develop extended programs. Benefits were cited that could be expected from such a move. Several problems and issues that would need to be addressed in the transition were discussed.

The AACTE report apparently stimulated considerable interest in extended programs among schools, colleges, and departments of education. AACTE's *Report to the Profession* (1983d), for example, notes that approximately one-fourth of the reporting institutions have one or more programs that extend beyond four years. While many of these undoubtedly are the sparsely populated master of arts in teaching programs left over from the 1960s, several are known to be newly designed five-year programs.

Further evidence that interest is mounting in extended programs can be seen in the Holmes Group Consortium of Education Deans' Interim Report #2, *Goals for the Education of Teachers as Professionals* (Lanier 1985). The report recommends that the curriculum for prospective career teachers should not permit a major in education during the baccalaureate years and that, instead, undergraduates should pursue more serious general/liberal study and a standard major in an academic subject normally taught in schools. The report recommends also that the curriculum should require a master's degree in education and a successful year of well-supervised internship (apparently not unlike the five-plus-one year, master's degree plus internship) model described in AACTE's 1983 task force report on extended programs.

The report of the National Commission on Excellence in Education (1983) recommended that all prospective teachers, as a part of their liberal education, should be educated in at least one academic major, that a minimum of four years be devoted to the liberal arts components, and a minimum of five years to the total program.

A statement by the Research and Policy Committee of the Committee for Economic Development, *Investing in Our Children: Business and the Public Schools* (1985), recommends that teacher candidates complete a bachelor of arts or sciences program with a major other than education and take courses in education that will develop professional knowledge and professional skills (presumably at the postbaccalaureate level).

Several public statements attributed to NEA President Mary Futrell and AFT President Albert Shanker suggest their support of the extended program concept. Also supporting the establishment of extended programs are Arthur Wise of the Rand Corporation (1986) and Marc Tucker, executive director of the Carnegie Foundation on Education and the Economy (1986).

The movement is more than rhetoric. Several schools of education have five-year programs in operation, at least two of which are not completely new. The University of New Hampshire has had a five-year teacher-education program since 1974. [See Chapter 3.] Austin College (Texas) Professor John E. White, writing in *Education Week* (1985), chided newcomers to the five-year program movement by noting that a successful five-year program has been in operation at his institution since 1968. [See Chapter 2.]

Within the past three years extended programs have become operational at three large institutions: The University of Kansas [see Chapter 6], the University of Florida [see Chapter 7], and Memphis State University. The models used in these programs are described briefly in the following section.

Alternative Models of Extended Programs

There are at least seven programmatic configurations that can be designed under the rubric of extended programs. This section contains a brief description of the various patterns and then presents a fuller description of the program model now in use at Memphis State University. The Memphis State model is used as the primary illustration because the author helped conceptualize, develop, and implement that program and, also, because the program's chief features are similar to those in the several other proposed models.

The seven alternative models for the preparation of teachers range from five to seven years in length; each contains a somewhat different profile as described below. The descriptions are abstracted from the AACTE task force report on extended programs (1983).

FOUR-PLUS-ONE (B.A.). This model is a four-year program extended by one additional year of professional studies and practicum or internship. It culminates in the baccalaureate degree and typically includes studies in general education and in the teaching field(s) (customarily and appropriately taken in a college of liberal arts and sciences). Professional studies may include generic pedagogical and foundation studies, subject-specific professional studies, and clinical application of professional studies. The fundamental distinction between traditional teacher preparation programs and the program described in this model is one of degree (amount of study), rather than kind.

FOUR-PLUS-ONE (INTERNSHIP). Also culminating in the baccalaureate degree, this model calls for the first four years of study closely resembling traditional teacher education programs. The extended year involves a year-long internship with much more extensive professional practice than is the case in traditional programs. In the evolution of education toward full professional status, this model would be positive in the short term and negative in the long term. In other words, if a program for the preparation of educators emphasizes an experiential base to an inordinate degree, the field might be viewed as a skilled craft requiring an apprenticeship rather than as a full profession built upon an extensive knowledge base.

FIVE-YEAR (B.A. PLUS MASTERS). This model takes on a configuration significantly different from the above two models. It is based upon a five-year program in which the fifth year is closely integrated with the previous four years, allowing modest increases in the teaching field subject-matter and general education components. It may also provide the opportunity for a preprofessional component prior to engaging in professional studies. This component could include areas of study that bear upon education but are not professional education *per se,* such as rural sociology, urban sociology, cultural anthropology, and abnormal psychology. The model provides the opportunity for including substantial increased professional knowledge in the program.

FIVE-PLUS-ONE-YEAR (MASTER'S DEGREE PLUS INTERNSHIP). The five-plus-one-year model is similar to the five-year model in that it permits a slightly larger professional component. It is different in that it specifies a substantially larger clinical component. The model permits more sophisticated clinical practice based upon a larger knowledge base and, also, increased time for clinical application.

FOUR-PLUS-TWO-YEARS. The four-plus-two-year model implies major changes in the form and kind of teacher preparation. Entry and participation in this program assumes a strong background in general education and subject-matter preparation. A common preprofessional component is also required.

The entire professional program is postbaccalaureate, making it possible for SCDEs to function more fully as professional schools. Although requiring a more rigorous background, this model still permits schools of education to function more independently of colleges of liberal arts and sciences. The model would permit a slightly expanded professional knowledge segment beyond the models presented earlier, perhaps resulting in greater rigor within the professional component with the greater application of research findings to the teaching-learning setting. In addition this model would increase the potential for highly integrated professional knowledge and clinical components.

FOUR-PLUS-THREE-YEARS (DOCTORATE). This ultimate model culminates in the acquisition of a teaching doctorate and connotes the full professionalization of teaching.

The model is consistent with the one presented previously in that the entire professional study is postbaccalaureate. It has powerful implications for major changes in administrator preparation. It should be acknowledged that this model would be the most expensive model to implement. The question of whether the costs exceed or are less than the anticipated benefits has received little discussion, but the evidence at present seems obvious.

THREE-PLUS-THREE (DOCTORATE). A three-plus-three model program is also possible and has been proposed. Clearly, a variety of models can be developed based upon a professional program built upon three years of undergraduate study outside SCDEs. As is true for some of the other models, there may be variation in the configuration of the model among elementary, special, and secondary education programs.

In the first three years of the program, study in general education and the teaching subject matter areas would be completed in a college of liberal arts and sciences. During the second three years, emphasis would be upon study in foundational areas of education, generic, pedagogical, subject, and age-specific pedagogical content, and the clinical component of the program. It would be highly desirable for clinical components to be incorporated in virtually all aspects of professional study.

This program has the added virtue of making it possible to increase the time available in subject matter and general education study as well as preprofessional and professional education. Consequently, it should be possible to build not upon existing courses but to redesign programs in an effort to provide pedagogical knowledge consistent with the growing knowledge base on effective teaching and learning.

Extended Programs Currently in Operation

As noted earlier there are at least five extended teacher-education programs on the scene. The programs at Austin College in Sherman, Texas, and at the University of New Hampshire have been in operation for more than a decade. They have survived start-up problems and attest to the fact that extended programs can work in relatively small institutions.

Other extended programs are in large, multipurpose and complex state universities such as the University of Kansas, the University of Florida, and Memphis State University. Monahan (1984) describes both the common features of these programs as well as their differences. The next three paragraphs are based heavily on his description.

All three of these are extended programs—that is, they involve a period of overall study that goes beyond the traditional four-year period. Although similar in many ways, these programs are far from being alike. Some result in a five-year baccalaureate degree, others in a master's degree. All of them require a long internship or student teaching experience (typically, one full school year), and all of them also place more responsibility on the classroom teacher who supervises the on-the-job experiences of the trainee. Such programs vary greatly in the ways that content areas are designed and in the nature of the curricula that are followed.

The Memphis State program, for example, requires an undergraduate liberal arts degree or the equivalent for entry, and its pedagogical component is designed with an intensive summer session followed by a full academic year of internship, plus another intensive summer after that. The Florida program, known as PROTEACH, integrates all academic clinical experiences across a full five years. The program leads ultimately to the M.A. degree but provides for the awarding of the bachelor's degree at the appropriate time in the program when one has completed such requirements. Florida's initial program plan provides for three areas of certification—secondary, elementary, and special education. The Kansas University plan, on the other hand, has the bachelor's degree awarded at the end of approximately four years, but the student is not recommended for certification until the end of the fifth year.

At Memphis State the program is quite clearly linked with the state's recently enacted "Master Teacher" plan. In order to be successful over time, programs for teacher preparation, extended programs included, must make changes that are congruent with legislated reform movements. As was pointed out by Corrigan (1984, 16), "Anyone who doesn't think that these master-teacher programs and career-ladder programs being installed by states and school districts are teacher education and who continues to believe that teacher preparation can only be carried out in colleges and universities is very badly mistaken."

A fuller description of the program at Memphis State is provided for the reasons given earlier. This program is primarily a four-plus-one, M.A.T.-type program. Its dual entry options accommodate two viable groups into teacher education. One option permits entering freshmen who wish to prepare for a teaching career to enroll in an undergraduate preeducation curriculum (not unlike the nature and purpose of premed and prelaw configurations) and complete the baccalaureate degree in the chosen teaching field. Included in the preeducation curriculum is a small band of courses (ten semester hours for elementary and special education majors and eight for secondary majors) for preprofessional courses and field experiences. These few courses enable the undergraduate students to test their decision to pursue a teaching career, to validate their interest and aptitude, and to gain a preliminary understanding of schools and teaching.

The second entry option accommodates persons who have already completed an undergraduate degree with a major in one or more of the teaching fields ordinarily found in grades K–12. This feature is especially appropriate for schools of education in large urban areas where literally thousands of such persons reside and many of them, for a variety of reasons, decide later in life to embark upon a career in teaching. Some such persons are career changers who, in the late twenties or early thirties, haven't "found their niche" and seek a more fulfilling job. Others are second career persons such as a retiring engineer who at age fifty-five wants to work another ten to fifteen years and sees a second career as a physics/chemistry teacher as being both logical and practical.

At Memphis State, the M.A.T. program contains a generic core of pedagogical studies including the following five major areas of content:

1. The social, philosophical, theoretical foundations of education, with emphasis on current trends, issues, and problems in education, multicultural considerations and the role of schools and teachers in American society

2. Principles of human development and learning theory applied to teaching

3. Handicapping and exceptional conditions of students and their implication for teaching and learning

4. Interaction and intervention strategies with students, parents, teachers, and other professionals

5. Instructional strategies and materials (including computer usage and the utilization of other media and technology), reading in the content field, classroom organization and management, measurement and evaluation and curriculum planning, strategies and resources applicable to the field(s) of teaching specialization

A full-time, nine-month internship under a Career Level III "Master" teacher incorporates instruction in specialized curriculum and pedagogy concurrent with direct teaching responsibilities.

The M.A.T. degree program can be completed over a fifteen-month period. Students are admitted only once a year, in June, and proceed through the program in clusters of approximately twenty persons. Campus-based instruction occurs during the two summer sessions and in late afternoon-evening courses during the fall and spring semesters.

The minimum requirement for the M.A.T. is forty-five semester hours. Approximately half of the study is completed on campus in generic courses with certain laboratory applications targeted for completion during the full-year internship. College of Education faculty work with the interns and their level III teacher/mentors in ways similar to those typically employed in the student teaching programs. Faculty from the intern's teaching specialty serve on each intern's mentoring team. Interns are paid stipends of approximately half the salary of a beginning teacher.

As a condition of graduation from the program and in order to attain teacher certification in Tennessee, students are required to meet the state-prescribed minimum score on the "Core Battery Tests" of the National Teacher Examination. The appropriate "Specialty Area Test" of the National Teacher Examination probably will be required later. Interns whose stipends are paid by the state must teach two years in a Tennessee public school or repay the amount of the stipend. Graduates of the five-year program are eligible for employment as apprentice teachers, having been allowed to count the internship year as the probationary year now required in Tennessee of all graduates of four-year programs.

Risks, Issues, and Problems

It would be naive to assume that teacher-education programs can be substantially redesigned and extended beyond the traditional four-year model without experiencing several rather serious implementation problems and without confronting several realities that require serious attention. The AACTE task force report on extended programs (1983b) devotes an entire section to these several issues and problems and suggests ways that they might be dealt with effectively.

That report identifies at least five sets of issues and problems that will be involved in the extension of the current four-year curricula in teacher education. These include (1) questions as to the adequacy of the knowledge base in teacher education to justify an extension; (2) additional costs associated with the extension, both for students and for institutions; (3) difficulties encountered by colleges and universities, especially for institutions without graduate programs that want to continue to prepare teachers; (4) legal matters including program approval, accreditation, and certification; and (5) relationships with external groups such as employing agencies.

Additional issues and problems undoubtedly will surface as the movement continues. It should be remembered, however, that change in any professional preparation program is complex, controversial, and typically rather slow.

In our own field the transition from normal schools to teacher's colleges and university schools of education was a slow and difficult process, taking a full thirty years to complete. Conversion to extended models may move more rapidly, but perhaps with no less intensity in discussions and debate.

It is important to weigh the problems and difficulties against expected benefits—and benefits should be thought of as both immediate and long-term. In the next section the author projects nine benefits he believes will accrue if the initial preparation of teaching is moved to the postbaccalaureate level via an extended model.

Expected Benefits

1. Extended program models free up some of the life space at the baccalaureate level that normally would be devoted to professional studies. The additional space can be used to increase students' studies in their chosen teaching fields and in general education. At Memphis State, for example, the new program increases the liberal studies (general education and teaching field[s]) component of the curriculum by about 20 percent for secondary and 31 percent for elementary students when compared to the current B.S.Ed. and M.Ed. program combined. (This comparison is used because it is intended that the performance level of the graduate of the five-year extended program will be equal to that attained by students in traditional preparation models, that is, the traditional master's degree in addition to the traditional baccalaureate degree in education.) The internship/clinical component is increased by 70 percent to 133 percent for elementary students and 133 percent for secondary education students. The professional studies component (exclusive of the internship) in the five-year program is reduced by 31–41 percent for secondary and 29 percent for elementary teachers when compared to the current B.S.Ed. program. Professional studies are reduced 61–64 percent for secondary and 55 percent for elementary teachers when compared to the combined B.S.Ed. and M.Ed. program.

The reduction in professional education is justified largely by the belief that the students who have completed an undergraduate degree program with high marks can accelerate their pedagogical training and thereby use the freed-up life space in the undergraduate program for more studies in academic fields.

2. As implied above, pedagogical training is delivered at a higher level of sophistication and in a more accelerated fashion, thus enabling students to enter the teaching profession with performance skills higher than formerly attained by graduates in the undergraduate degree program, even though fewer credit hours will be devoted to studies in professional education.

3. A longer and more intensified internship under exemplary (role-model) teachers will enable students to benefit more from the internship than is typically the case with the shorter, less intense student teaching experience in undergraduate programs.

4. Teacher preparation will enjoy increased confidence and credibility with K–12 educators by their having become true partners in the preparation of preservice teachers.

5. Requirement of a bachelor degree in the teaching field followed by a graduate-level professional education component for initial certification

will signify that teacher education is rigorous, demanding, and substantive, thereby helping improve the image of teacher education with its many publics, making it more similar in this regard to preparation in law, medicine, veterinary medicine, clinical psychology, and others.

6. Some program models will sharply reduce (and eventually eliminate) the need for on-campus, specialized pedagogical courses for preservice students, thereby reducing or eliminating some rather difficult scheduling and staffing problems occasioned by small enrollments in some teaching fields. Under the plan at MSU, for example, the students receive their specialized methodology during the internship under the master teacher — one intern, one master teacher.

7. Completion of a liberal studies undergraduate degree for secondary teachers as a condition for admission to an intensive graduate-level teacher preparation component will elevate both the status and image of teacher education as it has for other professions that use similar models such as law, medicine, veterinary medicine, and clinical psychology.

8. Accountability for the preparation of teachers will be shared with many faculty throughout the university and with school practitioners, promoting increased levels of meaning, enthusiasm, and respect for teacher education through the university and in schools.

9. Teacher education is severely penalized at present by discouraging entry into the profession by anyone who doesn't elect to pursue it by the freshman year. By opening admissions to liberal arts and science upperclassmen and graduates, the applicant pool will be increased both quantitatively and qualitatively. The widened pool will attract many arts and science graduates in their late twenties and early thirties who haven't settled into fulfilling careers as well as persons in their fifties and early sixties who want teaching as a second career. Attracting these two cohorts will add quality and credibility to the teaching work force thereby enhancing the image of the teaching profession.

SUMMARY

There is increasing evidence that the traditional four-year model for the initial preparation of teachers is inadequate for the needs of even today's schools, not to mention the kinds of schools being envisioned for the future. Also increasing is the number of commission reports along with thoughtful and knowledgeable individuals advocating that the current model be extended by at least one year. Indeed, several reports have recommended an extension of two or more years. The growing body of literature on extended programs contains at least seven possible programmatic configurations (models) ranging from five to seven years in length.

There seems to be little doubt that five-year programs will increase in number during the next three to five years. Indeed, there is reason to predict with confidence that by the year 2000 teacher-education programs that exceed four years in length will be commonplace. This transition will be comparable to the way two-year normal schools were replaced with four-year programs.

Much of the current debate about the need for extended programs will very likely give way to debates as to which particular model is most effective and the most feasible. The four-plus-one master's degree could well emerge as the most popular model due to the political attractiveness of its liberal arts, baccalaureate degree base as a precondition for the fifth-year pedagogical component. The five-year, integrative model that terminates in the master's degree is likely to be popular as well.

One can hope that the extending of teacher-preparation programs and the benefits that accrue will be viewed as a professionalizing step. The chances are good that policymakers and legislative bodies in states that have serious reform efforts underway will interpret the movement as a sufficient basis for improving the attractiveness of the teaching profession including the restructuring of schools, the improvement of salaries, and the creation of better working conditions.

BIBLIOGRAPHY

American Association of Colleges for Teacher Education. *Educating a Profession.* Washington, D.C.: American Association of Colleges for Teacher Education, 1976.

―――. *Educating a Profession: Competency Assessment.* Washington, D.C.: American Association of Colleges for Teacher Education, 1983a.

―――. *Educating a Profession: Extended Programs for Teacher Education.* Washington, D.C.: American Association of Colleges for Teacher Education, 1983b.

―――. *Educating a Profession: Profile of a Beginning Teacher.* Washington, D.C.: American Association of Colleges for Teacher Education, 1983c.

―――. *Report to the Profession.* Washington, D.C.: American Association of Colleges for Teacher Education, 1983d.

Committee for Economic Development. *Investing in Our Children: Business and the Public Schools.* Washington, D.C.: Educational Commission of the States, 1985.

Corrigan, D. Paper presented at Leadership Institute, American Association of Colleges for Teacher Education, Gallaudet College, Washington, D.C., June 1984.

Lanier, J. *Goals for the Education of Teachers as Professionals.* East Lansing: Holmes Group Report, 1985.

Monahan, W. *Teacher Education in the '90's: A Working Paper.* Occasional paper 016, Occasional Paper Series. Charleston: Appalachia Educational Laboratory, 1984.

National Commission on Excellence in Education. *A Nation at Risk.* Washington, D.C.: U.S. Government Printing Office, 1983.

Tucker, M. *Presentation to Board of Directors.* Chicago: American Association of Colleges for Teacher Education, Feb. 24, 1986.

White, J. "How We Arrived at Five-year Teacher Education." *Education Week ,* 5, no. 3, Sept. 18, 1985:24,

Wise, A. Presentation at Annual Meeting of American Association of Colleges for Teacher Education. Chicago, Feb. 28, 1986.

6 | Launching Extended Teacher-education Programs in a Multi-versity: The Kansas Experiment

DALE P. SCANNELL

REFORM OF TEACHER EDUCATION has been one of the predictable topics to receive attention by educators and policymakers in response to the "crisis" in American education described by a number of review panels, most notable the National Commission on Excellence in Education report, *A Nation at Risk*. The responses have included a variety of recommendations: that teacher education be abolished entirely, that alternative ways to qualify for initial certification be used, that the traditional four-year program be made more rigorous, and that teacher-education programs be extended to enable the development of more comprehensive training prior to initial certification.

In a paper recently presented to the annual meeting of the Association of Teacher Educators, Cruickshank (1986) reviewed proposals for reform and noted that twelve of twenty-seven proposals for reform made recommendations about the length of teacher education and eleven of the twelve proposed expanding the curriculum and extending the program. Although several recommended programs exceeded five years, the most common recommended length was five years.

Recommendations for extended teacher-education programs have appeared in educational literature periodically for at least twenty-five years. During the 1960s, a period when this country was nursing its wounds caused by the launching of Sputnik by the Soviet Union, a number of writers suggested that teacher-education programs should be extended to

Dale P. Scannell is professor and dean of the College of Education, University of Maryland, College Park.

five years. The timing for such proposals, even with the Sputnik-stimulated concern about American education, was not favorable to the adoption of a program format that would delay the entry of new teachers into the field and perhaps reduce the number of students interested in pursuing teacher education. The 1960s were an era during which K–12 education was experiencing rapidly expanded enrollments, which in turn created a need for additional qualified teachers. In addition to the supply-demand problem, the knowledge base for justifying an expanded teacher-education program was extremely weak during the 1960s.

Even so, in the late 1960s Austin College in Sherman, Texas, developed a five-year teacher-education program that culminated in the award of a master's degree. [See Chapter 2.] This innovation remained a well-guarded secret in professional circles for many years, and only recently has the possibility of extended programs received widespread attention.

The current interest in extended teacher-education programs can be traced to the publication in 1976 of the report of the Bicentennial Commission established by the American Association of Colleges for Teacher Education (AACTE). The report, titled *Educating a Profession,* challenged teacher education leaders to take bold steps to move the field of teaching from a semiprofession to a full profession. Included in the commission recommendations was the expansion of the teacher-education curriculum to 150 hours, thus creating a five-year program. Even though AACTE and other professional organizations did little to encourage the debate on this recommendation or the implementation of more comprehensive teacher-education programs, *Educating a Profession* became the basic reference work for those in the profession who were considering ways in which teacher-education programs could be improved.

THE RATIONALE FOR EXTENDED PROGRAMS

The prevailing model for teacher education in the United States was adopted during the late 1920s and the early 1930s when the four-year baccalaureate program was implemented. Thus, for more than fifty years the same general model has prevailed. This is a longer period of time than any previous plateau in the evolution of teacher education. In addition it is a much longer period than will be found in the evolution of virtually all other fields of professional preparation.

The change from the two-year normal-school model to the four-year baccalaureate model was dramatic in its time. Not only was the time frame for teacher education doubled, but the change also recognized the importance of academic revitalization in teacher education. The baccalaureate program may have been adequate at the time of its adoption, but the nature of our society, the expectations for schools and teachers, and the knowledge base related to teaching and learning have changed in many remarkable ways since the initial adoption of this model. Fifty years ago most children completed schooling in the community where they started elementary school. The mores of a given community were relatively monolithic, and they were understood and accepted by most citizens of that community. In general, children grew up in homes with two parents, one who worked outside the home to earn the family livelihood, and importantly, one who was at home to greet children at the end of the school day. In 1930 teachers were among the best educated people in a community and were respected as dedicated contributors to the stability of the community. Expectations for schools were relatively narrow with an emphasis on the teaching of basic skills and academic subjects.

In contrast to these conditions our current society is much more complex. The child who attends school in the same district from kindergarten through grade twelve is no longer the norm. Many children attend schools in a number of communities during their K–12 careers, because mobility now characterizes our society. Most communities today have populations that include a variety of life-styles and value systems. The church as an institution, the community, and even the family provide less structure and nurturance for children and youth. Many children live with single parents or with parents in their second or third marriages. The role of the school has been expanded to include a major responsibility for implementing public policy and social change. In response to this relatively new responsibility school curricula have been expanded to include health education, economic education, career education, and parent education; the creeping curriculum includes substance abuse education and driver education among the many other topics for which schools have now been assigned responsibility. All of the changes noted above impact the role of teachers and should impact the way in which teachers are prepared to meet their responsibilities. However, teacher education has not evolved to keep pace with the rest of society and the four-year model continues to prevail.

The expansion of the teacher-education curriculum, and thus the extension of teacher-education programs, would not be justified unless the added course work contributed to better-educated teachers and more skillful instructional leaders. There are at least two ways in which this issue can be addressed. First, many recent studies have described the need to strengthen liberal arts in institutions of higher education. The reports cite the gradual erosion of the liberal arts component in the curricula for many professional fields including engineering, pharmacy, business, and architecture, as well as teacher education. As the knowledge base for the professional fields has expanded, the professional component has been enriched at the expense of the liberal arts. These changes have occurred at a time when the liberal arts are increasingly important for the graduates of institutions of higher education who will be assuming leadership positions in business, industry, and political endeavors. Recognizing the need for comprehensive coverage of both the liberal arts and the professionally oriented topics, the reports have recommended that many university curricula be expanded to a minimum of five years.

Second, the knowledge base for teaching, perhaps tenuous for a long period of time, has expanded rapidly during the past ten to fifteen years. We now know more than we can teach in the time allocated for professional course work in four-year teacher-education programs. Pedagogy cannot be taught in isolation from the world of practice. Thus, prospective teachers must be provided an opportunity to work in actual school settings and to learn applications of the theories taught in didactic settings. Teachers must know not only the structure of the content they are teaching, they must also be skillful in assessing student progress and the learning strengths and weaknesses of their students. Teachers must have a repertoire of instructional strategies and the skill to adapt various methodologies to the unique needs of individual learners. Teachers must develop skill in working with other adults including parents and school specialists. These are only samples of the pedagogy required to prepare effective professionals, and the material should not be covered in a perfunctory fashion within a seriously constrained professional curriculum.

The liberal arts are increasingly important to a well-educated society and require more time than is currently provided in professional programs. Subject matter content must be comprehensive in the teacher-education curriculum. Professional course work requires more time than has been provided in the traditional four-year program. All of these factors argue for the need to expand teacher-education curricula and to extend teacher preparation programs.

MODELS FOR EXTENDED TEACHER-EDUCATION PROGRAMS

Among the extended teacher-education programs now in operation and those currently being planned, two general models with variations are characteristic. One model includes the integration of professional course work with the liberal arts and teaching field content throughout the five-year period. The second model includes a baccalaureate program with a major in a liberal arts field followed by a year of professional study.

In some of the programs using the integrated model the first two years include only general education; the upper division course work includes both teaching-field content and professional study, and the fifth year is devoted entirely, or mostly, to professional study including student teaching. Some programs of this type include some early but limited introductory professional work at the lower division level.

Some programs of the second type adhere strictly to the model with no professional work prior to the fifth year. These programs generally include a requirement for work during the summers preceding and following the fifth year. A slight variation of this model includes a relatively small amount of professional work during the first four years, usually tied to field experiences.

THE EXTENDED TEACHER-EDUCATION PROGRAM AT THE UNIVERSITY OF KANSAS

One of the first extended teacher-education programs to be introduced by a doctoral granting school of education within a complex university was at the University of Kansas. The program became effective for students matriculating to higher education in the fall of 1981 with the first class from the extended program graduating in May of 1986.

The decision to embark on an extended teacher-education program was made by the education faculty as part of a planning process that had started in 1979. In the process of defining a role for the School of Education that would be consistent with the purposes and environment of the University of Kansas, the faculty decided that preservice programs for teachers should emphasize the research base for teacher education and should strive to provide a comprehensive professional program built on a foundation of the liberal arts and depth in teaching fields. High quality and experimentation were deemed to be more appropriate for the institution than attempts to graduate large numbers of new teachers.

A committee was formed representing faculty from all departments in the school. The committee was asked to develop a paper that described the characteristics the institution should strive to develop in its teacher-education students, a rationale for a new program, and a description of a program that might accomplish the goal noted above. The committee was asked to propose goals for the program and not to be constrained by the amount of time the program would require. With regard to a rationale for a new teacher-education program, the factors cited by the committee included:

1. Because of the constant expansion of knowledge and the changing perceptions by society on the role of education, educators are needed with the ability to adapt to change.

2. A teacher-education program should include a strong emphasis on the use of research findings.

3. Because individualized instruction was increasingly needed and emphasized in the schools, prospective teachers should be provided training and field experience to prepare them to individualize effectively for all students.

4. Prospective teachers should develop the capability to use educational technology to improve their instruction and to enhance student learning.

The concept paper also included fifty-three objectives related to nine major goals for a teacher-education program. The nine goals are:

1. The professional teacher possesses self-understanding.

2. The professional teacher has knowledge of human growth, development, and learning and applies this knowledge to teaching children and adolescents.

3. The professional teacher is skilled in human relations.

4. The professional teacher understands curriculum planning and is skilled in choosing and adapting instructional strategies to implement varying curricula.

5. The professional teacher manages a learning environment effectively.

6. The professional teacher evaluates student learning and uses educational research methodologies to improve instruction in student learning.

7. The professional teacher understands the scope of the teaching profession and the school as a social-political organization.

8. The professional teacher is a liberally educated person.

9. The professional teacher has thorough knowledge of the aspects of at least one subject matter area that is included in the public school curriculum.

Even though the concept paper did not attempt to specify courses or credits, it was clear that the goals could not be met adequately in a four-year program. However, the faculty approved the concept paper, without dissent, as a basis for revising the teacher-education program.

The next step in the process was to do a "reality check" by obtaining reactions from members of the school's off-campus advisory group comprised of local teacher leaders, superintendents, and representatives of state organizations. Copies of the concept paper were mailed with an invitation to meet on campus to discuss the implications of the paper. The discussion centered on the general nature of the program, the employability of graduates from such a program, and the feasibility of the program.

Though the reactions included cautions, support for the program was generally stronger than anticipated. Teachers praised the emphasis on K-12 classroom experiences throughout the curriculum and others applauded the breadth of the general education component. Questions were raised about the feasibility of asking students to spend extra time in completing a program leading to employment for insufficient salaries, but others observed that better preparation could lead to better salaries. In fact, superintendents in the group indicated willingness to modify salary schedules in recognition of the added training. Two major conclusions came from the discussion. First, the school was encouraged to develop the program. Second, the teachers and administrators volunteered to assist in program development and implementation.

Throughout the next three semesters committees worked on various aspects of the program: general education, subject-field requirements, the experiential component, professional education requirements, and student teaching. The general model derived included sixty semester hours of general education distributed across English, speech, the humanities, the social sciences, natural science, and mathematics. The teaching-field requirement was a major with a minimum of forty hours or two minors with minimums of twenty hours. Although course work from general education could be counted in the teaching field, the requirements ensured inclusion of upper-division advanced courses. The professional education component was sixty hours including all experiential and clinical activities.

The distribution of requirements was intended to accomplish several goals related to the premises of the program. All teachers, regardless of subject or level, should be models of liberally educated people and capable of relating concepts and issues across academic boundaries. Thus, prospective teachers should be engaged in a solid general education experience.

Teachers should have depth in the subjects to be taught and thus study in the teaching fields should ensure comprehension of how knowledge in the field is created and how validity of new concepts is determined. When teaching fields were all designed, the actual minimums turned out to be forty-three hours in the majors and twenty-five hours in the minors.

The professional component was designed to include frequent in-school experiences so that theory and practice could be articulated. In addition professional course work was based on the emerging knowledge base of scholarship and accepted good practice.

Two "escape" points were built into the program at the end of the sophomore and senior years. A small amount of professional course work was placed in years one and two so that students would have the opportunity to make an informed decision about their choice of education as a major. Follow-up studies have indicated that many teacher-education graduates from traditional programs discovered late in their programs that teaching was not a good career for them. The earlier exposure to schools, pedagogy, and the job of a teacher allowed students to transfer majors, if a change seemed appropriate at the end of the sophomore year, in time to complete a major in a different field within the normal four-year baccalaureate program.

At the end of four years students who had met the requirements of the program were granted a bachelor's degree but had not qualified for certification. Thus, those who became disenchanted with teaching as a career during their upper-division experiences could drop out of the program with a university degree and an education comparable to that of liberal arts graduates. The design of the program increased the likelihood that upper-division students were committed to teaching and virtually ensured that students in the fifth year were committed to, and confident of, their decisions to become teachers.

The professional component of the program was organized in a spiral approach to four major themes. These are (1) growth and development of children and youth, (2) self-concept and interpersonal relationships, (3) research, measurement, and technology, and (4) field experiences and application of theory to practice. Most of the course work in these themes is generic, required, and appropriate regardless of field or level of intended teaching.

The generic approach to pedagogy has several important implications. First, faculty with teaching assignments in these courses can concentrate personal professional development on the research in their area of assignment. As a result they can be expected to be up-to-date at all times with the best of what is known in the topics of their assignment. Second, students will be exposed to applicability of concepts across teaching fields and age levels and thus be better able to relate their own instructional planning to the total school curriculum. Third, subject methods instructors are freed from the responsibilities of trying to stay current in all aspects of pedagogy, and methods courses can focus on techniques and characteristics specific to their subject field.

Admission to the fifth year of the program requires students to have a 2.75 GPA on a four-point scale for provisional admission and 3.0 for clear admission. Since some of the work in the fifth year is at the graduate level, admission to graduate school is required.

The fifth year was designed to include two student teaching assignments and a period of study in advanced courses. The first part of the fall semester was a six-week student teaching assignment. This was followed by course work that could be more meaningful because of the student teaching experience. The spring semester was to be a second student teaching assignment in a different school, perhaps at a different level, and for some students in a second teaching field.

The design of student teaching ensured that students would experience the requirements of both the opening and closing of school, that is, the decisions and planning that occur as a year's work is initiated and evaluated. Students are encouraged to student teach in different types of schools — urban, suburban, rural, large, and small. By working with two different cooperating teachers, different styles and approaches could be experienced. This, it was predicted, would assist prospective teachers in developing a repertoire of skills and behaviors effective for them.

Secondary and middle-level students are encouraged to take two teaching majors or one major and one minor. Since most schools, even those midsize to large, must assign teachers to more than one subject, the completion of a planned teaching field would serve the students well both in seeking a position and subsequently in performing effectively.

Elementary students are required to take, as a minimum, two minor teaching fields. This approach was a compromise between the belief that depth in a field was intellectually appropriate and the recognition of the breadth of content for which elementary teachers are responsible. The two minors also would serve the student well if hired after graduation by a school in which some form of quasi-departmentalization occurs, an increasingly popular approach in schools.

Several aspects of the program were topics of heated debate among the faculty. Some advocated a requirement that students qualify for certification at two levels — elementary and middle school, middle school and secondary. Others recommended that students be encouraged, but not required, to certify at two levels — a viewpoint that prevailed.

Some advocated that secondary education students be required to complete two teaching fields; others wanted this to be a recommendation, not a requirement. The latter view prevailed.

The configuration of student teaching was debated at length. The major issue was the amount of time students should have uninterrupted by seminars, course work, or group meetings for other purposes. Some agreed that periodic seminars would allow close articulation between theory and practice. Others advocated very long periods of uninterrupted student teaching. The compromise leans very heavily in the latter direction.

The most serious disagreement among faculty was the nature of credit in the fifth year and thus the degree to be granted. The decision was to grant graduate credit for organized courses and, under very strict conditions, to part of the second student teaching assignment (sometimes referred to as a practicum or internship). Thus it is virtually impossible for students to earn a master's degree at the end of the fifth year. Summer session enrollments between the fourth and fifth years and after the fifth year would enable some students to complete the master's degree.

External reviewers of the program noted that the total program contained all of the elements, plus other features, of what normally comprises a bachelor's and a master's in education, even if some work technically in a master's degree is found in year four, and student teaching, normally in year four, is in year five. Representatives of departments that typically include practica as part of the master's degree program expressed surprise and even dismay at the attitude of other colleagues. For most students in the program, completion of all requirements will earn a bachelor's degree, about twelve to fifteen hours of graduate credit, and the institutional recommendation for certification.

EPILOGUE

In retrospect, the first step of the formal process that led to creating an extended program was absolutely critical, namely, achieving faculty consensus on the essential characteristics of students graduating in teacher education from the institution. The concept paper was developed by a committee with representatives of all departments in the school. The paper listed premises about the future, the skills and knowledge that students should possess by the time of graduation, and the goals of the teacher-education program. This paper not only provided a structure for future work, it also represented a commitment on the part of the faculty in the School of Education.

The commitment was absolutely critical for a number of reasons. First, careful program revision takes time and energy, and resolve weakens sometimes in the face of hours of tedious committee work. Second, even though faculty are most often guided by lofty motives, agreement to principles in abstraction is more easily achieved than getting agreement about changing a professor's course or teaching assignment. More than one person who endorsed the concept paper found reasons to oppose subsequent aspects of program revision, particularly when his or her course was to be changed to create generic courses in pedagogy.

The political aspects of major innovative program changes (both internal and external to the university) also test the commitment of faculty. From the time of initial planning through the first year of program implementation, the institution had three different people serving as vice-chancellor for academic affairs and three different people serving as chancellor. Deliberate efforts were made to gain support for the new program within the institution. Although at this institution faculty have autonomy in establishing degree requirements, support of the vice-chancellor is extremely important. The vice-chancellor during most of the planning started as a skeptic but became an advocate as he became more knowledgeable about teacher education and the reasons a major change was desirable. The strong support of the off-campus advisory committee was a clinching factor. A commitment was made to the school that no negative budget changes would be made if enrollment declined initially, as we and others thought would be the case. The vice-chancellor during the initial year of implementation was openly dubious of the wisdom of the new program and this added to the faculty anxiety that is typical during major unilateral recasting of programs.

During the period of program development a few members of the Board of Regents questioned our right to make the change without board approval. The vice-chancellor and chancellor were steadfast in defending our right to make the decision, but the very fact of board concern added to faculty anxiety. No pressures emanated from the State Board of Education or the State Department of Education. Both groups had been represented on the advisory committee and had allowed us to make presentations at several points during the decision process and subsequent program development. Presentations also were made to legislative committees, and although skepticism was expressed, support for more rigorous programs also was expressed.

Maintaining support, at least neutrality, among the political groups, and at the same time providing reassurance to faculty became major tasks for the administrators in the school. The attitudes can be described as a question. How can you be so sure that the change you're making is correct if there are so few other institutions (none in Kansas) making the change? And then came *A Nation at Risk* and all the attention it received. Almost overnight the attitudes of skeptics and critics changed. Campus administrators who had constantly put us on the defensive now asked us to publicize more widely the program we had initiated. *A Nation at Risk* would be a tenuous basis for deciding to implement an extended program (or many of the other changes that have been made since its publication), but it did stimulate additional studies and action in the states and made more acceptable those ideas that had little credibility as unilateral actions.

The first class of extended program students graduated in May 1986. It was a smaller class than the last to graduate in the discontinued four-year program. However, pipeline figures for the program were extremely encouraging. In addition, the students in the first extended program class were bright, talented, and committed, and many of them entered teaching. We believe that this program gave them the preparation necessary for initial teacher effectiveness and for continuing professional growth throughout their careers.

The discussion of and support for extended programs have increased markedly since the late 1970s. The debate now seems to be more on what kind of extended program than on whether to extend. No one knows the best format for teacher education, and the entry of many institutions into the extended model will provide opportunities for experimentation, evaluation, and comparative studies. These efforts will benefit schools and colleges of education and, more importantly, the children and youth who will be taught by more competent teachers.

Predicting the nature of teacher education in 1995 would be risky business, and research yet to be done will have a major impact on what becomes the normal or traditional program of 1995. However, value judgments also will play a major role. If it is true that all teachers should be models of liberally educated adults, have depth in teaching fields, and comprehend the knowledge base of effective classrooms, there seems little doubt that programs in 1995 will be more comprehensive and require more time than the four years provided as the common model of the 1980s.

BIBLIOGRAPHY

American Association of Colleges for Teacher Education. *Educating a Profession.* Washington, D.C.: American Association of Colleges for Teacher Education, 1976.

_____. *Educating a Profession: Extended Programs for Teacher Education.* Washington, D.C.: American Association of Colleges for Teacher Education, 1983a.

_____. *Educating a Profession: Profile of a Beginning Teacher.* Washington, D.C.: American Association of Colleges for Teacher Education, 1983b.

Association of American Colleges. *Project on Redefining the Meaning and Purpose of Baccalaureate Degrees.* Washington, D.C.: Association of American Colleges, 1985.

Berliner, D. "Making the Right Changes in Preservice Teacher Education." *Phi Delta Kappan* 66, no. 2(1984):94–96.

Cremin, L. A. *The Education of the Educating Professions.* 19th Annual Charles W. Hunt Lecture. Washington, D.C.: American Association of Colleges for Teacher Education, 1977.

Cruickshank, D. "Deciding What to Teach Teachers: A Synthesis of Teacher Education Curriculum Recommendations Derived from Twenty-seven Proposals."

Paper presented at annual meeting of Association of Teacher Educators, February 1986.

Gage, N. L. *The Scientific Basis for the Art of Teaching.* New York: Teachers College Press, 1978.

————. "What Do We Know about Teaching Effectiveness." *Phi Delta Kappan* 66, no. 2(1984):87–93.

Galumbos, E. C. *Teacher Preparation: The Anatomy of a College Degree.* Atlanta: Southern Regional Education Board, 1985.

Gideonse, H. "The Necessary Revolution in Teacher Education." *Phi Delta Kappan* 64, no. 18(1982):19–21.

Howsam, R., D. Corrigan, G. Denemark, and R. Nash. *Educating a Profession.* Washington, D.C.: American Association of Colleges for Teacher Education, 1976.

National Association of State Universities and Land-Grant Colleges. *Report of the Executive Committee of the Academic Affairs Council on Elementary and Secondary Education.* Washington, D.C.: National Association of State Universities and Land-Grant Colleges, 1984.

National Commission on Excellence in Education. *A Nation at Risk.* Washington, D.C.: U.S. Government Printing Office, 1983.

National Institute of Education. *Involvement in Learning: Realizing the Potential of American Higher Education.* Washington, D.C.: National Institute of Education, 1984.

Reynolds, M., ed. *A Common Body of Practice for Teachers: The Challenge of Public Law 94-142 to Teacher Education.* Washington, D.C.: American Association of Colleges for Teacher Education, 1980.

Sharpe, B., ed. *Dean's Grant Projects: Challenge and Change in Teacher Education.* Minneapolis: National Support System Project, 1982.

Smith, B. O. *A Design for a School of Pedagogy.* Washington, D.C.: U.S. Department of Education, 1980a.

————. "Now Is the Time to Advance Pedagogical Education." *Educational Theory* 30, no. 3(1980b):177–83.

Smith, D., ed. *Essential Knowledge for Beginning Teachers.* Washington, D.C.: American Association of Colleges for Teacher Education, 1983.

7 PROTEACH: The Content and Context of Change in Teacher Education at the University of Florida

ROBERT G. CARROLL

PROTEACH (Professional Teacher Program) is the new teacher preparation program of the College of Education at the University of Florida. It was implemented in the fall of 1984 after a six-year period of study, debate, and curriculum development. This chapter examines in five sections the various factors and philosophical positions that affected the development and implementation of PROTEACH. The initial portion briefly examines the primary reasons that brought most of the faculty of the college to the belief that some form of change in the traditional methods of training beginning teachers was justified. The second part focuses on the three most prominent positions taken by faculty members relative to teacher education and its philosophical underpinnings. Next, the social and political factors that affected PROTEACH are briefly described. The fourth section includes a description of the three separate PROTEACH teacher-education programs. The final part of the chapter summarizes some of the author's opinions concerning a few of the challenges that remain to be met.

THE DECISION TO CHANGE

The initial recommendation to investigate changing the format of teacher education at the University of Florida came from a faculty committee in

Robert G. Carroll is visiting assistant professor in the Department of Instruction and Curriculum, College of Education, University of Florida. He served for four years on the College of Education's Coordinating Committee, which had primary responsibility for the development of PROTEACH.

116

1978. A second faculty committee concurred with that recommendation a year later. This launched the college into an extended period of deliberations over not just what changes should be made but whether any changes should be made at all.

The preparation programs that existed in the 1970s and early 1980s at Florida commanded a great deal of loyalty from many faculty members. One program had been unchanged for a number of years and most of the faculty seemed content with it. A second program had undergone a significant curricular change some years before that had received national attention and acclaim. The third, due to the nature of its faculty, was in a constant state of self-examination and change and the faculty were confident they were moving in positive directions. Hence, the suggestion of extensively altering these programs did not meet with universal enthusiasm.

Furthermore, the loyalty to the existing programs appeared to be justified. In 1981 the National Council for the Accreditation of Teacher Education (NCATE) had examined the programs at the University of Florida. In its final report the visiting team wrote that Florida's programs were among the best that had ever been reviewed. A year later a State Department of Education review team also praised Florida's teacher-preparation programs, as did a Board of Regents report in 1984. Furthermore, the college was consistently receiving feedback from public school personnel that its graduates were doing quite well. These accolades supported the faculty in its belief that it had already developed strong programs that would continue to produce excellent teachers.

Yet, at the same time that this praise was being received the college was moving toward the reforms of PROTEACH and most of the faculty shared the belief that some form of change in the basic fabric of teacher education was appropriate. In fact, the strength of the existing programs made the PROTEACH reforms possible. Only strong programs and strong faculty can give birth to creative and innovative change.

The reasons that compelled the faculty to investigate making significant changes fell into two complementary lines of thought. The first related to the context of teaching in the foreseeable future and the second related to the status of the research base on teaching.

The demands placed on teachers today are greater than ever before. We continue to crowd the school curriculum with requirements and courses like consumer education, sex education, environmental education, drug and alcohol awareness, and suicide prevention. Certainly all of these are worthy of our attention. However, they are evidence that the schools are being forced to be all things to all people and every minute spent on these requirements is a minute not spent on mathematics, science, and language arts — the subjects in which most parents and the public at large seem to be interested. Furthermore, it is the latter group of subjects that has the more direct impact on SAT scores, the yardstick the public uses to judge the quality of education.

With increased demands for academic excellence and a crowded "cafeteria style curriculum" (National Commission 1983) it is essential that teachers be expert in the art of teaching, in the efficient use of time, and in the subject area(s) they will be expected to teach. This calls for better training of beginning teachers and better preparation for them in their teaching field than we have ever given them before.

Fifty years ago the possession of a bachelor's degree placed teachers among the most highly educated members of their communities. Today a much greater proportion of the population has graduated from high school, attended some college, obtained a bachelor's degree, or obtained an advanced degree. Meanwhile, the basic requirements for certifying teachers have not significantly changed. As a result, teachers have only slightly more training than a large portion of the public, and an equal amount or even less training than many others.

This deficiency is critical in an information age. The explosion of knowledge and the emphasis on information usage are having dramatic effects on teachers and their students. This can best be illustrated in the role that computers play in the schools. Fifteen years ago computers were esoteric instruments that were used by only a select few; today the schools are expected to help every child become computer literate and more classrooms are getting their own personal computers every day. In fact, many children are now doing their homework using microcomputers to write, edit, and print the final "hard copy."

The demands on teachers arising from life in American society are not limited to the fields of science, mathematics, and language arts; they extend to every facet of the curriculum. For example, the implications of the impact of minority cultures on mainstream America in the coming years are staggering. Social scientists and the teachers of social studies in the public schools must play a crucial role if we are ever to understand and be enriched by each other.

All of this implies that tomorrow's teachers have to be better than yesterday's. They must be better not because yesterday's were bad, but because tomorrow's will be required to know so much more, to have access to so much more, and to display greater expertise in imparting so much more to their students. Yet we are training teachers in essentially the same way and for the same length of time as we did fifty years ago. Surely this justifies a careful examination of the content and processes of preparing beginning teachers.

The preceding argument for investigating change was compelling enough for many faculty members, but for others it merely raised other questions. No one argued that we do not have to do a better job of training teachers. Professionals are always seeking better ways to do their jobs. However, do we really know any more about teaching than we knew before? Does a knowledge base for teaching and teacher education exist?

An early step in the PROTEACH curriculum development process was to investigate these questions. A series of task forces was appointed in 1981 to conduct extensive reviews of the literature to identify that knowledge which is essential for beginning teachers to have relative to effective pedagogy and to the various academic teaching fields. The task forces worked for about a full year and produced a number of research syntheses. Naturally, any series of documents done by committees working almost exclusively on their own time will be of varying quality. However, their combined effect convinced many faculty members that a knowledge base for teaching does exist. Since that time, numerous publications have added to that conviction (e.g., Good 1983; Smith 1983; Wittrock 1986).

In the state of Florida, in particular, the conviction that a knowledge base for teaching exists has had profound implications. An exhaustive search of the professional literature has given birth to something called the Florida Performance Measurement System, or the FPMS (Florida Coalition 1983). This system has codified the knowledge base into six domains of teaching, about three dozen generic teaching competencies, and seemingly hundreds of descriptors and behavioral indicators of effective practice. The result is a series of formative and summative observational instruments, which is intended to help university and public school personnel lead prospective teachers to a high degree of initial professional competence.

The recognition that an emerging knowledge base exists and the legislated requirement that beginning teachers in Florida must be able to demonstrate mastery of the FPMS competencies combined to convince many faculty members that some curricular reform was appropriate. Certainly, if such a knowledge base exists then colleges of education are honor-bound to insure that their students learn it. The further combination of these arguments with the increased demands of teaching convinced most faculty that change of some nature was needed. The shape of that change, however, was heatedly debated.

THE SHAPE OF CHANGE

Agreeing that change is justified and reaching consensus on the theoretical and philosophical stances that should provide the foundation for that change are two decidedly different matters. On a faculty of over one hundred individuals it would have been remarkable if any single vision of teachers and teacher education was acceptable to all. At Florida there were a number of positions that were avidly defended by their proponents. However, it is fair to say that most of the faculty held beliefs that represented one or more of three different conceptualizations of the function of teacher-education programs.

The first position was taken by a decided minority within the faculty, but they were among the most vocal. Furthermore, their arguments made sense, once their basic premises were accepted. In fact, several prestigious universities had accepted them and acted upon them. Therefore, this group received much attention and some serious consideration, and their ideas ultimately helped to shape PROTEACH as it is today.

In effect, they argued that colleges of education should get out of the preservice teacher-preparation business and become primarily graduate-level research centers. These proponents contended that prospective teachers should seek a liberal arts education while taking a few courses in education that focus on effective communication skills and the learning process in young persons. Later, after spending some time in the classroom, the teachers may then choose to pursue advanced degrees in education. Pedagogy would make more sense to them at that point and the university could help them refine their skills and teach them about the workings and philosophies of their profession.

This vision of colleges of education abandoning preservice preparation programs was held by a small minority of the college's faculty. Most of the faculty believed that it is a legitimate mission of colleges of education to train preservice teachers and that such a mission should be guided by one of two philosophical orientations, or a combination of them. In this chapter the terms "child-centered" and "process-centered" will be used to describe those orientations.

The philosophy of the child-centered approach was embodied at Florida in its Florida Childhood Education Program (CEP), which had received considerable national attention. One of its better articulations was in a thoughtful little book by Wass and her colleagues (Wass et al. 1974). One paragraph from that text clearly illustrates its philosophical position.

> The Florida Childhood Education Program (CEP) sees good teaching as a highly personal matter. Its theoretical base is derived from perceptual-humanistic psychology which locates the causes of behavior in the belief systems of the behavior. Beginning from those understandings, it follows that teacher education is, not a question of learning "how to teach," but a matter of personal discovery, of learning how to use one's self and surroundings to

assist other persons to learn. The Florida program is a humanistic one designed to help each student find his own best ways of teaching. As such, it represents an alternative model to the traditional behavioristically oriented thinking currently in fashion in many colleges and state and federal agencies. (p. i)

On the opposite end of the spectrum was a group of faculty who argued that "personal discovery" and "using one's self and surroundings to assist other persons to learn" is all well and good but, unless it is translated into cognitive gains and skill development, it is just so much wasted effort. They insisted that the schools are entrusted by the nation to impart a body of knowledge to its young. The function of colleges of education, therefore, is to train teachers in the most efficient means of communicating that knowledge. They focused their attention on the vast quantity of process-product research being completed by educators. They acknowledged that there would never be a direct one-to-one relationship between teacher behavior X and student outcome Y. Nonetheless, they asserted, knowing that teacher behavior X contributes to student outcome Y in the presence of context variables $A, B,$ and C gives teachers a powerful teaching tool, that is, one that it would be irresponsible to ignore.

The mission of colleges of education, therefore, is to insure that graduates (1) could recognize critical student and context variables, (2) understand the research base as it applies to those variables, (3) are aware of the teaching behaviors that are most likely to succeed in the presence of those variables, and (4) have mastered those behaviors to the extent that they can be used effectively in the classroom.

Most faculty actually held beliefs that were a synthesis of the child-centered and process-centered positions. But the pull of the two emphases was exerted on the PROTEACH curriculum development process from its inception. At times PROTEACH was tugged toward the affective domains and the child-centered philosophy; at others it was tugged toward the cognitive domains and the process-centered philosophy. Not surprisingly, the program that resulted represented a blend of both. In the end a few saw PROTEACH as being somewhat "schizophrenic," a product having two personalities with an attendant lack of philosophical consistency. However, most of the faculty seemed to believe that an appropriate combination of consensus and compromise had been reached, preserving the best of both philosophies and avoiding their extremes.

Whichever of these viewpoints proves to be more accurate remains to be seen, but one thing is abundantly clear: the professional and political climate in Florida was calling for teacher-education reform and was favoring change in the process-centered direction.

THE CONTEXT OF CHANGE

Earlier it was noted that the impetus for PROTEACH began in 1978 and the actual process of deliberation and study in 1980. This preceded by a few years the national concern for teacher education that commanded so much attention after the publication of *A Nation at Risk* (National Commission 1983). However, in 1982 and early 1983 when the actual design and plans for implementation of PROTEACH were being made, the criticism was already being felt in some key places.

For a few years prior to 1983 key individuals in the central administration of the University of Florida had been hearing criticisms of the state of teacher education nationwide. The reply usually given was that at Florida we were doing something creative about that situation. But PROTEACH was a long time in coming and pressure for concrete change was mounting. In fact, on at least two occasions one administrator reminded college faculty members that at some universities "the unthinkable has been done; colleges of education have been abolished."

It should be noted here that PROTEACH exists today largely because of the consistent and informed support of that same administration. That support surfaced in numerous ways including moral support, the protection of faculty lines when they became vacant, and political support within the university community. However, it was clear that business as usual was no longer acceptable.

Other forces were also impinging upon the college's efforts and had a significant impact on PROTEACH. Since the early to mid-1970s the Florida legislature has been very active in the reform of public education. Over the years it has raised minimum performance standards at all levels of education, enacted specific and rigorous requirements for passing from one level of education to the next and for graduating from high school, lengthened the public school day, mandated new performance standards for school administrators, adopted a merit pay plan for teachers, required that all first-year teachers be able to demonstrate proficiency in the thirty-five generic competencies of the FPMS, and so on through a long list of legislation. Aside from the fact that a more rigorous curriculum means more demands being placed on teachers (and therefore on their training), the legislation concerning the FPMS and its use in the Florida Beginning Teacher Program (FBTP) probably had the greatest impact on the college's curriculum. The faculty was well aware that the proportion of its students who were successful in the FBTP would ultimately reflect on the quality of the preparation program it had received at Florida. Fortunately, the domains of teaching identified by the FPMS and the college's task forces were almost identical in that there was a large amount of overlap in the research base that was thought to be vital to the success of a beginning teacher. Hence, that which was believed to be important by one group was indirectly mandated by the other and the curriculum changed accordingly.

THE CONTENT OF THE CHANGE

The final scope and sequence of the PROTEACH programs fell together in a four-month period from January to April 1983. However, the groundwork for the final design began at what has come to be known as the PROTEACH I Conference in May of 1980. It brought together over seventy educators representing every level of public education including classroom teachers, principals, and district administrators; representatives of the Florida branches of the American Federation of Teachers and the National Education Association; representatives from the State Department of Education and the various professional organizations within the state; and College of Education faculty members. Together they addressed three questions.

1. What does a beginning teacher need to know?
2. What does a beginning teacher need to be able to do?
3. What kind of person should a beginning teacher be?

The answers to these questions developed during PROTEACH I served as guideposts for the future direction and development of the program.

In general, the answers pointed to at least five categories of knowledge and skill that should make up the content of a teacher-preparation program. First, prospective teachers must have a broad-based general background of knowledge that they bring with them to their professional training. Second, they must have an in-depth knowledge of the subject(s) they would be expected to teach. Third, they should have a firm grasp of the research base on teaching, the theory that undergirds that research base, and the history and philosophy that provides a foundation for the profession. Fourth, they must have the pedagogical expertise needed to apply the findings of research and to maximize student learning. Fifth, they must possess the knowledge and skills necessary to interact effectively with students, parents, and fellow professionals of all kinds. These five criteria were eventually translated into a curriculum of general and professional studies that would, in the opinion of most faculty members, contribute to the development of highly effective beginning teachers.

The specifics of PROTEACH have been described extensively elsewhere (Carroll, unpublished; Carroll and McMillin 1986; Carroll and Soar 1987; McMillin et al. 1986; Smith 1984; Smith et al. 1984; Smith et al. 1983; Smith et al. 1985) so the program description presented here is relatively brief.

PROTEACH is an extended, integrated, five-year program of general and professional studies leading to initial teacher certification and the master of education degree. It is built on a broad-based general background knowledge component. Students come to the College of Education after completing at least sixty-four semester hours of work. The university has set some parameters for thirty-six of these hours in order to guarantee that they be distributed among English; the physical, biological, and mathematical sciences; the social and behavioral sciences; and the humanities. This component is further delineated by the preprofessional requirements of the individual programs within PROTEACH. They each list specific courses that can be used to fulfill some of the general component and others that expand upon it.

As the background knowledge component provides students with a broad base of general information, the PROTEACH foundational component provides a strong basis in some critical areas of professional knowledge. The foundational component includes thirteen hours of study in the social and historical foundations of education, child development, learning and cognition, measurement and evaluation, and mainstreaming. All students take a course in instructional computing and students in the elementary and special education programs also share a course in parent education. Taken in its entirety, this component provides all PROTEACH students with a shared background of professional knowledge and skills that is essential to the development of prospective educators.

The elementary education program comprises five years of preparation including six semesters of professional study leading to the master's degree and initial certification. Students in this program are required to complete a twelve-hour specialization in an academic teaching field outside of the College of Education. A second specialization may also be taken outside of the college or inside of the college in a professional specialization such as early childhood, middle grades, special education, or the teaching of reading. The academic specializations were developed in close cooperation with faculty in other colleges in the university, and they represent specific sequences of study beyond that which may have been taken in the general education component.

Students become members of a clinical seminar immediately upon their entry into the college and begin their fieldwork at that time. Ideally, students remain in the same seminar with the same seminar leader throughout their program. The seminar and its members then become a support system, a laboratory for practicing skills, and a forum for feelings and new ideas.

The elementary program emphasizes a dedication to research and to a holistic evaluation of student progress. Courses in educational diagnosis and evaluation and in the research base for teaching are taken early in the program to provide students with a basis for reading and analyzing the professional literature in subsequent courses. A master's level seminar provides each student with the opportunity to pursue a research interest of his or her own that is related to teaching practice. Evaluation practices include a student portfolio that contains written and videotaped evidence of the student's mastery of the FPMS competencies, evaluations from university and school-based personnel, and the students' own logs, journals, and personal reactions to their fieldwork.

The special education program requires that all students work toward certification in two of the four areas of exceptionalities (mental retardation, emotional handicaps, learning disabilities, and motor disabilities). Students must also opt for either the mild- or severe-handicapping track. During their program they are further required to complete an eighteen-hour academic specialization outside of the College of Education.

The Department of Special Education faculty follows a precision teaching model. It has developed a data-based, computerized evaluation system that allows faculty members to track their students' success in teaching exceptional children on a skill-by-skill basis. The result is a diagnostic and prescriptive process that is much more precise than is normally even attempted.

Students in special education are expected to become familiar with the FPMS observational system and are required to use it to analyze their own and other students' teaching. Each advanced student acts as a peer counselor and support system for one beginning student. They work together to improve each other's teaching and the fifth-year student helps the new student survive some of the rough spots in the first year of a rigorous program. Fifth-year students are also assigned to work with a graduate-level student in the Department of Counselor Education to develop an individual educational plan for a specific student. These sessions are videotaped and later analyzed by the students and their professors, thereby helping them to work effectively on an interdisciplinary staffing team.

The secondary education program is unique among the other PRO-TEACH programs in that it does not include a bachelor's degree in education. Instead students are expected to complete their bachelor's degree in a teaching field in the College of Liberal Arts and Sciences. They are also required to complete the foundational component described above prior to their entry into the College of Education for a year of professional studies.

During that graduate year students take an additional nine hours in their teaching field, a requirement that grows out of a commitment to in-depth training in the subject area and one that exceeds the minimum requirement set by the graduate school at the university.

The graduate year in secondary education is spent primarily in professional preparation for teaching. It features a unique spiraling curriculum and flexible grouping patterns. For example, broad generic teaching competencies such as those in the FPMS are introduced in large interdisciplinary classes. The subject-specific applications of those competencies are then elaborated upon in subject area methods classes. Next, students are sent into the field in teams of two persons from the same subject area to look for specific instances of those competencies learned in their methods classes. Finally, students practice the competencies in microteaching labs with five to eight students from various subject areas. The curriculum and grouping patterns provide a progression from theory to practice and a support system for students as they work towards mastery of each skill.

The foregoing discussion of PROTEACH is only a cursory one but it illustrates the influence of each of the three major philosophical positions held by most of the faculty. Each program has an element that is skill oriented and that requires the mastery of specific competencies. Each program also has some form of support system built into it to provide for some of the affective needs of its students. The individual course work also reflects both schools of thought in that much attention is given to both the cognitive and affective learning and growth of students. Furthermore, the heavy emphasis on sufficient academic training and on the graduate research function of the college can be seen in the academic specializations, the expansion into the graduate level, and the abandonment of undergraduate degrees in secondary education. Clearly, PROTEACH reflects compromise among the positions, and the overwhelming vote of the faculty to adopt the program indicates a high degree of consensus as well.

THE CHALLENGES THAT REMAIN

It may be self-evident to say that the work of curriculum development does not end with the implementation of new courses. On the contrary, implementation should mark the beginning of a new stage of development and refinement. However, in many cases the real challenge of implementation is to continue the development process once faculty burnout sets in following the strenuous efforts of the design process.

PROTEACH may be subject to such burnout on a greater scale than some other reform efforts because of its overall six-year duration, the intensity of the year-long literature reviews and syntheses, the extended debates, and the concentrated efforts that led to the final design of the program. Whether PROTEACH is typical or atypical in that regard, it is clear that some work remains to be completed. In the opinion of the author at least three critical challenges remain to be met.

PROTEACH offers few concrete assurances that its courses are not offering old wine in new bottles. Certainly, the faculty has done extensive work in reshaping its programs, creating new courses, and identifying the critical knowledge and skills its students must possess. Yet there is no systematic collection of evidence to either support or refute the claim that all of that work has resulted in significant changes in course content and in the methods used to train prospective teachers. Therefore, the first challenge for the college is to monitor the implementation of each new course to insure that its content reflects the research base that has received such strong verbal commitments.

The monitoring of course content is actually a portion of the second challenge. The college must pursue a vigorous agenda of both formative and summative program evaluation. It cannot be presumed that because so much work went into the new program it must necessarily produce better teachers. Only the systematic collection and careful analysis of objective data can answer the hard questions that must be asked in the years ahead. The college has an obligation to the profession and to its students, who are making a substantial commitment of their own to PROTEACH, to assess and to report its successes and failures.

Finally, one of the most exciting aspects of the PROTEACH effort was the amount of constructive conversation that occurred among faculty from the various departments. During the deliberations that led to the establishment of the thirteen-hour foundational component, the special education faculty agreed to reduce the mainstreaming course from three to two hours if they could in turn spend some time each semester helping methods instructors build mainstreaming units into their courses. This kind of cooperation enriched the PROTEACH effort, fostered a strong sense of collegiality, and broke down traditional barriers of turf protection. Unfortunately, no mechanism currently exists for facilitating continuous communication among the three program areas. As a result, the successes and failures of each program go virtually unnoticed in the others. The third challenge, therefore, is to find the means of encouraging the exchange of ideas and strategies among the program areas. If this can be accomplished it is possible that a sense of PROTEACH as a collegewide effort that has three programmatic incarnations, and in the success of which all have a personal stake, can emerge in place of the belief that there are three distinctly separate programs that happen to share the name PROTEACH.

BIBLIOGRAPHY

Carroll, R. G. "Operation PROTEACH: Teacher Education at the University of Florida." Gainesville, Fla.: The College of Education, unpublished.

Carroll, R. G., and M. McMillin. "A Naturalistic Study of Curriculum Change: The Ethnographer as Participant Observer." Paper presented at the annual meeting of the American Educational Research Association, San Francisco, Calif., April 1986.

Carroll, R. G., and R. S. Soar. "PROTEACH: Student and Program Assessment at the University of Florida." In *Student Assessment in Teacher Education,* edited by J. R. Rosario and B. J. Soldwedel. Jacksonville: The Florida Institute of Education, 1987.

Florida Coalition for the Development of a Performance Measurement System. *Domains: Knowledge Base of the Florida Performance Measurement System.* Tallahassee, Fla.: Office of Teacher Education, Certification, and Inservice Staff Development, Florida Department of Education, 1983.

Good, T. L., ed. "Research on Teaching." Special issue. *The Elementary School Journal* 83, no. 4(1983).

McMillin, M., D. C. Smith, and R. G. Carroll. "PROTEACH: An Overview." Paper presented at the annual meeting of the Association for Teacher Educators, Atlanta, Ga., February 1986.

National Commission on Excellence in Education. *A Nation at Risk.* Washington, D.C.: U.S. Government Printing Office, 1983.

Smith, D. C. (1984). "PROTEACH: Teacher Preparation at the University of Florida." *Teacher Education in Practice* 1, no. 2(1984):5–12.

Smith, D. C., ed. *Essential Knowledge for Beginning Educators.* Washington, D.C.: American Association of Colleges for Teacher Education and the ERIC Clearinghouse, 1983. ERIC Document Reproduction Service No. ED 237 455.

Smith, D. C., M. McMillin, and R. G. Carroll. "Extended Teacher Preparation at the University of Florida." Paper presented at the annual conference of the American Association of Colleges for Teacher Education, Denver, Colo., February 1985.

Smith, D. C., R. G. Carroll, and B. Fry. "PROTEACH: Professional Teacher Preparation at the University of Florida." *Phi Delta Kappan* 66, no. 2(1984):134–35.

Smith, D. C., S. M. Kinzer, S. L. Krogh, and D. D. Ross. *Reconceptualizing Teacher Education at the University of Florida.* Gainesville, Fla.: University of Florida, College of Education, 1983. ERIC Document Reproduction Service No. ED 232 976.

Wass, H., R. A. Blume, A. W. Combs, and W. D. Hedges. *Humanistic Teacher Education: An Experiment in Systematic Curriculum Innovation.* Fort Collins, Colo.: Shields, 1974.

Wittrock, M. C., ed. *Handbook of Research on Teaching.* 3rd ed. New York: Macmillan, 1986.

8 | The Transition to an Extended Teacher-preparation Program

RICHARD WISNIEWSKI

THE HISTORY OF TEACHER EDUCATION reveals a steady line of development. Expectations of teachers, certification requirements, and the length of preparation have all increased over a hundred-year period. Educational leaders argue that the next step in this process is the extension of teacher preparation to a postbaccalaureate level. The reports of the Carnegie Forum on Education and the Economy and of the Holmes Group in the mid-1980s are but two expositions of this view. These documents advocate the postbaccalaureate preparation of teachers as well as fundamental changes in teaching conditions and the structure of the profession.

Like all ideas, these proposals have a much longer history than their exposition in a particular document. Just as the Flexner report altered medical education, one of several current statements may indeed guide the future of teacher preparation; or such a touchstone treatise may yet have to be written. In any event, it is likely that history will characterize the 1980s as a period when fundamental change in teacher education began to take place. This era is a reprise of the uneven and contentious change from two- to four-year patterns of preparation fifty or more years ago. As is already clear, the change to extended programs will take place on an institution by institution basis. Only gradually will states mandate new requirements predicated on postbaccalaureate programs. The state of California remains unique since its shift to a fifth-year process is now over twenty years old.

Advocates of continuing four-year patterns of preparation are, for the most part, one or two generations removed from the controversy over the

Richard Wisniewski is professor and dean of education at the University of Tennessee-Knoxville.

elimination of normal schools. Hence, the four-year pattern is what most professors of education experienced in their own training. Calls to abandon are heretical. As a result, it will take a generation or two before five-year programs become the norm. And at some future date five-year programs will themselves be challenged by changing times.

Suggesting a historical perspective is of little help in the day-to-day debates that characterize faculty life, however. Like most professionals, our concern is with our careers, in our own institutions, in our own time. Being reminded that we are part of a historical process suggests a loftiness not in keeping with reality. Nonetheless, the extension of programs to five years is meaningful only in historical terms.

Judging by the spate of reports and debates within their national associations, a small but growing number of teacher educators realize that the profession is enmeshed in a gridlock insofar as squeezing improvements out of four-year programs is concerned. In my view, teacher education reached a dead end decades ago. All the subject matter and professional preparation compromises common to four-year programs have long been evident. A more fundamental factor also needs to be considered. The baccalaureate level of preparation once placed teachers at a level of educational attainment above much of the general populace. This is no longer the case. The time when a baccalaureate with a smattering of education courses was sufficient training for the demanding role of teaching is long past. Unless this pattern is dramatically changed the quality of public education can only be further weakened.

AN EXTENDED PROGRAM AT THE
UNIVERSITY OF TENNESSEE-KNOXVILLE

In response to debates on these matters the University of Tennessee at Knoxville (UTK) began to implement a five-year teacher-preparation program in 1987–88. The goals of the extended program include (1) stronger subject-matter preparation for elementary and secondary teachers; (2) stronger professional preparation including an internship; and (3) a level of preparation consistent with needed changes in teaching conditions, salaries, and the overall status of teaching. An additional long-range goal of the program is to increase the quality base of future educational roles as graduates of the extended program progress in their careers.

These goals are counterbalanced by arguments against extending the length of teacher preparation including (1) teacher education can be improved within a four-year context; (2) the additional expense of a five-year program will not be supported by individuals or the state; (3) persons will not choose five-year programs given poor teaching salaries; and (4) if teacher education is wanting within a four-year context, what guarantee is there that a fifth year would not be more of the same.

Another more guarded fear is the impact of five-year programs on the livelihood of teacher educators. Clearly, such a major change requires a careful assessment of enrollment implications, new recruitment strategies, and other prudent considerations. At its core the debate reveals a moral and professional dilemma: do we advocate what is professionally sound and in the best interest of the profession? Or do we submit to fears regarding a decrease in enrollments and job security in the transition to extended programs? The faculty at Tennessee has taken the highroad in making its decision.

Those familiar with teacher education will understand the difficulty in summarizing the major components of any new program. Several factors complicate the matter including (1) intricate certification codes; (2) well-established four-year programs with strong distinctions between elementary and secondary education; and (3) unique requirements in specialized fields such as art, music, and special education. The five-year program at UTK is breaking new ground but it also includes components with more than seventy-five years of history.

The strength of established practices sometimes appears ignored in the often-heard recommendation that teachers should earn a bachelor's degree prior to any professional education requirements. I share this goal but it is difficult for teacher educators to abandon well-established preparation patterns, most of which are embedded in a four-year context. The power of tradition and the specificity of certification requirements are such that even strong proponents of postbaccalaureate preparation may falter. This is particularly the case in elementary education programs. The debate over appropriate academic majors for elementary teachers continues to rage. In contrast, postbaccalaureate programs are easier to achieve at the secondary level and this truism is reflected in UTK's program.

The UTK program includes several options in order to achieve three goals: (1) to provide options to students who wish to become teachers at various points during or after their baccalaureate work, (2) to expand the pool of potential teachers, and (3) to allow for needed variations because of certification code requirements until those codes are somewhat relaxed. The program is designed primarily for persons who begin their baccalaureates at UTK (or transfer from a community college). For persons already holding a baccalaureate degree a summer induction program is a vital part of the plan. The summer program consists of an intensive minor in education to prepare persons for the fifth (or professional) year of preparation. By including the latter provision the college will encourage persons to enter teaching whether they begin at the university, transfer from a community college, or come to UTK after they have completed a baccalaureate elsewhere.

A major decision in planning the new program undergirds the fact that the program will not culminate in a master's degree. Students will complete the program with a "leg up" toward a graduate degree, that is, twelve graduate hours toward a master's degree in education. This is only possible for persons fully admitted to the Graduate School. Consideration was given to granting a master's degree at the conclusion of the fifth year. The prevailing view argued that this decision would "cheapen" the master's degree since the program prepares persons for initial entry into the profession. A master's degree, in contrast, should signify a higher level of specialization. This was not an easy decision. Market concerns as well as the fact that a sister institution, Memphis State University, is offering the MAT as part of its program made the issue difficult to resolve. I share the faculty's view that our decision is professionally sound, but the goal of making the master's degree the entry degree for teaching is appealing. We will need to monitor the impact of our decision to determine its wisdom.

My concern here is not with the details of the program, however. I am intrigued by what such a change means to a college faculty. What is truly being changed by extending the preparation process? Will it merely be old wine in new bottles? What does such a change do to the dynamics of a faculty? Will the new program influence the broader profession? These and other vexing questions surround the transition to a five-year program at Tennessee.

My attempts to understand these issues are, at best, observations. Systematic research on such questions would require a team of skilled observers. Many forces and traditions impinge on the matter as well as the views of many people. I suspect my observations are not unique and know that other faculties are dealing with similar issues. At the same time, each institutional decision takes place in a unique context. This chapter discusses the context in which the change is taking place at the University of Tennessee-Knoxville. The changes possible, as well as the context in which they occur, will vary from institution to institution. Those noted here appear to be salient factors in the UTK context. It is possible that other factors are not recognized by this writer or that undue emphasis is placed on matters colleagues see as being less critical.

EDUCATIONAL FERMENT IN THE STATE

Educational reform has been taken seriously in Tennessee in the 1980s. For me, as a newcomer to the state, one of the attractions of moving to Tennessee was the opportunity to be involved in major educational reforms. In his second term as governor Lamar Alexander made the improvement of education his highest priority. His efforts culminated in legislative approval of a Better Schools Program within the Comprehensive Education Reform Act of 1984. Among the provisions of the act is a career ladder for teachers, the most controversial aspect of the law and one hotly debated into its fourth year of implementation.

Other aspects of the Better Schools Program are not vital to this discussion. It is important to underscore, however, that UTK and other higher education institutions benefited from the attention paid to education. Centers of excellence, many endowed chairs, and additional funding accompanied the new legislation. Higher admissions standards are being implemented by the university. The efforts of the College of Education to strengthen its programs were influenced and accelerated by a sense of ferment. This observation suggests that it might have been impossible to change to a five-year program if educational reform was at a low ebb. It certainly would have been more difficult. There is no doubt that the new legislation, the leadership of the governor and key legislators, and a host of related factors facilitated proposals to strengthen teacher preparation.

The UTK decision to begin an extended program took place in a state with thirty-eight teacher-training institutions. Only one other institution had already made the decision to implement a five-year program, Memphis State University. (See Chapter 5.) Thus, UTK is the second Tennessee institution to develop an extended program. It goes without saying that teacher educators at the other institutions are assessing the actions at Memphis State and at UTK. At this writing there are signs that one or two other universities are contemplating a five-year process. There is no compelling reason for other institutions to do so, however. The 1988 plan for teacher education adopted by the State Board of Education encourages institutions to initiate internships or to enhance their student teaching program. The former option, in effect, extends teacher preparation to a five-year pattern; the latter option is likely to be chosen by most institutions. The state plan is, of course, far more comprehensive than this brief comment suggests.

UNIVERSITY-LEVEL SUPPORT

A major facilitating factor has been the support of the university's central administration. University officials have made it clear that they support the college's efforts to strengthen its programs and to provide leadership for the improvement of teacher education statewide. Faculty in the College of Liberal Arts have also been strongly supportive of the changes being instituted. Such support is a critical contextual factor, whatever the mood of the state as a whole. Support for the college has been consistent and clear. The decision to move to a five-year program could not have been implemented without universitywide encouragement. Support may not have been forthcoming, however, if the college had delayed in addressing the quality of its programs.

Being familiar only with the college's recent history, I am dependent on the observations of colleagues with longer careers at the institution. If their assessment is correct, there is little doubt that the future of the college was precarious if changes were not made in the quality of teacher preparation. This assessment does not mean the college was in danger of being closed. Rather, colleagues say that if the College of Education did not institute reforms, it would be passed over by central administration in the competition for funds and other forms of support. In effect, the college would lose faculty positions over the years; it would not receive new monies or program development incentives; it would be relegated to a backwater position on campus.

The belief that the college's future was bleak encouraged a number of faculty members to participate on task forces charged with finding ways to strengthen the quality of teacher preparation. Extending the length of teacher preparation was at best a tangential part of those debates; it was not initially a prime focus. The extended program concept was grafted onto a number of other needed reforms recommended by various committees.

While some faculty members were convinced reforms had to be instituted, others did not agree with negative assessments of the college's quality or future. Tension between advocates of each view was apparent over several years though it never broached collegial friendships. The debate is not over; it will be part of the college's folklore long after the five-year program has become the norm. It is in the nature of faculty dynamics that closure is seldom achieved on fundamental issues. Hence, the question remains: would the college have survived if it had maintained the four-year pattern or was the transition to an extended program vital to its future? An answer satisfactory to all concerned is unlikely.

As in any large college, teacher education is only one of this college's missions. While preparing teachers is the bedrock of the college, graduate and scholarly functions as well as professional programs outside of education have their own needs and purposes. It would be wrong, therefore, to communicate the impression that all 140 faculty members devoted time and energy to the changes discussed here. A large number of the faculty have indeed been so engaged. For some faculty members outside of teacher education, the focus on undergraduate reform is viewed as being restrictive. Overall, however, the faculty recognizes that the college is first and foremost an institution of teacher preparation. Most of the other professional roles for which persons are prepared in the college, as well as its other missions, derive from this fundamental purpose.

It should also be noted that the changes discussed here were instituted during exceptionally busy academic years. Quarters of instruction began and ended with all their advisement and enrollment rhythms. Committee work, merit, tenure and promotion decisions, changes in leadership posts, and a host of other collegiate affairs engaged the faculty. The press of these activities seriously hampers planning and implementing change, yet there is no way to slow the pace of modern university life. As someone has quipped, reforming education is akin to repairing an airplane's wing while in the air. As an added overlay that required much faculty effort, the college was engaged in preparing for a transition from a quarter to a semester system of instruction. In short, the years since 1985 have been exceptionally busy, a time of many transitions. Operating all the established programs and simultaneously implementing a number of changes required a heavy commitment on the part of all concerned.

OLD WINE, NEW BOTTLES

The new five-year program is taught by the same faculty members who have operated four-year programs. The new program is operational within the same university, within the same college, within the same certification code, and within all the other conditions of professional life that characterize the four-year pattern. Skeptics rightly argue that extending the length of a program in and of itself does not guarantee an innovative, rigorous approach to teacher preparation.

There is merit to such skepticism. Compromises had to be made in order to achieve consensus on courses, requirements, and other issues. As a result, the new five-year program will not be that different from the four-year program. Not at first. It will take some years before truly altered norms of faculty (and student) behaviors and expectations are fully visible. The change from any old to new pattern is never quick. New bulletins, organizational charts, and course descriptions are not the substance of reform. That substance will be confirmed by positive answers to questions such as the following: (1) Has the overall academic quality of education students increased? (2) Have expectations for student performance been raised? (3) Are new patterns of faculty and student interaction resulting in stronger professional competencies? (4) Has the intellectual rigor of the program been strengthened? and (5) Have strong partnerships been developed with local school systems? Happily, the answers beginning to emerge are encouraging.

The UTK extended program is designed to enhance the likelihood of achieving positive answers to such questions. It must be underscored that progress toward these goals is uneven. Faculties do not change years of established habits, traditions, and procedures overnight. No profession does. Indeed, one is tempted to suggest that education faculty may be more amenable to fundamental changes than is the case in other disciplines. This observation may be more hope than fact, but there is some reason to posit it as a serious possibility. Over the years education faculty has demonstrated a willingness to implement new programs, especially when federal and foundation funding were available. Virtually all the components of the new program have been demonstrated in pilot or experimental programs over the past twenty years. The new components are hardly untested. This fact does not ensure that the new program will indeed be a new wine. The latter goal may more likely be attained because of the overall approach to reform at UTK.

A SET OF INTERLOCKING CHANGES

The change strategy guiding UTK's efforts is simple: a number of interlocking changes have been introduced simultaneously. To do anything less would be ineffectual. If anything has been learned from pilot programs over the decades it is that no single change, no matter how important, is sufficient to reform teacher education. If the transition to a five-year program was the only change being undertaken, it would not be worthwhile. As an advocate of extended programs, I would object to their implementation. The change to a five-year process must be accompanied by a series of other interrelated changes, each designed to escalate the level of professional attainment in teacher preparation. The other escalations must go beyond extending the time required in the program.

ADMISSION STANDARDS

Among these escalations are increased admissions standards. Like all the changes noted below, the new standards were a prelude to the five-year program. General education, academic major, and grade point requirements were increased. Although I believe that they should be increased even higher, the new requirements are encouraging. The academic achievement norms for education students are now clearly within university norms. But even more important, meeting minimum test and academic admission's criteria does not guarantee admission to the college. Each program area sets enrollment limits or goals; preference is given to students who exceed minimum criteria for admission. An active recruitment program has also been implemented, and affirmative action goals are a major concern. A true professional school can only achieve its goals if all its admissions procedures are carefully crafted.

"ONCE-A-YEAR STARTS"

A second major change has been dubbed "once-a-year starts;" that is, each sequence of courses will begin only once per year, as is the case in law and medicine. Beginning a new class each year is a fundamental characteristic of a true professional school. A fundamental weakness of teacher preparation has been the drudgery imposed on faculty who offer the same required courses quarter after quarter so as to make entrance into teaching as convenient as possible. This longstanding tradition has severely weakened the preparation process. It has made difficult the development of student cohorts moving through a program as a class of 1989, of 1990, and so on. Given an essentially open admissions tradition, it will take another year or two for once-a-year starts to be fully implemented. This is inevitable since students in the old pipeline must be served. In effect, the new and old programs will coexist for several years.

ADMISSIONS BOARDS

Admissions boards are another major change. Since the initiation of the boards in 1985 not one undergraduate has been admitted to teacher preparation without being interviewed by an admissions board. Approximately twelve hundred interviews have already taken place. The boards consist of faculty members in education and liberal arts, a senior student in the program, and a practicing professional from the field. The teachers serving on admissions boards are appointed as faculty associates and receive a small stipend for this service. At this writing the faculty associate roster consists of about sixty individuals, with plans to increase such appointments until a cadre of about 150 persons is established. The faculty associates are becoming thoroughly knowledgeable about the teacher-preparation process as they help select students for the college. They will also be the only teachers with whom student teachers and interns will be placed.

INTERNSHIPS

A major component of the new program will be an internship during the fifth year. Such internships have been prototyped by the Lyndhurst Program, an alternative path to certification for persons already holding baccalaureate or higher degrees. With the support of the Lyndhurst Foundation this program is in its third year of operation and approximately fifty interns have earned teaching certificates. The program includes a ten-week, full-time summer preparation process, followed by an internship mentored by an experienced teacher as well as by university professors. This program has provided an opportunity for a number of education and liberal arts faculty to work with a group of applicants with strong subject-matter orientations. The interns are fully responsible for three classes in secondary schools during their internships. Because these interns are jointly selected and mentored, a new partnership between several school systems and the college is being forged. Such partnerships are critical to the five-year program, and the college was fortunate to have an opportunity to develop the internship concept before the extended program became operational. A fourth cycle of the program will test assumptions related to the preparation of elementary school teachers.

MENTORING TEAMS

Another innovation in the college, though hardly new in teacher preparation, is the development of mentoring teams. Such teams consist of five or six professors who serve on admissions boards and work with students in the core courses in teacher education. Because a group of professors work with the same cohort of students throughout the program, the articulation of content with clinical experiences is greatly facilitated. Working together on mentoring teams is a new experience for many faculty members, though there have been such attempts earlier in the college's history. This is the first time that the entire teacher-education program is predicated on cohorts of students working with groups of faculty. This structure calls for new working relationships among professors with far more joint planning and evaluation activities. There is some evidence that such relationships are evolving with students on several mentoring teams. An Institute of Teacher Education was created to coordinate this and other aspects of the extended program.

TEACHING SIMULATION LABORATORY

The college has opened a teaching simulation laboratory. A key finding in this process was that the research and materials related to simulation activities that evolved in the sixties have been largely disregarded by teacher educators. Only a handful of colleges appears to be effectively utilizing simulation techniques (including microteaching) as part of a clinical preparation process. The revised four-year program in the college, a prelude to the five-year process, is predicated on the utilization of simulation activities as an integral part of teacher preparation. It is difficult to understand how a methods course can be taught effectively unless it utilizes simulation activities. This has not been the norm in the college nor is it a norm in the teacher-education profession. Hence, simulation is a major component of the transition to a five-year program and it is being gradually accepted by the faculty. The rate of adoption is slow; this particular change has not progressed at a rate consistent with its potential.

CORE PROFESSIONAL COURSES

The development of a core of professional courses is another major accomplishment. This is hardly an innovation; many institutions have had such cores for generations. In some colleges, however, each department operates its own teacher-education program. No agreement on a core of knowledge existed, and this was the case at UTK. Key faculty have begun to identify the knowledge areas and skills common to all teachers, that is, a professional core. The full articulation of content and clinical experiences has not been achieved since the core courses and mentoring teams are in their first stages of operation. By the time the extended program is fully in effect the articulation of field and clinical work will be much further advanced than at present.

CHANGE AND FACULTY DEVELOPMENT

As these changes take hold, they demonstrate an approach to faculty development on a grand scale. Faculty development is usually defined as what a given faculty member might do to enhance his or her skills. At UTK a growing number of faculty are involved in a variety of activities that a year or two ago existed only as discussion points. As the number of students in the five-year program increases, virtually all of the teacher-education faculty will have worked on mentoring teams, in the simulation lab, on admissions boards, with faculty associates, and with other components of a program designed to dramatically increase the quality of teacher preparation. If Dewey was right, learning by doing applies to all of us, neophytes and experienced professionals alike.

AN ON-GOING PROCESS

It is clear that these efforts will never be complete. This is a difficult concept for some colleagues to accept. It is an understandable reaction. Most professors of education have spent their lives as students, then as teachers or administrators, and eventually as professors. The schooling process and all its routines (calendars, credit hours, schedules, and formalized behaviors) are a routine part of each day's work. For many persons the certainty of knowing exactly which three classes will be taught, at what time and on what days, is the epitome of security.

The changes at UTK require flexible and deeper involvements with students on the part of the faculty. Simply teaching one's courses is not sufficient. A collection of even well-taught courses leaves to chance the impact of each course on the professional competence of students. The reforms described here are designed to insure that the issues of competence and quality are addressed at many points from admission to certification. They cannot be left to chance, as has been the case for generations even in the best of programs.

UTK is a large institution. Like any bureaucratic structure, communication about these matters is uneven. There are daily criticisms, quips, and inquiries regarding the wisdom of the five-year program and the other changes being implemented. This fact leads to perhaps the only important observation I can offer. While it is a truism that nothing is more difficult than change, there is a very positive side to the process for many faculty members: the revitalization of people deeply involved in the process. It is clear that faculty members who have carried the brunt of planning and implementing these changes have a new lease on their professional lives. They see themselves as making a contribution to strengthening the college and their professional futures. They enjoy occasional accolades for being in the forefront of educational reform. They enjoy talking about their work to colleagues at other institutions or at national meetings. In short, they take pride in their work.

Other individuals who also take pride in their work see nothing but the disruption of well-ordered routines. They are not comfortable with the changes described. They do not see how the new program will benefit them, their students, or the profession. They do not appear to connect what they do in their classrooms with the new research on teacher education or with the calls to reform teacher education. They do not foresee the erosion of teacher education as a profession if it does not dramatically reorganize its work. The number of individuals in this group appears to decline with each additional year of experience with the new program.

Fortunately, a strong tradition of goodwill characterizes the UTK faculty. A strong sense of friendship and colleagueship developed over many years keeps the debate in bounds. As an advocate of change and as one concerned with the future of the profession, I am committed to those willing to experiment on both sides of the debate. Happily, there are signs in the college, in national associations, and in the literature that a growing number of teacher educators see an opportunity to revitalize teacher education. That is the mood that characterizes the UTK faculty engaged in reform activities; with that faculty lies the hope for a positive future for the college.

These comments are not intended to extol changes at UTK as a model for teacher preparation. On the contrary, what is desperately needed in teacher education is a willingness to innovate and experiment on a broad scale. Higher expectations of performance is the goal but the paths to this end are many. Teacher education is stultified because of the lack of innovation. The intellectually numbing processes of schooling have overcome the research and development that characterize a first-rate professional college. Any college that offers the same programs and utilizes the same procedures decade after decade contributes to the stultification of a profession.

At the University of Tennessee-Knoxville fundamental decisions have been made that challenge the status quo. Halting but apparently effective steps toward reform have been taken. A voyage has been begun by the commitment to implement an extended program. From the viewpoint of one participant the future of teacher education looks positive on this campus. It is a future consistent with the educational reform movement writ large.

BIBLIOGRAPHY

Adler, M. *The Paideia Proposal.* New York: Macmillan, 1982.

Alexander, L. *Better Schools Program: Tennessee Master Teacher Program, A Summary of Governor Lamar Alexander's State of Education Address.* Nashville, Tenn.: Department of Education, 1983.

Boyer, E. *High School: A Report on Secondary Education in America.* New York: Harper & Row, 1983.

Flexner, A. *Medical Education: A Comparative Study.* New York: Macmillan, 1925.

Lanier, J. *Goals for the Education of Teachers as Professionals.* East Lansing: Holmes Group Report, 1985.

National Commission on Excellence in Education. *A Nation at Risk.* Washington, D.C.: U.S. Government Printing Office, 1983.

Sizer, T. *Horace's Compromise: The Dilemma of the American High School.* Boston: Houghton Mifflin, 1984.

3 | Teacher Education: A Tradition of Excellence and Diversity

9 | Developmental Education: La Salle's Rationale and Program for Integrative Teacher Education

PRESTON D. FEDEN

GARY K. CLABAUGH

THIS CHAPTER BEGINS WITH A BRIEF HISTORY of how teachers were trained and children were grouped in American education, and describes how elementary and special education teacher-training programs emerged as two distinctly separate processes. The authors contend that a relatively recent knowledge base has emerged that permits all teachers to understand and meet the educational needs of individual children in the context of their developmental levels and stages using both general and specific information. This new breed of developmentally oriented general educator is described, and the need for such teachers is addressed. It is suggested that elementary and special education teacher-training programs be combined into a single program using developmental theory as the unifying theme. The program currently being implemented at La Salle University, Philadelphia, Pennsylvania, is described.

A HISTORICAL PERSPECTIVE

In the late colonial and early national period of American educational history, elementary education was characterized by individual instruction

This essay was published under a different title in 1986. Preston Feden and Gary Clabaugh, "The 'New Breed' Educator: A Rationale and Program for Combining Elementary and Special Education Teacher Preparation." *Teacher Education and Special Education* 9(1986):180–89. Copyright 1986 by Special Press. Reprinted with the permission of the Teacher Education Division of the Council for Exceptional Children and Special Press.

Preston D. Feden is associate professor of education and chair of the Department of Education at La Salle University, Philadelphia, Pennsylvania. Gary K. Clabaugh is an associate professor of education and director, graduate program in education at La Salle.

using drill, practice, rote memorization, and the birch rod (Meyer 1967). This instruction echoed the "memoriter" methods of three thousand years of educational history during which the teacher called on each child in turn and asked questions that were to be answered from memory (Graves 1913). Much of the teacher's time was devoted to hearing individual recitations and deciding where to start and how fast to proceed with each child's studies.

As classes and schools grew in size, the inadequacy of this type of individualized instruction became increasingly apparent. At the same time, American society was undergoing radical transformation from cottage industries and private artisans to factories characterized by specialization, bureaucratization, and mass production. Inevitably, the schools began to reflect these new trends, particularly when they were confronted with a rising tide of children of the "common man" (Pessen 1962). The method of group instruction based upon organizing "grades" of children by chronological age became increasingly popular. One natural by-product of this method was that children who did not fit handily into preestablished grades became even more problematic than they had been in earlier times. Many of these children were ultimately to receive grades and labels of their own such as mentally retarded, emotionally disturbed, and more recently, learning disabled.

The education of teachers for these early schools was either primitive or nonexistent (Potter and Emerson 1858; Tanner and Tanner 1980). Coincidental with the advent of chronologically aged group instruction, this began to change. By the end of the Civil War the idea that teachers should be provided with some sort of formal training was widely accepted, and the numbers of normal schools for this training grew rapidly. Much of the philosophy and methodology that characterized these normal schools was provided by Pestalozzianism (Graves 1914; Knight 1940). The remainder was provided by faculty psychology (Tanner and Tanner 1980).

Johann Heinrich Pestalozzi (1746–1827) held that education must be based upon developmental principles and that there are certain wholly natural elements unfolding within the life of each child that the teacher must understand as fundamentally important to successful instruction. This position ultimately was to have a profound influence upon American primary education, making it far more child centered than its secondary education counterpart. Faculty psychology advocated strengthening the whole of the individual's powers through mental exercise and stressed that these powers had critical periods of development (Spurzheim 1883). Ironically, Pestalozzianism and the influence of faculty psychology began to be felt at the same time that elementary schools had to cope with very rapid growth in the number of youngsters attending school by adopting the chronologically derived, deindividualized classification and instruction of students described earlier. The result was an assembly-line method of grouping and instruction animated by a profoundly developmental and humanistic philosophy—an impossible marriage if ever there was one.

Miraculously, children were generally able to muddle through such a system, and there is evidence that "the graduates of grammar schools were able to spell, write, or speak effectively" (Tanner and Tanner 1980, 245). Partially protected from the more grotesque implications of assembly-line education by the more developmental and humanistic orientation of their teachers, youngsters at least learned to cope; not so incidentally, they also learned a lot about surviving in the world of work awaiting them. There were, however, youngsters who simply could not cope. They were too different to fit into the uniform flow of things, and they defied traditional chronological classification.

For many years these youngsters either clung unprofitably to the fringes of the system or were systematically excluded from it altogether. Ultimately and very belatedly, following initial experiments with institutionalization and compulsory sterilization for the more severely handicapped, special education programs for exceptional children began to appear. The first college programs for the preparation of special educators soon followed (Reynolds and Birch 1977).

Two distinctly different teacher-training processes have emerged from these beginnings, one leading to certification as an elementary educator and one leading to certification as a special educator (Morsink 1984; Reynolds and Birch 1977; Stainback and Stainback 1984). Teacher training was, from its inception, accomplished in separate programs, each with its own faculty, journal, knowledge bases, and the like. The so-called special educators, compelled by the nature of the pupils to reject chronological-age classifications, turned instead to classifications based on handicapping conditions. This did not correspond to reality either, but the deficiencies of this classification system were more easily ignored than the deficiencies inherent in a chronological-age system.

Elementary and special needs children were educated in the tradition described above until the 1960s. As the human rights movement took an ever stronger hold on our culture, laws were passed that both recognized and specified the rights of children who were labeled as handicapped and in need of special attention. These laws mandated, among other things, that handicapped children be educated in the least restrictive environment. This mandate led to the current practice of mainstreaming, which places handicapped children in regular classes for as much of the school day as they can manage. Mainstreaming upsets many elementary educators, who feel ill-prepared to teach handicapped youngsters because their own professional preparation has not included much, if any, study of or work with children who differ significantly from the norm (Gickling and Theobald 1975). They fail to recognize, as many teacher educators fail to realize, that customary elementary education practices may deprive even "normal" children of a "least restrictive environment" by refusing to accommodate or even recognize the individual differences of these children.

The Pestalozzian individualism that animated the philosophy and practice of early elementary educators had been largely subordinated to the more concrete demands of the classificatory system based on chronological age and to educational methods oriented to the broad masses to maximize "efficient" production. Except for brief misadventures with progressive and open education, it remains so to this day.

As special education practices came under increasing criticism, some special educators began to question the wisdom of using traditional categorical labels to design instruction for handicapped children. They also began to question the use of self-contained classrooms as the most effective organization for delivering instruction. A movement started to base instruction on the observed needs of handicapped children rather than on the perceived needs engendered by stereotypical conceptions of what it means to be mentally retarded, emotionally disturbed, or learning disabled (Dunn 1968). This movement also led to what was at the time called cross-categorical certification of special education teachers, a procedure many states adopted. In effect, the feeling was that handicapped children, when viewed developmentally, were more similar than different, and therefore teachers qualified to teach in one area of certification (for instance, mental retardation) should be qualified in other areas as well (Blackhurst 1981; Reynolds and Birch 1977).

One wonders precisely what it was that encouraged these reconsiderations, since similar deficiencies associated with the chronological classification of "normal" children have plagued elementary education without bringing about a corresponding demand for reform. Perhaps it is easier to ignore the fact that some nonhandicapped four-year-olds are really more like five- or six-year-olds than it is to ignore the fact that some retarded children also insist on being emotionally disturbed or even learning disabled.

EMERGENCE OF A NEW KNOWLEDGE BASE

It is this history that has led us to a time in American education when serious consideration should be given to preparing generically competent teachers to teach children, whether handicapped or nonhandicapped. Stainback and Stainback (1984) have stated that "there are not . . . two distinctly different types of students, that is, those who are special and those who are regular. Rather, all students are unique individuals, each with his/her own set of physical, intellectual, and psychological characteristics" (p. 103). This uniqueness requires educators to accommodate differences and adjust curriculum and instruction to maximize learning of subject matter.

What makes teaching in this manner more possible is the emergence of an increasingly sophisticated knowledge base about human growth and development that relates to learning. The relatively recent acceptance of Piaget's work by American psychologists and the current extension of his ideas to educational practice by Kuhn (1979), Hooper and DeFrain (1980), and many others have contributed significantly to the level of sophistication of this knowledge base. Building upon this work and the work of other cognitive structuralists, information-processing theorists such as Bartlett (1932) and Spiro (1977) have placed even more emphasis on the learner than on the content to be learned, and have added a great amount of information to our knowledge of how children develop and learn. Very recent and admittedly speculative work by Wittrock (1978), Bogen (1977), and others on the implications of the functions of the right brain and of the left brain for teaching children shows promise of increasing this knowledge base still further. Finally, the work on learning styles that is currently finding renewed interest has the potential to help teachers appreciate and value the individual differences found among children in their classrooms.

The general orientation of all this work is its focus on the development of the human being and its attempt to understand the individual's role as an active agent of his or her own learning at various stages of that development. The principles derived from this knowledge base can be used to understand and organize learning theories, teaching strategies, and the measurement and evaluation of instruction, thereby lending coherence to bodies of knowledge too often viewed as discrete and practiced in isolation from one another. Adopting what we shall generally label developmental theory as a basic organizing theme, it is possible to understand the educational needs of any child and, in effect, give every child "special education," that is, an education designed to meet his or her unique needs, abilities, and learning styles.

Therefore, elementary and special education should not be thought of as being so different as we are sometimes led to believe. It is the task of all teachers, regardless of job title, to facilitate learning. This task is formidable, and its complexities are often either misunderstood or not fully appreciated by the American public. It requires informed judgments made within a complex that involves the teacher's own classroom, the larger school setting, and the world beyond the school. It requires a new breed of educator.

GENERAL VS. SPECIFIC INFORMATION

To make these informed judgments or decisions on behalf of their students, teachers use both general and specific information as guides. Sometimes the differences between general and specific information, their sources, and the way they are used, is not properly understood even by the teachers who use them. In fact, failure to understand the ways in which general information should be used has itself perpetuated the separation of elementary and special education. For example, during their training elementary educators are often led to believe that they cannot teach handicapped children. It is as if the label mental retardation or learning disability connotes a mysterious inner deviation that somehow makes the child very different from other children. In fact, a child is a child first and handicapped second, and the methods used to teach such children need not usually differ substantially from those used with normal children (Gardner 1977).

Special educators are slowly learning to use handicapping labels as sources of general information only, since children sharing a given handicapping condition differ from one another in the same way as do nonhandicapped children. That fact makes the label itself inadequate for developing instruction to meet any given child's needs. Knowing that a child is trainable mentally retarded (TMR) gives an informed teacher some limited but useful general information. For example, one would expect that if the child is properly labeled his or her mental age will be significantly lower than that of his or her chronological-age peers, that social skills also will probably be less well developed compared to those of nonretarded peers, and that adaptive behavior will be impaired when the TMR child is compared to others of the same chronological age. In short, a child labeled TMR will be developing more slowly than his or her age peers and is less likely to be totally self-sufficient at adulthood. While all of these bits of general information are significant for general educational programming, they tell us little about any given child as an individual. A TMR child is, after all, not developing very differently from other children. All children are qualitatively different from one another. The major difference between a TMR child and other children is a quantitative one. He or she is simply developing more slowly and is unlikely ever to equal a more typical child in total development.

The label learning disabled (LD) also provides only general information for special education teachers. LD children are, by definition, of average or above average intelligence. Customarily they have a specific disability or several specific disabilities, often in language or language-related areas. These cause gaps in their learning profiles. We would expect that if the child is properly labeled, he or she might excel in one subject but fail miserably in another. Such problems as hyperactivity, perceptual disorders, and inability to attend may characterize these children. But again, these children are not so different from non-LD children. Their behaviors are a bit more extreme, perhaps, but the notion of significant qualitative differences, the feeling among elementary educators that somehow this disorder transforms the child into some different kind of being who can be handled only by a specially trained educator, is more fallacy than fact. What this child really requires is not a special educator but a properly trained educator.

More examples could be given of the ways in which handicapping levels are used as sources of general information among special educators. However, the main point is that handicapped children are not as different from nonhandicapped children as many educators have been led to believe.

While special educators use labels such as emotional disturbance and mental retardation, it has already been noted that elementary educators use their own labels such as sixth grade, third grade, or kindergarten. In actuality, these traditional grade labels serve elementary educators in much the same way that categorical labels serve special educators: they communicate very general information about the children. Most fourth graders are 9 or 10 years old, read from fourth-grade readers, are capable of cursive writing, and are able to work productively in groups. However, these grade labels do not give elementary educators specific information about any one child's strengths, weaknesses, preferred learning styles, and the like. Thus, while the point was made earlier that handicapped children are not so different from nonhandicapped children as many have been led to believe, it should also be apparent at this point that nonhandicapped children in the regular grades are not as similar to one another as many have previously believed. Even when we consider a fifth-grade class with a perfectly normally distributed range of intelligence quotients (IQs of 90–110), we would expect to find a two-year spread of mental ages from approximately 9 to 11 years. In reality, few classes are so normally distributed.

THE NEED FOR DEVELOPMENTALLY ORIENTED TEACHERS

This all leads to the logical conclusion that, in order for teachers to do their job properly and professionally, using general information about children is simply insufficient. The teacher must go beyond general information and delve into specific information about the students. This necessitates a solid grounding in developmental theory and its translation into classroom practices. Since handicapped children are not so different from nonhandicapped children as many believe, and since nonhandicapped children are not as similar to one another as many would like to think, the distinction between special education and elementary education is more apparent than real (Martin 1976). Detailed knowledge of developmental theory and its application in the classroom would make either regular or special education teachers much more effective and would also correspond to classroom realities now made unmistakably obvious by the practice of mainstreaming. So, why do we educate elementary and special education teachers in separate programs?

It is true that individuals are sometimes trained in both elementary and special education simultaneously and that it is customary to issue the two different teaching certificates. This seems to suggest that many teacher-education programs are not so artificially delimited as we suggest. Unfortunately, what appear at first glance to be generally oriented programs that synthesize all the elements of effective teaching of younger children usually turn out to be Siamese twins — two truly different organisms joined together through an unnatural connection. They lead parallel existences joined only at the skin level by the bond of bureaucratic convenience.

This reality is reflected in the fact that if one wishes to be certified in both elementary and special education the most common requirement is for the future teacher to take both training programs and perhaps even additional student teaching. In other words, the assumption is still made that elementary and special educators are very different in the tasks they perform and the children they teach and that they therefore need very different programs.

This approach to training perpetuates the myth that elementary teachers cannot teach handicapped children and that special educators cannot teach nonhandicapped children presumably because the needs of the children are so different. It also encourages the miseducation of these future teachers. In fact, educating elementary and special educators apart from one another keeps each group from reading the other's literature, from sharing the other's methods and techniques, and, most importantly, from developing an accurate understanding of children (Lortie 1978; Panko 1984).

The distinctions between elementary and special education teacher training are often perpetuated by firmly entrenched teacher interest groups, not the least of which are the universities and professors who train teachers. Education professors have become markedly territorial and parochially wedded to the narrow disciplines in which they specialize. Thus, the departments of elementary education, special education, secondary education, and early childhood education, to name a few, have grown apart and become very protective of their individual provinces. Unfortunately, this

Balkanization of teacher education does not reflect the way children grow and develop or the knowledge teachers need to teach them (Stainback and Stainback 1984).

Such artificially divided teacher-training programs seem to encourage an overly methodological approach to educating teachers that puts too much stress on "how to" courses and too little on understanding how all children develop and learn. They also promote the development and perpetuation of course sequences lacking in articulation and intellectually stimulating content. These practices are at the heart of the criticisms recently leveled at teacher-education programs by several national commissions.

Specific information about learners is absolutely essential in order to effectively individualize instruction in the classroom. Individualized instruction is instruction directed to the levels, needs, abilities, and learning styles of the learner. It may take place in individual tutorial settings, small-group settings, large-group settings, or even as independent work initiated by either the teacher or the pupil. In any case, the intent of the individualized instruction is to maximize the probability that learning will take place. Implementing individualized instruction is no easy task and cannot be done by teachers who do not know how to operationalize the term "individual." A solid grounding in developmental theory affords the teacher a knowledge base that permits the operationalization of the term and therefore enables the teacher to truly individualize instruction. This knowledge provides a compass that directs other decisions as well.

Whether to move ahead to a new concept or to review an old one, what kind of question would be most effective, whether pupils have the prerequisites necessary to tackle new learning, what type of objective will best accomplish a given purpose, which test will yield valuable information for any given question—these and many more questions can be framed within the context of a developmental orientation and provide the teacher with an intelligent and consistent decision-making schema. Furthermore, such a framework would help teachers in the following ways:

1. As the needs of children change during the year—and change is especially obvious among the mildly handicapped and nonhandicapped—developmentally oriented teachers will be able to understand clearly the implications for classroom activities and will adjust lessons accordingly.

2. As children's potential and limitations become more obvious, as is usually the case with moderately and severely handicapped youngsters, developmentally oriented teachers will understand the implications for broader curriculum change for these children such as a shift to practical life-skills activities.

3. As children progress through the educational system, developmen-

tally oriented teachers will understand from where the children they now teach have come and to where they are going, since development is never static and has a predictable flow.

Consider the following example of the way a generically trained teacher with a solid grounding in developmental theory will be able to supplement traditional classificatory information such as this — TMR, IQ of 50, chronological age of 14; and Grade 2, IQ of 100, chronological age 7. A generically trained teacher will understand that both youngsters have mental ages of 7. However, social ages might not be quite so similar since the TMR child has lived for 7 more years than the second grader. Of course, retarded children have poor adaptive skills and are usually socially immature, so the TMR child is unlikely to be as socially adept as his or her chronological-age peers. Further, the teacher would recognize that while the second grader is progressing "normally" through school, the TMR child at 14 years of age should no longer be in the second-grade reader. Rather, the need for adjustment to the postschool world has become an important educational goal for this adolescent; therefore the curriculum cannot be the same one that is used for a second grader even though their mental ages are equivalent. A developmentally oriented teacher would be knowledgeable enough to realize that for the TMR child a switch to a more practical life-skills curriculum too soon in the child's educational career would be imposing limitations on the child that might be premature and prove unjustified. Still, too late a shift would also be detrimental.

Making decisions on behalf of children is a formidable task. It should never be taken lightly, and it should never be done by the poorly informed. A developmentally oriented teacher would be in a unique position to make well-informed decisions for any child that he or she teaches.

Moving from general to specific information, the very kind of information needed to make wise decisions for the children discussed above, developmentally oriented teachers will view children in terms of their levels of cognitive, social, moral, sexual, physical, and emotional functioning. Further, they will understand children's behaviors from an ecological perspective, which necessitates understanding the interrelationships among the components of their environments and the effects of these components on the learning process. Viewing children in such a way no longer mandates that elementary and special education teachers be educated and certified in separate programs, since all children develop qualitatively in the areas named above and in identifiable and verifiable sequences.

What distinguishes a developmentally oriented, generically trained teacher from a psychologist is that such a teacher must be able to translate theory into educational practice. The concept of conservation is interesting for educational researchers, but it is also essential that teachers understand it if they hope to assist children to learn the concept of number. Further, teachers must understand this concept in terms of whether or not it can yet be taught, what new concepts cannot be meaningfully learned by a child unable to conserve, and so forth. Thus, knowledge of developmental theory leads to methods that are effective and efficient in facilitating the learning process among children. Even more importantly, these methods have a philosophically consistent foundation and are therefore articulated and not simply patchwork. They focus on the child himself or herself. These methods no longer focus on our perceptions of what sixth graders or fourth graders or learning disabled or emotionally disturbed children should be doing. Instead, they focus on the needs of individual children who also happen to be sixth graders, fourth graders, learning disabled, or emotionally disturbed.

THE CONTEXT OF CULTURE

Of course we must be careful not to assume that schools serve only individual needs or that the teacher properly operates only as a facilitator and enricher of personal development. Clearly, much of the "hidden curriculum" of the school necessarily involves teaching children lessons about group life, being patient, obeying rules, and ignoring or suppressing their own interests in order to please external authority (Friedenberg 1959; Goodman 1964; Nasaw 1979; Silberman 1970). Whatever else they are, schools are also people-processing organizations with strong tendencies to depersonalize and even objectify students (Parelius and Parelius 1978). They are social organizations with the same needs for collectivism and cooperation as the larger society.

The fatal error of the neoromantic educational reform movement of the 1960s and 1970s was its simpleminded neglect of the elemental reality that in order to enjoy the benefits of the culture that enriches them, children must learn to curtail as well as to express, to fulfill obligations as well as to claim rights. What encouraged this neglect was that neoromanticism was based more on wishes and hopes than on the rigors of science.

An educational reform movement spearheaded by a new breed of developmentally oriented teachers need not share this flaw. Clearly, the developmental process is given its context via culture. A scientifically derived view of human development must necessarily consider the social aspects of human existence in precise fashion.

Political meddling, folk wisdom, and appeals to human conceit have always hampered the advancement of education. Our teachers will not improve until their education is reformulated to take maximum advantage of what has been learned about the development of children. Only when it is clearly recognized that education's real advance is inextricably interwoven with collateral developments in the scientific understanding of learning and development will true progress be made. A scientifically oriented teacher-education program such as the one outlined below promises such progress.

THE PROGRAM AT LA SALLE UNIVERSITY

The Department of Education at La Salle University is in the process of implementing a program that combines elementary and special education teacher preparation using developmental theory and its applications as the theoretical orientation. Following an extraordinarily successful eleven-year history of preparing special education teachers through a cross-categorical, developmental approach, La Salle University extended its developmental orientation to the graduate level (Clabaugh, Feden, and Vogel 1984). At this level, elementary, special, early childhood, and secondary education teachers were enrolled in the same core courses. It was strongly felt that this was consistent with the notion that all educators must be knowledgeable in the area of human growth and development. It is also consistent with Goodlad's (1984) finding that practicing teachers feel well prepared in subject areas, but much less well prepared in pedagogy. They perceive their problem to be one of knowing what to teach but not how to teach it. This graduate program has proven to be very popular among the teachers enrolled in it and among school administrators who employ these teachers.

The La Salle University Department of Education has very recently extended this developmental concept to the preservice elementary education level, while simultaneously restructuring the way its preservice special education teachers are educated. The curriculum by which this new elementary and special education (ESE) program was used to educate an essentially new breed of general educator was already largely in place, thanks to the existing cross-categorical special education program with its decidedly developmental orientation. The required courses appear in Table 9.1, and all elementary and special education students take the same courses.

It is difficult to reflect the nature of each course in a title; however, faculty have carefully articulated the content of the various courses, and every course shares the developmental orientation. For example, the course entitled Mathematics for Teachers is a study of the ways in which mathematical thought develops and the methods teachers might use to foster this development. An example of the noncategorical and developmental nature of the program is the course Human Exceptionality, which stresses the

Table 9.1. **Courses required of elementary and special education majors**

Number	Title	Credit hours
Ed. 101	The Role of the Developmentally Oriented Teacher	3
Ed. 102	Foundations of Education: A Developmental Approach	3
Ed. 103	Educational Psychology: Learning and Development	3
Ed. 201	Human Exceptionality	3
Ed. 203	Educational Psychology: Curricular and Instructional Applications	3
Ed. 217	Mathematics for Teachers	3
Ed. 218	Geography	3
Ed. 301	General Methods and Management: A Developmental Perspective	3
Ed. 302	Instructional Media and Technology	3
Ed. 303	Developmental Reading	3
Ed. 343	Developing and Adjusting Instruction to Meet the Needs of Elementary and Special Needs Learners	3
Ed. 344	Assessing the Learning Abilities and Disabilities of Elementary and Special Needs Learners	3
Ed. 475	The Professional Year-Student Teaching	18
Ed. 476	The Professional Year-Specific Methods (Includes reading, math, science, social studies, health, and physical education)	12

uniqueness of all human beings rather than focusing simply on the traditional categories of exceptionality. All syllabi include the competencies expected of students upon exit from any given course.

A unique feature of this ESE program is the professional year concept, which includes one entire academic year of student teaching and also includes specific methods delivered in module form. The year of student teaching insures that each graduate will have had closely supervised practice teaching with a variety of children. This usually includes a placement in the regular elementary grades and placement in at least two different special education settings representing different levels of disability. It also permits the preservice teachers to enroll in specific methods course work while they are engaged in student teaching and after they have mastered basic developmental theory. This enhances the probability that information gained will be incorporated into teaching practice in a way that has practical utility as well as theoretical integrity. All of this is accomplished without sacrificing the liberal arts courses required of all La Salle University students.

Through implementation of this program La Salle University hopes to improve upon the way in which elementary and special education teachers are currently trained by preparing teachers who

- Are decidedly developmental in orientation and philosophy
- Are able to apply this orientation in the classroom, thereby making their students the center of the educational enterprise

- Are able to meet the individual needs of a variety of children by effectively individualizing instruction
- Are prepared for a lifetime of professional service because they have internalized the attitudes, abilities, and research skills necessary for effective instruction in a changing world
- Are prepared to apply intelligently secondary technologies such as microcomputing and telecommunications to enhance learning for any student
- Are prepared to meet competently the challenges for all teachers inherent in PL 94-142, PL 93-112, and PL 94-103
- Are prepared to do what is educationally sound for the individual child, rather than relying upon stereotypical classifications incapable of reflecting the true complexities of human development

These objectives have been operationalized in 167 specific competency statements that appear in appropriate course syllabi.

Plans for evaluating the effectiveness of the ESE program are now under way. Table 9.2 shows the proposed scheme for both formative and summative evaluation based upon evaluation procedures used by the department in past years. If data indicate that this program is successful, then the secondary education program also will be reformulated to bring it into theoretical consistency with the developmental approach that characterizes all other teacher-education programs at La Salle University.

In short, the faculty at La Salle University believes that teacher education in America is beyond tinkering; it needs reformulating! Rather than simply criticizing and adding fuel to the philosophical fires that currently burn, we are actualizing our philosophies by developing programs consist-

Table 9.2. Program evaluation scheme

Type of Evaluation	Students	Evaluators/ faculty	Employers/ others
Formative	Evaluation of each course Meeting with program director once each semester	Evaluation of students in each course Evaluation of course outcomes in terms of objectives	Advisory board meetings
Summative	Evaluation of total program three years after graduation	Pre/post data taken from beliefs inventory Evaluation of student teaching performance of each student	Employer evaluations of graduates on dimensions indicated by program competency statements

ent with them. We firmly believe that, in the end, those who benefit most will be the children whom we serve.

Stainback and Stainback (1984) discuss the implications of merging regular and special education. They conclude that "with careful planning, it should be possible to meet the unique needs of all students within one unified system of education — a system that does not deny differences, but rather a system that recognizes and accommodates for differences" (p. 109).

Indeed, that is our goal.

BIBLIOGRAPHY

Bartlett, F. *Remembering*. Cambridge: Cambridge University Press, 1932.

Blackhurst, A. E. "Noncategorical Teacher Preparation: Problems and Promises." *Exceptional Children* 48(1981):197–205.

Bogen, J. "Some Educational Implication of Hemispheric Specialization." In *The Human Brain,* edited by M. Wittrock, 133–52. Englewood Cliffs, N.J.: Prentice Hall, 1977.

Clabaugh, G. K., P. D. Feden, and R. Vogel (1984). "Revolutionizing Teacher Education: Training Developmentally Oriented Teachers." *Phi Delta Kappan* 65(1984):616–17.

Dunn, L. M. "Special Education for the Mildly Retarded — Is Much of It Justified?" *Exceptional Children* 35(1968):5–22.

Friedenberg, E. Z. *The Vanishing Adolescent*. Boston: Beacon, 1959.

Gardner, W. *Learning and Behavior Characteristics of Exceptional Children and Youth*. Boston: Allyn and Bacon, 1977.

Gickling, E., and J. Theobald. "Mainstreaming: Affect or Effect." *Journal of Special Education* 9(1975):317–28.

Goodlad, J. *A Place Called School*. New York: McGraw-Hill, 1984.

Goodman, P. *Compulsory Miseducation*. Boston: Beacon, 1964.

Graves, F. P. *A History of Education before the Middle Ages*. New York: Macmillan, 1913.

Graves, F. P. *A History of Education in Modern Times*. New York: Macmillan, 1914.

Hooper, F., and J. DeFrain. "On Delineating Distinctly Piagetian Contributions to Education." *Genetic Psychology Monographs* 101(1980):151–81.

Knight, E. W. *Twenty Centuries of Education*. Boston: Ginn, 1940.

Kuhn, D. "The Application of Piaget's Theory of Cognitive Development to Education." *Harvard Educational Review* 49(1949):340–60.

Lortie, D. "Some Reflections on Renegotiation." In *Futures of Education for Exceptional Students,* edited by M. Reynolds, 235–44. Reston, Va.: The Council for Exceptional Children, 1978.

Martin, E. "Integration of the Handicapped Child into Regular Schools." In *Main-*

streaming: Origins and Implications, edited by M. Reynolds, 5–7. Reston, Va.: The Council for Exceptional Children, 1976.

Meyer, A. *An Educational History of the American People.* New York: McGraw-Hill, 1967.

Morsink, C. V. *Teaching Special Needs Students in Regular Classrooms.* Boston: Little, Brown, 1984.

Nasaw, D. *Schooled to Order.* Oxford: Oxford University Press, 1979.

Panko, J. S. *Communication between Special and Regular Educators.* ERIC Document Reproduction Service No. ED 243 851, 1984.

Parelius, A., and D. Parelius. *The Sociology of Education.* Englewood Cliffs, N.J.: Prentice-Hall, 1978.

Pessen, E. "The Working Men's Movement of the Jacksonian Era." In *Jacksonian Democracy: Myth or Reality?* edited by J. Bugg, Jr., 83–91. New York: Holt, Rinehart and Winston, 1962.

Potter, A., and G. B. Emerson. *The School and the Schoolmaster.* New York: Harper, 1858.

Reynolds, M. C., and J. W. Birch. *Teaching Exceptional Children in All America's Schools.* Reston, Va.: The Council for Exceptional Children, 1977.

Silberman, C. E. *Crisis in the Classroom.* New York: Vintage, 1970.

Spiro, R. "Remembering Information from Text: Theoretical and Empirical Issues Concerning the 'State of Schema' Reconstruction Hypothesis." In *Schooling and Acquisition of Knowledge,* edited by R. Anderson, R. Spiro, and W. Montague, 137–65. Hillsdale, N.J.: Erlbaum, 1977.

Spurzheim, J. G. *Education: Its Elementary Principles Founded on the Nature of Man.* New York: Fowler and Wells, 1883.

Stainback, W., and S. Stainback. "A Rationale for the Merger of Special and Regular Education." *Exceptional Children* 51(1984):102–11.

Tanner, D., and L. Tanner. *Curriculum Development: Theory into Practice.* New York: Macmillan, 1980.

Wittrock, M. "Education and the Cognitive Processes of the Brain." In *Education and the Brain: The 77th Yearbook of the National Society for the Study of Education, Part II,* edited by J. Chall and A. Mirsky, 61–102. Chicago: University of Chicago Press, 1978.

10 | PROBE: Problem-based Teacher Education at the University of Colorado, Boulder

RICHARD J. KRAFT

JOHN D. HAAS

MORE THAN A FEW POLITICIANS, members of the general public, and even some teacher educators would have suggested in 1986 that the title of this chapter be the Problems in Teacher Education, rather than Problem-based Teacher Education. The federal and state governments have placed the reform of teacher education high on their agendas over the past few years and although the current critics may not be as strident as Lyons, who stated that "teacher education . . . is a sham, a mammoth and very expensive swindle of the public interest, a hoax, and an intellectual disgrace" (1979, 125), they are, nevertheless, seeking a major overhaul of the system.

Among the major reforms being discussed and implemented in various states are: the elimination of the undergraduate education major (allowing only liberal arts subject majors), the movement of all basic teacher education to fifth-year programs (i.e., postbaccalaureate), "fast-track" entrance to the profession by "testing out" of required certification courses, the use of multiple tests for both entrance to and exit from teacher certification programs, recruitment of better-quality teachers through scholarships and payback fellowships, new public school/university partnerships, and other organizational and structural reforms. Few of the political or educational reformers, however, have probed beneath the surface of these "convenient" policies that merely tinker with existing rules, regulations, and administrative structures. In their haste for the quick fix rarely do they confront the

Richard J. Kraft is professor of education, former director of teacher education and the PROBE program at the University of Colorado-Boulder, and vice-chairman of the Colorado State Board of Education. John D. Haas is professor of education at the University of Colorado at Boulder.

161

philosophical and methodological underpinnings of the teacher-education process itself. Without examination of basic assumptions it is doubtful that effective and lasting changes in teacher-education programs will occur. What is more likely is a set of cosmetic, political alterations of present arrangements similar to those that emerged from *A Nation at Risk* — longer school years and school days, more credits for high school graduation, more homework, and more frequent testing.

HISTORICAL BACKGROUND

Five years ago, prior to the current outcry over the need for reform in teacher education, the University of Colorado, Boulder (CUB) took a critical look at its program. After a year of careful analysis and planning a new experimental design emerged that has come to be known as PROBE, an acronym for Problem-based Teacher Education.

Traditionally the teacher-education program at the University of Colorado at Boulder has been similar to those found in most American colleges and universities, with theory preceding practice, courses in educational foundations and psychology, general and special methods, special education, and communications coming in advance of school-based student teaching. During the late 1960s and early 1970s there were efforts at CUB to add more humanistic components to the program, which in turn was followed by an influx of federal funds to implement a module approach to competency-based teacher education. By the time of the school reform movements in the early 1980s the CUB program had reverted to its traditional, course-based model. These efforts, however, were not without some lasting changes. CUB abolished its undergraduate majors in education in 1980, several years prior to the call to do so by many state and national commissions. It placed students in alternative student teaching settings in addition to traditional public school classrooms. Many CUB instructors attempted to tie the university classroom instruction to the realities of the public schools through teaching their university classes in the schools and assigning observations and tutoring experiences in public school classrooms. Still, the basic university-based, course-based program remained the dominant mode. That program is still in place and handles the majority of teacher certification students, while the new PROBE experiment involves only twenty to thirty students each year.

The failures of previous attempts at reform and the felt need for a different program for older adults (ages twenty-five to fifty or older) who were returning to the university to obtain secondary school teaching certificates prompted a group of faculty to meet extensively during the 1982–83 school year to design a new program. Many factors led to the PROBE model, but among the most important were the previous history of reform at CUB, the nature of the research university environment, the outstanding intellectual quality and maturity of returning students, the desire to model a teaching/learning environment that could be used in the schools, and the university faculty members' skills, interests, and philosophies.

PHILOSOPHICAL RATIONALE

The faculty working on what was to become the PROBE model recognized the need for a philosophical rationale early in the planning stages and discussed a range of orientations and positions. The philosophical ideas of Alfred North Whitehead and John Dewey seemed most appealing to the group, and the educational theories of these two writers became the infrastructure for the PROBE model.

Whitehead's theory of education is based on the concept of "the rhythm of education," by which he means that there are appropriate times for students to study particular "subjects and modes of study." These periods or stages, however, are not to be considered "as a uniform steady advance undifferentiated by change of type or alteration in pace." He observes that life is cyclical, comprising alternating periods, as in night/sleep and day/awake or seasons of the year. Rhythm conveys the concept of "difference within a framework of repetition" (Whitehead 1929, 15–22).

Similar to Hegel's theory of change in which there are three stages (thesis, antithesis, and synthesis), Whitehead's theory of human "intellectual progress" suggests renaming Hegel's stages "romance," "precision," and "generalization." In the first stage, romance, the learner experiences novelty, a situation that is fascinating yet perplexing. In PROBE this situation is the reality of a school and a classroom, and the many interactions one encounters in observing life in this context. What is apprehended here is not systematic knowledge but the romantic emotion and excitement "consequent on the transition from the bare facts to the first realizations of the import of their unexplored relationships." After the PROBE student has the feel of school and classroom, problematical case studies are viewed as both real and worthy of further exploration. The student is now ready to pursue new knowledge in order to try to set in order "a ferment already stirring in the mind" (Whitehead 1929).

The next stage is that of precision, where the student now must use rigor and analysis to come to grips with the problems inherent in the real world of school and classroom and the corresponding contrived world of the problem case study introduced to PROBE tutorial groups. The student attempts to be more precise in formulating a problem as well as more systematic in pursuing data, facts, and concepts to illuminate the problem. For Whitehead (1929) this leads to "both a disclosure and an analysis of the general subject matter of the romance."

The final stage is generalization, a synthesis of the fruits of both romance and precision. It is the emotional and intellectual satisfaction of achieving integration, of seeing the new creation, of solving, albeit tentatively, a perceived problem. For the PROBE student the satisfaction of closure is vicarious and experiential. The individual student and his or her tutorial group successfully come to grips with the contrived problem case study and the PROBE student returns to the school/classroom to test by experience if the solutions work in practice (Whitehead 1929).

John Dewey is the philosopher without peer of the American republic, a founder of the only school of philosophy unique to the United States, pragmatism, and one of the few theorists who saw the intimate and essential relationship between the ideas of democracy and education. In applying the tenets of pragmatism to education Dewey (like both Hegel and Whitehead) saw that, at root, education is a process of change. He coupled this insight with his faith in democracy as the ideal form of cooperative living and his faith in science as the best-evolved method to date of creating dependable knowledge. For the PROBE planners the most appealing aspects of Dewey's philosophy were that learning is rooted in experience and that knowledge derives from a process of inquiry (Dewey 1916).

PROBE attempts to combine these two critical aspects throughout the program. Since Dewey believed that inquiry was spurred into action by a bothersome state of affairs encountered in the course of normal living, PROBE students are immediately placed in contexts where educational problems constantly occur: the school/classroom. Since problems need to be formulated and reformulated in order to make them amenable to inquiry, PROBE tutorial groups use problems observed by students in the schools as well as written problem case studies created a priori as springboards to the process of inquiry (Dewey 1910).

As Dewey emphasized that experience (both virtual and vicarious) is the basis of education, PROBE begins with student contact. As will be seen later in the program description, PROBE seeks to have practice precede theory, to have PROBE students in contact with school students and teachers prior to, during, and after discussions of educational theory. While there are many teacher-education programs that attempt to carefully direct students in their student teaching experiences, PROBE follows Dewey's admonition that

> such practice teachers should be given the maximum amount of liberty possible. They should not be too closely supervised, nor too minutely and imme-

diately criticized upon either the matter or the method of their teaching. Students should be given to understand that they not only are permitted to act upon their own intellectual initiative, but that they are expected to do so, and that their ability to take hold of situations for themselves would be a more important factor in judging them than their following any particular set method or scheme. (1904, 269)

In the same work Dewey suggested several characteristics, or dispositions as he called them, of the ideal teacher-education student. These five dispositions form the key to much of what PROBE is attempting to do. The future teacher should be (1) a thoughtful student of education, (2) intellectually independent and responsible, (3) one who exhibits initiative, (4) skilled in scholarship, and (5) possessed of a spirit of inquiry.

Methodologically, Dewey calls for "observation, insight, and reflection," and the "inspiration and constant criticism of intelligence." He states that a teacher-education program should emphasize "convergence and concentration, thinking rather than drill" and that teachers see growth in terms of certain laws and principles (1904, 15–25).

Dewey's *Experience and Education* (1938) was a particularly influential volume to the PROBE planning group. It took seriously many excerpts from this work, such as the following:

To imposition from above is opposed expression and cultivation of individuality; to external discipline is opposed free activity; to learning from texts and teachers, learning through experience; to acquisition of isolated skills and techniques by drill, is opposed acquisition of them as means to attaining ends which make direct vital appeal; to preparation for a more or less remote future is opposed making the most of the opportunities of present life; to static aims and materials is opposed acquaintance with a changing world. (pp. 19–20)

MODELS OF TEACHER-EDUCATION PROGRAMS

After the PROBE faculty planning group concluded its discussions and debates concerning philosophy, it proceeded to considerations of alternative models of teacher-education programs. Zeichner (1983) summarizes four "alternative paradigms" in teacher education, and although the article in the *Journal of Teacher Education* was published after the PROBE model had been developed, he captured the essence of much of the discussion that took place in the planning stages. He defines a paradigm as a "matrix of beliefs and assumptions about the nature and purposes of schooling, teaching, teachers and their education that gives shape to specific forms of practice in teacher education" (p. 3). The PROBE planners and staff agree that there is no such thing as value-free education either for children or future teachers and that there is an underlying ideology, whether that of a total program or of an individual teacher educator. We thus sought a paradigm upon which the staff could agree, while in no way saying that other paradigms were necessarily inferior. Figure 10.1 summarizes the four paradigms of Zeichner and describes two of the most important dimensions along which one can differentiate models of teacher education. The four models are then placed in the appropriate quadrants.

The received/reflexive dimension refers to the degree to which the curriculum of the teacher-education program is specified in advance. Within the received perspective the teacher-education curriculum is specified in advance and is generally nonnegotiable with the prospective teachers as passive recipients of the program. The on-going program at CUB was basically received, while the PROBE staff sought a model that was more at the reflexive end of the continuum, in which the prospective teachers would be actively involved in the development of the curriculum.

Fig. 10.1. Four paradigms in teacher education

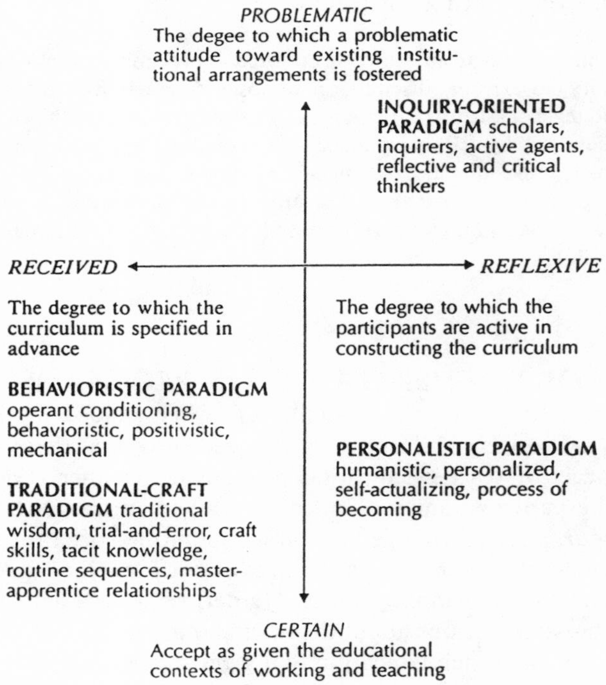

PROBLEMATIC
The degee to which a problematic
attitude toward existing institutional arrangements is fostered

**INQUIRY-ORIENTED
PARADIGM** scholars,
inquirers, active agents,
reflective and critical
thinkers

RECEIVED ← | → *REFLEXIVE*

The degree to which the
curriculum is specified in
advance

The degree to which the
participants are active in
constructing the curriculum

BEHAVIORISTIC PARADIGM
operant conditioning,
behavioristic, positivistic,
mechanical

**TRADITIONAL-CRAFT
PARADIGM** traditional
wisdom, trial-and-error, craft
skills, tacit knowledge,
routine sequences, master-
apprentice relationships

PERSONALISTIC PARADIGM
humanistic, personalized,
self-actualizing, process of
becoming

CERTAIN
Accept as given the educational
contexts of working and teaching

The second dimension in Zeichner's model, problematic/certain, concerns the degree to which teacher education views the form and context of schooling as problematic. Most teacher-training programs accept as given the educational and social contexts in which prospective teachers are to work. It is the question raised a half-century ago by George Counts, when he asked, "Dare the schools build a new social order?" The PROBE staff was not presumptuous enough to believe that it could build a new social order through a small teacher-training program, but it did come down solidly on the problematic end of the continuum, holding that future teachers should be trained to help in the transformation process of the schools. The staff felt it was difficult to justify the maintenance of the status quo. Thus, a model was sought that would foster a problematic attitude on the part of teacher-education students towards the institutions in which they would be working.

The first of Zeichner's paradigms explored by the PROBE staff was the behaviorist or competency-based model with its positivistic epistemology and emphasis upon specific and observable skills. As mentioned earlier, the University of Colorado, Boulder had explored aspects of this model in the 1970s under a grant with the National Science Foundation, but by 1983, with the exception of one educational psychology course, not much evidence of this model could still be found. The PROBE staff rejected this model as being too mechanistic and unsuited to the target population of teacher candidates and the PROBE faculty itself. The model specifies the curriculum in advance and treats the teacher candidate in a generally passive fashion. It also tends to accept the current institutional and societal patterns as givens rather than as a situation susceptible to change. It is thus a model or paradigm that fits neatly into the received/certain quadrant of Zeichner's model.

Also in the received/certain quadrant is a model Zeichner calls the Traditional-Craft Model. In this approach teaching is considered to be a craft and teachers are craftspersons. The normal schools strongly held to this model in which an apprenticeship played an extensive role, and prospective teachers learned by trial and error and through the wisdom of practitioners. Several teacher-education institutions in the 1960s explored extensive lists of skills needed by teachers, some lists in excess of two thousand discrete items. The PROBE staff rejected this model also, for a range of reasons, not the least being that there is little evidence that the mastery of such an array of skills adds up to the sum of a good teacher. In addition, the apprentice role tends to feed into the perpetuation of those structures that already exist rather than the problematic mode sought for PROBE students.

Some PROBE faculty planners have been and continue to be active in the open, alternative education movement, so that for them a personalistic/ humanistic model was most appealing. This model involves the students in designing their own curriculum to meet their own needs, something to which the PROBE staff was committed. But the model's general acceptance of schools and society as they currently exist and its emphasis upon the individual rather than the group were seen to be serious shortcomings. The planning group did not want to add to the narcissistic tendencies already too prevalent in American society. Although the staff valued "process" and "becoming," it also valued "product" and "competence." While the individual needs of students continue to be paramount in the PROBE program, they cannot be the sole basis upon which to build a program.

The rejection of three of the Zeichner paradigms left only what he terms the Inquiry-Oriented Model. PROBE staff had been active in the development of inquiry-oriented curriculum materials in the various disciplines throughout the 1960s and 1970s and so had a natural affinity for developing such a model in teacher education. The reflective nature of this model and the teacher as active change agent appealed to the PROBE staff. The reflective action of which Dewey spoke, and the praxis of action and reflection of which Freire writes, are focal points on which the PROBE staff agreed and which led it to develop an inquiry-oriented, problem-based model.

Having reached this agreement after a long struggle, the search was begun to find an extant inquiry-oriented model. While numerous teacher-education programs contain elements of such a paradigm, as of course they do of the other paradigms discussed above, the staff was unable to find any single teacher-training program containing all the elements that were felt to be essential. One of the staff members, however, had worked with the Harvard Business School case study approach, which he described to the planners. At the same time it was discovered that in residence at the University of Colorado was a member of the McMaster University medical faculty from Hamilton, Ontario. McMaster had recently created a carefully developed inquiry-oriented approach to the education of medical doctors that included the use of case studies. These fortuitous circumstances led the group to decide to adapt the Harvard and McMaster case study models to an inquiry-oriented PROBE program. Both approaches will be discussed in detail in the following pages.

GOALS AND OBJECTIVES

One of the basic characteristics of PROBE is its continuing evolution as a program, and this necessitates the constant review of goals and objectives.

The following list has been developed over the three years in which the program has existed but is regularly scrutinized and revised.

1. To identify and define educational problems and to search for information to resolve and manage them
2. To think critically about education and schooling and gain a knowledge and skill base to resolve problems
3. To become a competent member of a small group and to function productively as part of that group in learning, research, and teaching
4. To develop self-awareness and the ability to cope with the emotional reactions of self and others
5. To become a self-directed learner with abilities in the selection and use of appropriate resources, the management of personal working time, and self-evaluation skills
6. To be aware of and be able to work in a variety of educational settings
7. To develop the skills and to learn the methods required to diagnose learning needs and to manage the educational problems of learners including their cognitive, physical, emotional, and social aspects
8. To be aware of the "culture of the classroom" and of the school and the role of the teacher as a professional in this environment
9. To become aware of the stresses and demands placed upon teachers and to develop strategies for coping with them
10. To participate in the life of the school community as an active member and to perceive one's self as an educator
11. To identify the forces operating on the classroom and on the school and to conceptualize the school as part of the broader society
12. To move through the stages of teacher-as-person, teacher-as-learner, teacher-as-teacher, and teacher-as-member-of-the-broader-society

In addition to these broad goals the PROBE program has a range of more specific objectives too numerous to list here but all related to the goals presented above.

STUDENT SELECTION

In its initial year, 1983–84, PROBE admitted a range of students from twenty-one-year-olds in their senior year to mature adults who were seeking to change occupations. While all the students succeeded in completing the program, the staff felt that the younger students had a more difficult time adjusting to the self-directed nature of the program, while the mature adult learners were, for the most part, able to adapt rapidly to this significantly different learning model. The relatively unstructured learning environment was too great a shock for those who had been institutionalized for sixteen consecutive years, and the staff had a difficult time weaning them away from their expectations of lectures and tests. It was as a result of this experience that the program decided to limit PROBE students to age twenty-five or older, generally with experience in other professions or with children in the home or other settings.

The range of students in the three years of the program has been exceptional with a median age of thirty-two and students up to the age of fifty-five. All candidates must present at least a bachelor's degree, and many have presented master of arts degrees with several having the doctorate. Work in one's major discipline must have been completed prior to coming into the program, although students are permitted to take one course concurrently as long as it does not interfere with their participation in tutorial groups or work in the schools. A majority of the students have come from the sciences and mathematics, and this has made them most desirable to the schools in the region, many of which are facing shortages in these areas. Like students in the regular teacher-education program, they must pass a basic skills examination, but they must also have a 3.00 grade point average for acceptance (yet most have a 3.5 average or better). The following occupational and educational groups were represented in the first three PROBE classes: engineering, business, homemaking, law, veterinary medicine, airline hostessing, herpetology, philosophy, chemical engineering, outdoor education, environmental education, and the military.

At least as important as the paper requirements for admission are the personal characteristics and abilities of applicants. Using a mock tutorial case study all candidates are screened for such demonstrated abilities as independent learning, imaginative problem solving, and ability to work productively in a small group. Such characteristics as emotional stability, capacity for self-evaluation, responsibility, and motivation to enter the teaching profession are weighed prior to admission. The mock tutorial case study experience is used in combination with the more traditional academic criteria to determine admission to the PROBE program. The tutorial has proven to be an excellent device for revealing motivation, personality, and interpersonal skills.

EXPERIENCE-BASED LEARNING

A deep commitment to the role of experience in learning underlies PROBE, as was pointed out in the section on the philosophy of the program. The

PROBE faculty takes seriously the need for practice or experience to precede theory. PROBE candidates are thus placed in the schools from the first day of the program and are in and out of the schools on a daily basis throughout the full nine months. While initial placements are with the help of the university staff, the candidates themselves soon move into the role of structuring their own visits, observations, tutoring, miniteaching settings, and student teaching settings. If students are unable or unwilling to rapidly move into this pivotal role of finding their own learning environments, the staff will initially aid them but soon suggest that they are not functioning well in the self-directed learning mode expected of PROBE students. In three years only a handful of the seventy-five participants have had much difficulty in this arena.

While students are encouraged to begin their school/classroom experiences in regular public secondary schools, since this is the final destination for most of them, they are also encouraged to range far beyond the confines of suburban, white, Anglo-Saxon junior and senior high schools and visit preschools and elementary schools as well as inner-city secondary schools. Visits to alternative private and public secondary schools provide another view on the practice of schooling as do observations in teen parenting centers, juvenile delinquent homes, and parochial schools. Wherever children and teenagers are to be found in our society is where the PROBE candidate is encouraged to observe, aid, teach, and reflect. Since by state law all teachers must have completed a four hundred-hour student teaching experience, there is the expectation that sometime during the fall or spring semester such an intensive experience will take place. For most candidates this occurs in the spring semester, but program flexibility permits it to occur whenever the individual is ready, and it may begin as early as November or as late as April. While PROBE candidates, according to an evaluation done after the second year, appear to be considerably more at ease about their intensive student teaching experience than the younger, more traditionally trained undergraduate, they did ask for more actual teaching experiences prior to being immersed for eight weeks in a student teaching setting. With this request in mind, in the third year of the program a miniteaching week was instituted in early October so that students could experience a fuller range of responsibilities, from lesson planning to classroom management, than was the case in the observational and tutorial settings.

The experiential aspect of the PROBE program, then, consists of continuous contact with schools, children, and learning environments from the beginning of the academic year in September until the end of the program in May. The PROBE students thus get to experience the full academic year in the schools with its planning, organizing, teaching, examining, and other activities. Such a field-based component is often not possible in programs geared more to the university setting. There is also the opportunity to do observation and mini-unit teaching in a range of different settings and to do in-depth student teaching in at least two different environments. Students have taught in regular public junior and senior high schools, parochial schools, juvenile justice centers, teen parenting schools, alternative public and private schools, outdoor education centers, Indian reservation schools, and overseas dependent schools.

Dewey spoke constantly of the need for the interaction of experience and reflection, while the Brazilian philosopher, Paulo Freire, speaks of the praxis of action and reflection. Experiences in the schools and other settings can be educative or miseducative. With this and other considerations in mind PROBE planners included the "tutorial group" as a component of the program. This has become that critical place where the teacher candidates reflect upon their experiences, react to each other's experiences, and apply old and new experiences to the analysis and solutions of case studies.

TUTORIAL GROUPS

A critical part of the PROBE model is the small-group tutorial. Twice a week in the fall term and once a week in the spring the teacher candidates meet with eight to ten fellow students and two tutors. The pair of tutors consists of a regular faculty member of the university and a teacher on leave from the schools. The tutorial group serves a variety of functions. It is a laboratory where students develop interpersonal skills and look at their own personalities and abilities. It is a place for peer evaluation in which students regularly critique each other's presentations and overall involvement in the program. Traditional teacher-education programs seldom teach persons how to listen or to give or receive criticism, but these are important components of the PROBE tutorial group. The ability to give accurate and candid feedback within the safety of the tutorial group aids the future teachers for the day when they must evaluate and give feedback to their students in the schools. Since individually and collectively the students are responsible for their own learning, educational planning is also learned as part of the tutorial group process.

Not only is the tutorial process new to the vast majority of students in the program, it is also new to the professors, or tutors, as they are called. One of the major reasons that the tutorial model was chosen was to change the teaching behavior of faculty members. Many teacher-education reform movements have faltered when individual faculty members insist on continuing their particular classes in a lecture mode even though the rest of a program might have adopted a very different mode. One of the first decisions made by the PROBE planners was to eliminate all courses in the regular teacher-education program and move to the small tutorial groups in their place. This of course meant that in many cases the tutor/professor would not be an expert in the many topics to be dealt with in the case studies and thus would be forced into the role of generalist and facilitator rather than lecturer on his or her area of expertise. The tutor becomes a model of the self-directed learner and problem solver rather than the expositor of a fount of knowledge, so ubiquitous in regular university classrooms.

The tutorial role is often difficult for both the tutors and the students. It is always easier to just "tell them the answers" than to help the students to define the problems and find the answers for themselves. The facilitation role, which has become such an important part of the counseling movement, is rarely seen in academic classrooms so there are few examples from which to learn. Such roles as hinting, shaping, reinforcing, and encouraging, while occasionally part of more didactic approaches used in higher education, are not the major focus of a professor's teaching behavior. The tutorial approach is what might be called "guided discovery," and the tutor permits the student to make mistakes, but does not let the frustration reach a level at which learning becomes paralyzed.

It is through the tutorial groups and the experiences in the schools that the teacher candidates receive regular course credits from the university and complete all the state requirements for certification. Although the students do not take specific courses in methods, evaluation, foundations, psychology, and others, they do cover all these topics in their tutorial groups and/or in their school/classroom experiences. Since the springboard for analysis and discussion in the tutorial group is the case study, these are intentionally general encompassing many related topics and suggesting many others.

PROBLEM-BASED CASE STUDIES

Once it had been decided to develop an inquiry-oriented model for teacher education, the problem-based case study was a natural vehicle on which to focus the process of inquiry. The Harvard Business School has used the case study method successfully for many years, but uses highly detailed cases developed at great cost and containing most of the information needed by the student buried within the case. The McMaster Medical School cases, however, are very short, often only a paragraph or two, and the student researcher is forced to find the information needed to analyze and solve the problems in a wide range of learning resources. The PROBE staff, working with no special or external funding, decided that for both practical and philosophical reasons the McMaster model was more suitable. The case studies for PROBE have been written by faculty tutors, graduate students, teachers in the schools, and some by PROBE participants.

Although each case study is short (usually a page or two), embedded in the problem situation are many interrelated topics. Some of the topics are obvious while others can be inferred from a careful reading of the narrative and still others uncovered by the students were not even imagined by the authors. The solutions are seldom few or simple, and students bring to the tutorial groups evidence for their preferred solutions from a wide-ranging variety of sources: their own background of experience, recent experiences in schools/classrooms, and material from their readings in books and journals. Among the many resources that students consult in dealing with the problems are the following:

1. The PROBE library of books donated by faculty members along with two or three texts purchased for each participant
2. The PROBE tutors
3. Public school teachers, counselors, and administrators
4. The university library
5. The School of Education faculty and resource center
6. Fellow students at the university
7. School children and sometimes their parents
8. Other educative agencies in the society such as churches, youth centers and clubs, courts, migrant programs, juvenile homes, city and county agencies, cultural centers, and others
9. Preschools and elementary schools, even though PROBE is currently a secondary teacher-training program
10. Rural schools, alternative schools, inner-city schools, and others that have special characteristics
11. Videotapes, tape recordings, films, and other media

Students or groups of students bring their findings back to the tutorial group for presentation and discussion. Some of these presentations are videotaped for critique by the tutorial group or for use as models for succeeding programs. Following the completion of each case, the tutor and tutorial group discuss which of the PROBE objectives and which state certification objectives have been achieved and at what level.

The search for solutions to the various problems is carried out individually, in pairs, or even by a whole tutorial group. Students are encouraged to work together to seek out information and to consult a wide range of resources. Once they have analyzed a problem in depth and have marshaled evidence to support their tentative solutions, they must organize a mode of presentation for delivery at the next scheduled tutorial group meeting and be prepared for reactions and critiques by the tutors and their fellow group members.

In order to illustrate this use of case studies, we first present a sample case, that of "Sam"; then a list of case studies to show the scope of topics; and finally a matrix that indicates how program objectives are keyed to particular case studies.

Sam: A Case Study

Sam's third period chemistry class was an odd mixture of students. Most of them were of average ability, but there were several who did not match the norm. Sharon, for example, was a very gifted ninth-grader who had been accelerated in science and mathematics. Kris, on the other hand, had an IQ of 80. Then there was Tom who had cerebral palsy and was confined to a wheelchair. Sam, the teacher, suspected Rich and Mark both had some sort of learning disability. When first faced with this class, Sam had wondered how he would be able to meet the needs of all these students.

Today, Sam had scheduled a short written test on the periodic table for this class, accompanied by a second "hands on" test on flame tests. He expected that the results of the two tests would parallel those of previous tests this semester: Sharon would "max" them both in minutes; Kris would fail the written test but do reasonably well on the lab test; Tom would do well on the written test, but as usual be awkward at manipulating the equipment for the flame tests; Rich and Mark would score poorly on the written work even though Sam knew they would earn passing grades if he allowed them to answer the questions orally. The rest of the class of thirty students would receive B's or C's, except for one or two who along with Sharon would get A's.

By dividing his tests into written and lab parts, Sam hoped to obtain a better indication of the students' learning. He wanted to be known as a teacher who graded fairly, and thus felt he could do even more to reach the diversity of students in this class. Yet he was at a loss to know what more he could do.

In Table 10.1 this case appears along with eleven others, each followed by a brief listing of potential objectives that could be pursued and achieved by using the case. Next, in Table 10.2 the matrix lists the same twelve case studies across the top, while the program's major objectives are listed down the left margin, allowing for cross-checking of emphasis or neglect.

Table 10.1. Selected probe case studies

Case study	Potential Objectives
1. Sam	Diagnostic-prescriptive techniques, measurement and evaluation, individual differences and mainstreaming
2. Andrea Friesen	Interaction with social groups, parent-teacher cooperation, class management, interaction with peers and colleagues
3. Ann	Same as #2, plus mainstreaming, community relations
4. John	General teaching strategies, content-specific methods, presenting information, program planning
5. Emily	Community relations, curriculum theory, program planning and evaluation, district/school organization
6. Joan	Exceptional students: characteristics, teaching of, mainstreaming, class management, school organization
7. The Field Trip	Finances and logistics, community relations, school organization
8. Tony	Facilitating learning, teacher-student interaction, classroom management, small-group processes
9. Stanley	Teaching reading, mainstreaming
10. Rob	Theories of learning, child/adolescent development, curriculum theory
11. Media	Instructional media, colleagial interaction, curriculum theory
12. Leslie	Classroom management, general methods, unit/lesson planning, presenting classroom information

Table 10.2. Case studies and objectives

OBJECTIVE: INTERACTING WITH SOCIAL GROUPS; FACILITATING PARENT-TEACHER COOPERATION; EDUCATOR AS LIAISON WITH COMMUNITY; INTERACTING WITH COMMUNITY; INTERACTING WITH PEERS & COLLEAGUES; EDUCATOR AS FACILITATOR OF LEARNING; TEACHER-STUDENT INTERACTIONS; FACILITATING GROUP PROCESS IN THE CLASSROOM; DIAGNOSTIC-PRESCRIPTIVE TECHNIQUES; CURRICULUM THEORY; CLASSROOM MANAGEMENT; MEASUREMENT; METHODS OF INDIVIDUALIZING INSTRUCTION; GENERAL METHODS; CHILD DEVELOPMENT; INSTRUCTIONAL MEDIA; EVALUATION OF INDIVIDUAL PUPILS; EXCEPTIONAL CHILD: CHARACTERISTICS; ADOLESCENT GROWTH; LEARNING THEORY; ORGANIZING CLASSROOM INFORMATION; TEACHING STRATEGIES; METHODS OF TEACHING READING; SPECIFIC METHODS; PRESENTING CLASSROOM INFORMATION; TEACHING EXCEPTIONAL CHILD IN REG. CLASSRM.; THEORY OF TEACHING READING; PROGRAM PLANNING; PROGRAM EVALUATION; SCHOOL ORGANIZATION; ORGANIZATION OF PUBLIC SCHOOLS; PROFESSIONAL ORGANIZATIONS; FOUNDATIONS OF EDUCATION; HISTORY OF EDUCATION; PHILOSOPHY OF EDUCATION; FINANCING OF EDUCATION

Rows (blank grids): Sam, Andrea Friesen, Ann, John, Emily, Joan, Field Trip, Tony, Stanley, Rob, Media, Leslie

/ = Covered somewhat
x = Covered thoroughly

The case study approach represents an alternative to the traditional ways of viewing knowledge. Instead of individual courses with bodies of knowledge and prescribed textbooks, the PROBE model uses problem case studies from which the students derive, analyze, and present the same topics found in the required courses in the regular program. The major differences are that the knowledge topics do not occur (come up) in tidy parcels such as educational psychology or communications and that knowledge is acquired to analyze and solve problems rather than in a logical typology. This approach to learning is much like that described in Robert Pirsig's *Zen and the Art of Motorcycle Maintenance* in which each hypothesis opens up countless other hypotheses and problems are never solved, but rather the learner is involved in a continuous search.

EVALUATION

Evaluation occurs throughout the PROBE academic year as continuous feedback is critical to both the students and the tutors. The basic purposes of evaluation in this program are to facilitate student learning and to modify the program, not to compare students or rank order them. Although students receive grades at the end of each term as required by university regulations, the evaluation is continuous and not an anxiety producing "final examination." Students are actively involved in regular self-evaluation, as this is consistent with the self-directed learning format used in PROBE. Tutorial group members also evaluate each other, and of course the tutor gives regular and systematic feedback throughout the term.

Observation of the students in the tutorial groups and in the various school settings become part of the evaluation process as do the various written products of the students. Formal and informal presentations in the tutorial group along with a range of activities in the school setting are part of the overall evaluation. Precise definitions of satisfactory and unsatisfactory performance are not stressed in the program, but after three years' experience in the program, there appears to be extremely high correlations among the evaluations of fellow students, the tutors, and teachers in the schools. Except for a few cases, these external evaluations are similar to those given by the students themselves. Rather than emphasize performance levels on tightly specified learning criteria, PROBE prefers a descriptive profile on how each student is achieving and what needs to be done in the future.

CONCLUSION

PROBE is in its fourth year and it is still too early to proclaim it an unqualified success. Graduates from the program seeking teaching positions have all been employed, most in school districts with vast numbers of applicants for each opening. Student evaluations of the program have been overwhelmingly positive, with the few negative criticisms serving as prods to change. Numerous school districts have sought to work closely with PROBE, and the U.S. Department of Education selected it for one of its grants as a special demonstration project. Formative and summative evaluations of the program keep it in a state of change, but the overall model appears to be sound. No single component of PROBE is unique, but we believe that the combination of ingredients in a single year-long program is worthy of consideration as an effective alternative to current teacher-education programs.

BIBLIOGRAPHY

Counts, G. *Dare the Schools Build a New Social Order.* Salem, N.H.: Ayer, 1969.

Dewey, J. *Democracy and Education.* New York: Macmillan, 1916.

_____. *Experience and Education.* New York: Macmillan, 1938.

_____. *How We Think.* Boston, Mass: D.C. Heath, 1910.

_____. "The Relation of Theory to Practice in Education." In *The Relation of Theory to Practice in Education,* 15–25. Third Yearbook of the National Society for the Scientific Study of Education (Part I). Bloomington, Ind.: Public School Publishing Co., 1904.

Freire, P. *Pedagogy of the Oppressed.* New York: Herder and Herder, 1970.

Lyons, G. "Why Teachers Can't Teach." *Texas Monthly* 7(1979):122–28, 208–20.

National Commission on Excellence in Education. *A Nation at Risk.* Washington, D.C.: U.S. Government Printing Office, 1983.

Pirsig, R. *Zen and the Art of Motorcycle Maintenance: An Inquiry into Values.* New York: Morrow, 1979.

Whitehead, A. *The Aims of Education.* New York: Macmillan, 1929.

_____. *Process and Reality.* New York: Harper & Row, 1960.

Zeichner, K. "Alternative Paradigms of Teacher Education." *Journal of Teacher Education* 34, no. 3(1983):7.

11

Futures Studies and Teacher Education: A Theoretical and Structural Assessment of the Program at the University of Houston at Clear Lake, Texas

JAMES BOWMAN

FRED D. KIERSTEAD

THE UNIVERSITY OF HOUSTON AT CLEAR LAKE is an upper-level institution that began operation in 1974. The campus is located between Houston and the port of Galveston. With NASA's Johnson Space Center on one side and Armand Bayou Nature Preserve on the other, the campus setting is a stimulus to reflective thought and the study of change. Although this orientation has contributed to UHCL's program planning structure, it is particularly evident in the master of science program in studies of the future. This essay will explain the theory and structure of the program—its philosophic rationale, normative aims, curricular goals and strategies, and interdisciplinary course content.

THEORETICAL ASSUMPTIONS

Futures research is intrinsically interdisciplinary. Although this concept is often used in academic planning, it is usually applied within specific disciplines or in a multidisciplinary framework. Our approach, however, assumes that faculty participants should be drawn from all disciplines; and

James Bowman is associate dean of the School of Education, Morehead State University, Morehead, Kentucky. He is vice-president of the education division, World Future Society. Fred D. Kierstead is professor of educational foundations, University of Houston at Clear Lake, Texas.

students at the graduate level should represent a wide array of experience in formal and informal education. Although most of our students have academic experience in business, education, and government, we continue to seek to enroll students from other disciplines. In accord with John Dewey's view of instrumentalism this interdisciplinary approach helps students and faculty to perceive futures studies in different contexts.

Although it is possible that America is transcending the industrial era, there is an important need for specialized knowledge. Some authors have argued that education will become more comprehensive or general in orientation. This prediction is a significant consideration in our program, but we contend that there is also a need for content-specific skills. Thus, the program is designed with a core of information and skills that supports a general or global perspective for problem-solving/analytic skills. In addition to this students are expected to take discipline-specific courses relevant to employment expectations. The needs vary in accordance with previous skills and the expected future skills of individual students. Some students enter the program with no expectation of career changes while others expect to make substantial career changes. Individualized programs are necessary even though numerous models of study have been constructed for discipline-specific skills. We want to provide both comprehensive and specialized knowledge with a core of common courses complemented by individualized studies for individual needs.

The core courses are designed to build upon interdisciplinary and instrumental learning through the development of problem-solving skills. O. W. Markley in *Changing Images of Man* identifies a broad range of societal problems at several different levels of significance.

1. *Substantive* problems lie at an immediate or operational level and are usually identified as immediate targets for corrective attention or increased allocation of money or other resources.

2. *Process* problems are those that impede the methods and procedures of collectively setting priorities and strategies to solve substantive problems.

3. *Normative* problems concern the appropriateness and effectiveness of one's values, preference goals, and so forth, that are the basis for planning and priority setting.

4. *Conceptual* problems are difficulties that seem to be intrinsic to the way we think, the words we use—in short, to the particular vision or understanding of reality that is dominant in a culture—thus affecting our ways of perceiving and doing and also affecting the formation of our normative values. This inescapable circumstance necessarily affects our perceptions, our valuations, and our actions.

Substantive problems may be examined at two operational levels. First-level substantive problems include population growth, decreasing food supplies, decreasing fossil fuels, diminishing underground water resources, and a whole host of environmental problems (chemical dumping, acid rain, etc.). Second-level substantive problems result from and reinforce the problems mentioned above. They tend to be more obvious or immediate concerns that include conditions such as inflation, higher unemployment (and unemployability), increased debts, increased welfare expenses, higher military expenditures, and increased crime. Although it is possible to isolate problems for analysis, operational solutions to problems will necessitate an understanding of the interrelationships between substantive problems.

Normative views depict our notions about values, goals, and priorities, which include but extend beyond substantive problems and result in "quality-of-life" decision making. Most normative problems result from alienation. Melvin Seeman (1969) has defined alienation as a troubling human situation involving one or more of the following:

1. *Powerlessness.* The individual perceives himself or herself as having no power in what he or she considers to be important areas of decision making.

2. *Meaninglessness.* The individual finds no purpose, no value, and no meaning in tasks. There is a lack of feeling of accomplishment.

3. *Anomie.* Anomie is a state of normlessness. Goals are ambiguous. The future is uncertain.

4. *Isolation.* The individual feels alone in the world. His or her goals are different from those that he or she perceives others to be following.

5. *Self-estrangement.* This form of alienation is identified as an individual who is isolated from herself or himself. One's expectations of oneself are different from one's perceived self.

As with substantive problems, it is easier to classify alienation as a first-level problem that is related to societal expectations as well as individual goals. For example, as higher divorce rates become acceptable societal norms, it would seem that personal alienation would be reduced. When a normative problem becomes the norm, the result is social change but not necessarily social invention. This operational consideration is of major importance in futures studies. It is easier to address second-level normative problems. The latter include concerns that seem more immediate or specific such as sexual abuse (of children and adults), pornography, alcoholism, and drug abuse.

Our futures program is designed to link substantive problems and normative problems in order to ascertain developments in social invention and social change because a social *invention* has higher predictability value in its application than does social change. Thus, a social invention also tends to have more predictable impact on society in general. Examples include the creation of the House of Commons in 1300, the Red Cross in 1864, and Alcoholics Anonymous in 1934 (Conger 1973). Social inventions may also be distorted to the point that they result in less predictable social change. The I.Q. test was a social invention that resulted in unplanned social changes. It has been used to ascertain qualities of leadership, creativity, and monetary success. To this extent the test produces less predictable social change that is different from its original intent. The educational purpose in this kind of study is to provide students with conceptual and process skills that enhance abilities in strategic planning and priority setting.

STRUCTURE OF THE PROGRAM: HISTORICAL AND CURRENT

When the program first began in 1975, there were few precedents for how futures education should be offered. Neither the type of students it would draw nor the type of curriculum it would come to embody were known in any detail. Consequently, the initial thrust of the program consisted principally of famous futurist writings and methodologies as they may have been found in and outside the field. Alvin Toffler's *Future Shock* and *The Futurists,* Bertrand de Jouvenal's *The Art of Conjecture,* Donella Meadows et al.'s *The Limits to Growth,* and Herman Kahn's *The Next 200 Years* are examples of the works that were studied. The Delphi technique, trend extrapolation, the use of a cross-impact matrix, and content analysis were some of the methodologies studied for the purpose of comparison. Gradually, however, it became clear that most students wished to use futures studies for professional as well as personal reasons. It also became clear to us as a faculty that certain skills would be more useful than others, and thus core courses were developed in each of the two programs being offered.

There are two interrelated master's degree options in futures studies; one is a master's degree in education related sciences and the other is a master's degree in behavioral sciences with a concentration in studies of the future. Both programs have core courses but provide different bases for knowledge and varying skill dimensions, depending on the student's selection of optional courses.

These programs have undergone a pattern of continuing development with a current enrollment of approximately thirty-five total students, half of whom are attending full-time. All required core courses in both programs are offered in the evening in order to accommodate the majority of working students. Approximately ten faculty members from various backgrounds teach the principal courses for the program. Additionally, cooperative arrangements between the schools of professional education, humanities and human services, and business and public administration make it possible for students to formulate a variety of approaches to future-oriented preparation, whether or not they are formally matriculated in the futures programs. Most of these approaches are oriented toward one of the following objectives:

- teaching and/or educational planning and administration
- professional employment as a researcher, forecaster, planner in business, government, think tanks, or action-oriented public interest groups
- journalistic involvement in futures studies
- preparation for the pursuit of the Ph.D. in many different disciplines
- intellectual and/or aesthetic enjoyment of futures studies

From the program's inception these master's degrees were not designed to give a person all new job skills, but rather were oriented to "futurizing" knowledge already attained at the bachelor's degree level. The master's degree program in education related sciences is designed to give teachers expanded skills in futures methodologies, research, and planning. It is assumed from the beginning that the student in this program is going to remain in the classroom or in educational administration. The master's degree program in behavioral sciences is more general in its orientation but was originally designed to enhance skills already developed at the undergraduate level. As the need for futurists in business, government, and the private sector increases, the behavioral sciences program is becoming more structured in offerings, emphasizing skills in forecasting, systems thinking, and strategic planning.

Table 11.1 shows the similarities, differences, and interrelationships of the two master's degree programs as they exist today. Optional courses in both programs allow the students to take courses in their present fields (i.e., education, sociology, economics, history, etc.) that are oriented to a futures perspective or that give them new skills and knowledge. Students in the education related sciences program are strongly encouraged to take the core courses in the behavioral sciences program particularly if they are considering educational administration and planning.

Table 11.1. Model programs in education related sciences and behavioral sciences

M.S. in education related sciences (Concentration in futures studies)	M.S. in behavioral sciences/ futures studies
Core courses (12 hours mandatory)	
EDUC 6333 History and Philosophy of Education EDUC 5931 Utilization of Computers in Education EDUC 6132 Educational Evaluation SOCI 6731 Seminar in Futures Studies	SOCI 5432 Study of the Future SOCI 6734 Futures Research and Forecasting SOCI 6733 The Systems Approach SOCI 6731 Seminar in Futures Studies
Optional courses (18 hours)	
Strongly recommended courses (9 hours)	(See "Relevant Electives" under M.S. in education related sciences)
SOCI 5432 Study of the Future SOCI 6734 Futures Research and Forecasting SOCI 6733 The Systems Approach	
Relevant Electives (9 hours)	
ADMN 6132 Educational Administration SOCI 6338 Strategic Planning EDUC 5531 Educational/Societal Futures EDUC 5931 Futures Teaching Methodologies SOCI 6335 Technology and Ethics in the Future PSYC 5435 Visionary Futures STAT 5031 Data Analaysis Techniques SOCI 6735 Advanced Futures Research and Forecasting SOCI 6431 Demographic Projections ECON 5135 Resources in the Future	
Master's Thesis or Project (6 hours)	Master's Thesis, Project or Internship (6 hours)

A brief description of the core courses in both programs is presented in Table 11.2. Even though each degree program has required courses, both are flexible enough to provide the inclusion of optional courses that may enhance already-acquired specializations. The core courses denote what we as a faculty at UHCL believe to be the minimal competencies and knowledge needed for a person to speak intelligently about futurism and futures research. Individual tailoring of programs to meet more specific needs, skills, and employment objectives is an integral part of our program. Faculty in futures studies advise students individually as to the optional course

Table 11.2. A description of core courses in education and behavioral sciences futures program

M.S. in Education Related Sciences[a]

History and Philosophy of Education
- History and overview of education, with emphasis on the philosophic systems that have influenced the purposes of education in America
- New and old issues facing education including the possible changing definition of an educated person
- Qualitative research and analysis

Utilization of Computers in the Classroom
- The strengths, limits, and applications of computers and educational technology in the classroom
- Introductory programming, gaming, simulations, and evaluation techniques
- Human/machine partnerships in education

Educational Evaluation
- Quantitative research techniques, analysis, and evaluation
- Case studies, significance, validity, and reliability
- Limits and strengths of quantitative research

Seminar in Futures Studies
- Survey of emerging topics in the field
- Critical assessment of the field
- Overview of personal and professional styles and strategies
- Discussion of the ethics of practicing futurism
- Completion of an integrative project

M.S. in Behavioral Sciences/Futures Studies[a]

The Study of the Future
- History and overview of the field of futures studies
- Overview of the philosophies and perspectives of different futurists
- Introduction to the major schools of thought and the major activities that comprise the field
- Introduction to key topics of concern to futurists
- Exercise in alternative futures thinking

Futures Research and Forecasting
- Introduction to and exercises in information retrieval
- Overview of principle methodological approaches — e.g., strategic planning, input assessment, monitoring, and issues management
- Survey of futures research and forecasting techniques
- Readings and critique of selected case studies

The Systems Approach
- Introduction to and exercises in integrative and synthesis skills
- Systems theory and thinking
- Applications of systems thinking in education, business, and government
- Dissection of a complex systems model

Seminar in Futures Studies
(See Education Related Studies program)

[a] Requires a project thesis or internship as a culmination of the master's degree.

work they may want to take and whether they do a thesis (for postmaster's preparation), project (application of knowledge), or internship (work with business, government, or private organizations doing futures research).

NEW SKILLS AND OUTLOOKS: REDEFINING EDUCATION

Because futures research is interdisciplinary, much of what our students learn consists in the interrelatedness and interdependence of problems and their resolutions. Problem solvers have to be interdisciplinary in order to understand consequences of alternatives. Table 11.3 lists some present and emerging knowledge/skills that a futurist would have to consider when anticipating possibilities or desirabilities. The amount of expertise needed and the prioritization of such a laundry list would depend on the kind of job one was doing and what kinds of alternatives were being considered. Our master's degree programs attempt to provide a preliminary acquaintance with these topics, methods, and skills, but in-depth concentration is decided by the student. A basic thirty-six-hour program will not develop all skills, knowledge of the topics, and methodological expertise listed in Table 11.3; but it is important that students understand what present and emerging skills, methodologies, and issues are being discussed and tested by futurists and others.

Simply identifying such topics and skills as important for study is quite a different matter than trying to teach and apply topics, methods, and skills that help one grapple with transformational change, societal turbulence, and uncertainty. The experience of doing so leads to a recognition that being a futurist requires a different approach to education and practice than traditional school preparation. Key aspects of this altered orientation ask students to develop different objectives in their education than mere accumulation of facts and methodologies. These skills include

- a curiosity about patterns of change, explanation, and emergence (there are no ready-made or extrapolative answers that obviate our analysis)
- a development of a qualitative image of quantitative data (a sense of "rightness" based on experiences and a normative set of criteria)
- an ability to gather information quickly and continually scan social indicators
- a tolerance for ambiguity (tolerance for complexity, short-term solutions, inadequacy of information, and information overload)

Table 11.3. **Present and emerging knowledge/skills of importance in futures studies**

Present	Emerging
Substantive topics	
Population/demography	Sustainability of society
Energy	Geopolitics
Education	War/militaristics/peace
Economics	Global resource allocation
Technology/technology transfer	Appropriate methodology
Resource allocation	Biological engineering
Leisure/entertainment	Holistic and behavioral medicine
Ecological degradation	Consciousness research
Changing sex roles	Reconstructionist models of education
Transformational futures	Weather/climate
Appropriate technology	NIEO—New international economic order
Transportation	Development alternatives
Values/life-styles	Specific transformational futures
Agriculture/food	Nonlinear transformation theory (Prigo-
Communications/electronics/microproces-	gine, Thom, others)
sor "revolution"	Paradigm/value change
Policy process	Alternative decision-making processes and
Future problems/opportunities education	systems for teachers
Interactions among the above	Artificial intelligence
	"Deindustrialization" of America
General aproaches and/or methods of inquiry	
Alternative futures/scenarios	Simulation modeling
Impact assessment	Strategic planning/management
Issue identification/monitoring/forecasting	Vulnerability analysis
Systems analysis/theory	Tele-/computer-assisted techniques and
Systems-oriented project management	systems
Time-series forecasting	Anticipatory democracy/citizen-participa-
Trend analysis/assessment	tion techniques
Simulation modeling	Investigative reporting
Long-range planning	Decision analytic planning
Policy analysis	Intuitive/visionary forecasting impact
Survey research (including Delphi)	assessment
	Bayesian statistics (of subjective probabili-
	ties)
Other skills that are not specifically methods skills	
Information retrieval	Explaining the futures field
"Number sense"	Networking
Analysis/synthesis/evaluation	Entrepreneurial problem solving
Spoken/written/graphic communications	Conflict management/resolution
Career development (interviewing, resume	Social systems design
writing, etc.)	Flexible use of state-specific skills
Understand "wild card" futures (unex-	Survival
pected)	Global perspective
Computer programming	

- an understanding of the need for complementary/systematic thinking (avoiding provincialism or tempocentric approaches)
- an ability to deal with error effectively (to treat errors and miscalculation as important elements in decision making)
- a willingness to deal with unpopular alternatives, possibilities, and results (Some findings have not yet had their time, and people often refuse to accept them.)

These skills are not a complete list of the needs for futurists, but they do reflect the mindset needed by students in our programs. Teaching these skills is, in part, done by the students themselves, but we as teachers also provide guidance through real-life projects, experiences, and simulations.

EMERGING EMPLOYMENT OPPORTUNITIES

Although we have not emphasized our programs to be more than an enhancement to the baccalaureate degree, many of our students in education, human sciences, and other fields have obtained jobs doing pure futures research. A majority, however, maintain present employment in administration, in the classroom, or in business/industry. There are, however, emerging job opportunities for our graduates beyond present descriptions. Table 11.4 shows some of the present and emerging opportunities for those reflecting the knowledge and skills offered in our program. Many of our graduates have created their own job descriptions because their employers are unaware of their skills. As futures research becomes more established as a viable and important field of study, even more opportunities for employment will emerge but, until that time arrives, most of our students will continue to work within more traditional employment patterns.

CONCLUDING REMARKS

Invention is neither static nor beyond revision. In looking at societal (or global) good we may determine that any given social or technological invention should be revised, reconstructed, or abolished. This assumes that individuals and groups are receptive to critical assessment of their work. Historically, this has not been easily achieved as John Dewey (1927, 170–71) noted:

> There is a social pathology which works powerfully against effective inquiry into social institutions and conditions. It manifests itself in a thousand ways; in querulousness, in impotent drifting, in uneasy snatching at

Table 11.4. **Present and future employment opportunities for futurists**

Present fields	Emerging fields
Business	
Forecasting	Strategic planning
Public relations	Issues management
	Simulation modeling
	Developing "expert" systems
Government	
Planning and program management	Impact assessment
Government informational services	
Public and/or private interest groups	
Monitoring and issues management	Future-oriented lobbying
Social networking (task forces, work-shops, institutes, switchboards, etc.)	
Education	
Teaching in futures *and* another traditional field	Programming "expert" systems
Educational administration	Impact assessment
Curriculum designers for gifted education, etc.	Teaching interdisciplinary approaches, including futures
	Educational technology and learning
	Strategic planning
	Educational testing of complex learning skills
Other areas of work	
"Think tanks" (contract research)	Social networking with other sectors
Consulting	Journalistic and other mass media involvement

Note: We would like to thank Mark Markley and our UHCL futures students in a graduate organization development class for the information in Tables 11.3 and 11.4.

distractions, in idealization of the long established, in a facile optimism assumed as a cloak, in riotous glorification of things "as they are", in intimidation of all dissenters — ways which depress and dissipate thought all the more effectually because they operate with subtle and unconscious pervasiveness.

Educational institutions are currently witnessing a kind of pathology much like that described by Dewey. There is abundant literature designed to promote schools as they used to be. This perspective offers an essentialist theory premised on back to basics and a market approach to education that assumes that learning can best be equated with earning. The orientation is to perceive the school as a basic-literacy/job-mill institution, modeling a kind of common school (from the 1850s) that is present centered and generally lacking in historical perspective or futures application.

In order to effect needed changes in educational goals, the structure of education (itself a social invention) must also be changed. Schools, at present, support more collection of data; for real evaluation, innovation, planning, and participation in learning to take place educational institutions must reflect problem-analysis and synergetic planning modes. Finding desirable futures requires normative interpretation of what is learned. Educators will be required to provide very different kinds of learning environments than what is expected today. Education, in the true sense of the word, must be an agency for change and provide a forum for synergetic resolution of problems and possibilities.

BIBLIOGRAPHY

Conger, S. *Social Inventions*. Saskatchewan, Canada: New Start, 1973.

Dewey, J. *The Public and Its Problems*. New York: Holt, 1927.

Markley, O. W., and other consultants, Center for the Study of Social Policy. *Changing Images of Man*. Stanford: Stanford Research Institute, 1974.

Seeman, M. "On the meaning of alienation." In *Toward a Philosophy of Education*, edited by T. Buford, 61–74. New York: Holt, Rinehart and Winston, 1969.

12 | Educating for Inner-City Schools: Hunter College's Field-based Training Tomorrow's Teachers Program

MAE V. GAMBLE

TEACHING IN NEW YORK CITY TODAY is more difficult than ever. At least 40 percent of public school children live in homes below the poverty line. Many children come from single-parent homes where the mother is a very young adult who never completed high school. Since housing is a major problem in New York, many children live in crowded dwellings with little privacy or calm. Drugs, alcoholism, unemployment, and crime are major social problems that impinge upon their daily lives.

Such social problems influence not only children's ability to learn but their motivation, attendance, home support, and so on. Add to this the fact that most public school children in New York City do not come from the dominant culture of the society. Many come from families that have immigrated to New York from places such as Puerto Rico, Haiti, Dominican Republic, Jamaica, Columbia, Guatemala, China, Greece, India, Pakistan, and Middle Eastern countries.

Other individuals come from the ghettos of black America. They have a distinct culture and language, also different from those of the mainstream society. Preparing teachers to work in the public schools of New York City is the challenge faced by all teacher-education institutions in the metropolitan area. It is the challenge that prompted the Hunter College Education Division to create in 1970 the Training Tomorrow's Teachers program.

Mae V. Gamble is professor and chairperson of curriculum and teaching, Hunter College, City University of New York. Professor Gamble helped to develop the Training Tomorrow's Teachers program in 1970–72, and from 1975–87, she directed the program.

191

The program, usually known by its abbreviated forms TTT or Triple T, is based in East Harlem, a ghetto of the inner city that is close to Hunter College. TTT was created in partnership with Community School District Four, which governs the schools of East Harlem.

The basic underlying philosophy of the program is that if faculty and students work in actual, typical public schools with real children, as opposed to abstract, theoretical constructs of children, they will not only be given opportunities to apply the knowledge they are discussing concurrently in course work, but they will also have opportunity to confront the major problems of teaching in a city such as New York. Problems abound: how does a teacher interest a child in learning content that the child does not see as a part of his or her world; how does a teacher overcome the communication gap that exists between teachers and books that use standard English and children who speak in dialects; how does a teacher interact with children who are used to an authoritarian power structure when the teacher wants to be democratic and in many instances finds such authoritarian behavior repugnant?

These are some of the frustrating questions that confront educators in urban centers in the United States. Such frustrations often lead to premature discouragement and burnout among teachers. Adequate and workable answers can only be found by faculty and students working in public schools.

It is not only appropriate for faculty and students to work in such centers — it is *necessary*. Such experience gives faculty opportunity for research and learning on a continual basis so that theory can be modified to accommodate changes in conditions and practice without the lag that customarily impedes these modifications. The field experience gives preservice students opportunities to face and solve some of the pressing problems facing teachers in New York City. Solving such problems prior to professional teaching experience makes the first year of teaching that much easier and succeeding years less stressful.

Has the program been successful? Fifteen years have passed since its inception. Over 350 students have graduated from the Hunter College program and many are now teaching in the schools the college used as field centers. The graduates of the field-based TTT program are quite successful as beginning teachers in inner-city schools. They enter the classroom with buoyant confidence and experience great success from the start. They have little difficulty with classroom management and they demonstrate competencies and skills that took previous novices 3–4 years of teaching to acquire. *And,* they do not burn out. A survey was made of the graduates of the program in June of 1985. In spite of the fact that during the late seventies there was a teacher glut and many graduates were forced to find work in other fields, the survey found that 83 percent of the graduates who responded are presently teaching! (This statistic is based on 45 percent return of the questionnaire.) Those who are not teaching are either on maternity leave or are working in other fields because of higher pay.

Compare this with the fact that of 6832 new teachers who accepted teaching jobs in New York City in September of 1983, 1393 quit within two weeks and 775 never appeared for work (Purnick 1984).

The survey also found that the vast majority of TTT graduates felt prepared for teaching, were able to apply theory to practice (unlike most graduates who move to a "practicality ethic" where survival concerns dominate [Joyce and Clift 1984]), and felt successful as teachers!

Tables 12.1 to 12.4 show specific responses. Compare these statistics with the results of a survey of 683 public teachers in New York State from both urban and suburban school districts in 1980, 1981, and 1982 (Farber 1984).

A comparison of the data from the two studies is most impressive. Even taking into account the fact that the average years of teaching was 5.4 for the TTT group compared with 13.4 for the Farber group, the TTT

Table 12.1. Summary of responses relating to effectiveness of preservice experiences as preparation for teaching

| | Percentage of respondents | | | | |
| | Least | | | | Most |
	1	2	3	4	5
Foundation courses	1	4	28	41	42
Methods course	0	3	8	43	42
Field experience	1	2	4	9	80
Liberal arts course	2	4	20	45	24

Table 12.2. Summary of statistics relating to success and satisfaction with teaching

Questions	Responses				
	Percentage of Respondents				
	Least				Most
	1	2	3	4	5
1. Was the program successful in relating theory to practice? Do you believe the theories you learned in the TTT program apply to your present teaching situation?	1	3	14	35	36
2. Have you maintained an interest in teaching and do you find it rewarding? (Effective involvement)	2	4	9	31	54
3. Do you feel successful as a teacher? (Commitment)	1	1	6	36	43

Table 12.3. Suburban and urban teachers' responses to selected items on Factor 3 (effective involvement)

Item		Percentage endorsing choice-point			
		Never	Rarely	Occ.	Freq.
I have dealt very effectively with the problems	Suburban:	2.0	14.5	36.0	47.4
of my students.	Urban:	3.0	18.2	46.0	32.8
I have accomplished many worthwhile things	Suburban:	2.2	17.9	38.9	40.9
on this job.	Urban:	4.4	27.3	33.2	35.0
I could easily understand how my students have	Suburban:	1.4	13.1	34.5	51.0
felt about things.	Urban:	3.8	20.6	36.1	39.5
I have felt I was postiively influencing students'	Suburban:	1.4	22.1	33.1	43.5
lives through my work.	Urban:	3.7	20.0	41.3	35.1
I have felt exhilarated after working closely	Suburban:	3.7	20.0	41.3	35.1
with my students.	Urban:	5.9	32.1	33.2	28.8

Table 12.4. Suburban and urban teachers' responses to selected items on Factor 2 (commitment to teaching)

Item		Percentage endorsing choice-point			
		Never	Rarely	Occ.	Freq.
I have felt that if I had to do it all over, I would	Suburban:	21.0	26.5	19.9	32.5
still choose to be a teacher.	Urban:	34.2	21.3	18.6	25.9
I see myself continuing to teach for the rest of	Suburban:	24.6	24.5	22.5	28.3
my career	Urban:	29.1	21.9	19.3	29.8
I have felt that, all in all, the benefits outweigh	Suburban:	6.5	28.6	33.4	31.4
the disadvantages of teaching.	Urban:	15.0	30.4	31.3	23.6
I have felt that my work has provided me op-	Suburban:	10.7	34.1	30.8	24.3
portunities for personal growth.	Urban:	18.0	30.7	28.9	32.5
I have felt satisfied with teachers' standing in	Suburban:	41.1	38.8	13.9	6.2
today's society.	Urban:	48.0	33.8	11.9	6.3

graduates are clearly more successfully involved and satisfied as teachers.

Equating the category "frequent" with the categories labeled "4 (much)" or "5 (most)" in the TTT study, one can make comparisons. The TTT group had 85 percent of those responding selecting 4 or 5 as their answer to the question "have you maintained an interest in teaching and do you find it rewarding?" (Commitment to teaching). In the Farber study 32.5 percent of the urban teachers responding said that teaching frequently provided them opportunities for personal growth, and 29.8 percent of urban teachers saw themselves continuing to teach for the rest of their lives.

In the area of successful involvement 79 percent of the respondents in the TTT study indicated feeling successful as a teacher much or most of the time, while the Farber study showed an average of 33.5 percent of the urban teachers stating they frequently felt effectively involved in teaching.

Why is the Hunter College program so successful in training teachers for inner-city schools? What are the special characteristics that contribute to its success?

PROGRAM

Students enter the TTT program as freshmen and immediately are enrolled in two field-based education courses as a part of their first semester's program. In each course the students spend four hours a week in an elementary school in East Harlem: two hours in the classroom observing and working with the classroom teacher in an apprentice role followed by two hours of lecture and discussion with the Hunter College professor on the school premises. In the classroom component the students observe, teach, and work with individual children and small groups of children. The college professor who is teaching the course is also in the school, going from classroom to classroom in a supervisory role. Since there are usually about twenty-five college students in a group, the college professor does not have the time to observe each student for more than two or three minutes at a time. But that is enough time to make sure the student is present, is relatively at ease in the learning environment, and is engaged in a meaningful activity that is a learning experience. It is also enough time to touch base with the cooperating teacher who has taken the responsibility of assigning tasks to the student and often wants to share information and give feedback.

Immediately following the classroom experience activity, students meet with their college professor for traditional lecture and discussion. Some of this class time is formed by discussion of problems and questions relating to what happened in the school that morning. Most of the class time is devoted to covering the traditional content of education courses. The crucial difference here is that as theory is discussed, the student can use the actual classroom experience as a referent point.

The same pattern is followed for the three following semesters, with students working under the supervision of an elementary school teacher for part of their morning and attending a class taught by the college professor for the second half of their morning. Students take the rest of their courses at Hunter College, completing general education requirements and a collateral major requirement in a liberal arts field.

As juniors, students take on more responsibility. During this year they take methods courses in science and social studies. (Sequence of courses appears in Table 12.5.) In the fall semester they are expected to plan and teach science to a group of elementary school children twice a week. This

Table 12.5. Sequence of field-based courses

Fall Semester	Spring Semester
Freshman Year	
Social Foundations of Education	Education of Minorities
Introduction to Education	Methods of Teaching Language Arts and Reading
Sophomore Year	
Math for Elementary Education Teachers	Methods of Teaching Math in the Elementary Schools
Child Development	Learning Theory
Junior Year	
Physical Science for Nonscience Majors	Methods of Teaching Reading in Elementary Schools
Methods of Teaching Science in Elementary Schools	Methods of Teaching Social Studies in Elementary Schools
Senior Year	
Student Teaching (Either Semester)	

calls for the development of a unit as well as individual lessons. Both the classroom teacher and the college teacher supervise. During the spring semester the Hunter College students teach social studies usually to the same group of students with whom they were working in the fall semester.

In the senior year students spend one semester as four-fifths-time interns. (Two afternoons are spent at the college campus.) At this period in their development they are coteachers in the classroom and are given a great deal of responsibility. They are supervised by the cooperating teacher, an administrative head from the school, and the college professor. The evaluation of their performance as teachers is made by all three, usually with the classroom teacher having the greatest input.

Notice in the suggested sequence of courses (Table 12.5) that there are liberal arts courses included among the courses that are taught in the elementary school. This is done in an attempt to make the content of those courses relevant to the needs of teachers in inner-city schools.

The sequence of courses basically follows the traditional model of foundation courses before method courses with the exception of the language arts and reading course, which is offered early because the students need it to help them with their teaching experience.

NECESSARY COMPONENTS

In addition to a sound sequence of courses with appropriate field experience there are other factors that contribute success to the Training Tomorrow's Teachers program.

Parity

TTT has always worked on a parity principle, which insures that all those who are involved in working in the program will also be included in setting policy. This means that liberal arts faculty, education faculty, public school personnel, and students come together periodically when decisions are to be made that affect them. As a result, everyone who is involved in the process understands the various objectives and priorities of each particular group, and accommodations are made accordingly. Also, as each team member identifies the group decision as his or her own, he or she takes responsibility for making it work. With the sharing of power comes the assuming of responsibility.

The classroom teacher, for instance, has input into deciding what the student will be doing in the classroom. The teacher, consequently, is very happy to have the student in attendance because the student can perform tasks that the teacher perceives to be important and useful. The elementary school teacher is willing and anxious to take responsibility for supervising the student and giving the teacher trainer instruction and feedback, when appropriate.

The college professor, whose ideas and objectives have been considered in the joint decision-making process, also feels responsibility for making things work. If the school is willing to "lend" its children to these teacher trainers for practice teaching, the college professor tries to insure that the experience for the children is of good quality and that positive learning is taking place. The college instructor cannot help but feel a part of the public school and, as such, feels responsibility for a smoothly functioning and productive learning environment.

The same is true for the college students. They frequently will put in extra time at the school, go on trips with children, and turn into professionals overnight as they are given increased responsibility in decision making.

Space

A second factor that is crucial for operation of the program is space. The Hunter College program has a room in each of its field centers that it can call its own. This allows professors to bring material and equipment to the school and leave it there. It also provides students and professors with a place to hold seminars and conferences and do tutoring and teaching. A home base in the school further contributes to the feelings of partnership, commitment, and ownership which are such important ingredients for success.

Communication

Open lines of communication between all participants in the Hunter College program is also an essential element for success. Since the program is spread out in three schools, and students are dispersed throughout the elementary school building, lines of communication can easily be broken. Awareness of this danger has led to the formulation of specific policies and strategies.

1. Scheduled meetings between public school teachers and professors, between professors and students, and between classroom teachers and students are arranged on a regular basis. It is not enough to allow face-to-face communication to occur on an informal basis. It may never happen. Scheduled group meetings help people focus on problems and discover solutions.

2. Written communications between group participants include frequent, but brief letters to the teachers and administrators of the public school throughout the semester indicating the student's schedule, strengths, suggested activities, and so on; periodical evaluation of student performance and of the program by cooperating teachers; and a newsletter for students.

3. Since college professors are in the school every week, they go into each classroom and talk to classroom teachers and students on a regular basis. It is crucial that the college professor communicates openly to both the cooperating teacher and student and encourages the same from them. Reluctance to communicate feelings and ideas can cause conflict and stress without resolution. Openness can also cause conflict and stress but an honest interchange of opinions and ideas will more likely lead to eventual change and harmony as the end result.

Definition of Roles

Since the establishment of a teacher-education program as a partnership program between public school and college was a new concept, there was initially a great deal of anxiety on the part of all participants. Working in team relationships means that one person does not take all the responsibility but the problem of which responsibility falls to whom has to be defined and spelled out. Otherwise, people feel very anxious, and frequently no one takes responsibility for fear of stepping on someone else's toes.

Through trial and error the Hunter College TTT program has developed successful methods. It became clear very early that one person had to take a leadership role, but the person in charge differs according to the boundaries. The principal is the chief authority in the school and takes major responsibility for all decisions that relate to school policy. The classroom teacher is the leader of the classroom, coordinating all activities and being informed and consulted by student and professor in relation to class activities. The professor takes chief responsibility for the planned educational experience for the student. The Training Tomorrow's Teacher program put together a handbook that defines roles and typical activities of all participants. This has been very useful, especially when new people join the program.

Extended Field Experience

The Hunter College students log over seven hundred hours in the elementary school classrooms. This quantity of experience is certainly one of the important reasons for the success of the program in preparing these students for teaching in inner-city schools. The length of the training is also significant.

The fact that the program is stretched out over a four-year period gives students an early opportunity to discover whether teaching is something they really want to do. If they decide it is not for them they can drop out after a year or two and pick another career goal. This early field experience is the most effective method for "weeding out" those individuals who are not suited for teaching. Since the investment is so small at this time, changing career goals is an easy task.

The four-year training has a second advantage. Extending the field experience over a long period of time gives the student the opportunity to grow and develop gradually. The teaching experience is minimal in the beginning, and there is time for reflection, thought, and growth. Students teach individuals or small groups of children for the first two years and also do some observation. As the student gains experience and skill, more responsibility is given. They work with larger groups or the whole class.

This gradual, controlled experience offers an improved chance of success at each step of the way. Of course, the student teachers make mistakes and sometimes fail; but the failures are minimal for most students. The preservice student gains confidence, skill, and maturity through continued success over a long period of time.

Reality Base

The Hunter College field centers are New York City public schools faced with all the problems of the inner city. The majority of teachers are capable, some are mediocre, and some are clearly inadequate. Hunter students are placed with good and poor teaching models, and thus they see what works and what doesn't work and why. They learn early that teaching is difficult, but they also learn that teachers are successful and children can learn even in poor neighborhoods where children have fewer advantages. They develop realistic expectations for themselves and for children. They do not go into teaching with an idealistic preconception that can never be implemented, thereby creating feelings of guilt and inadequacy as has been the case with so many of their predecessors. And the teacher candidates never accuse the college professors of being too theoretical. They can't be. The reality is always there as a reference.

Variety

Although the Hunter College program uses only three elementary schools, there are fortunately a variety of programs in each school. Two schools have minischools with open-education designs, one school has a program for the gifted, another has a bilingual program, and one houses a minischool that stresses the performing arts. Because of the variety of programs, the education students can experience all the approaches to reading instruction, for instance, and witness for themselves the strengths and weaknesses of each approach. They can observe that where one approach works for one child, it may not work for the next. They frequently witness children being moved from one program to another, and they have an opportunity to observe what such changes can mean.

The Hunter College program requires that the student spend time with a variety of age groupings and teachers. Thus, if the students are placed in a kindergarten one year, they may work in a sixth grade class the next year. Such diverse experiences help the prospective teachers decide on their teaching preferences and also afford a sense of the developmental differences inherent in varying age groupings. The exposure to many teachers makes the preservice teacher aware that there is no one ideal teacher but rather a variety of teaching styles, each effective in a different way. The student realizes that one must develop one's own style, working with one's own particular strengths and weaknesses. Techniques are picked up from the teacher models; and since there are so many, there is a wealth to choose from.

Theory into Practice

The field experience provides the college professor with an excellent laboratory to illustrate all the theory that is presented to students either through lectures or assigned reading. Significant incidents that occurred during the lab period are sometimes shared and discussed when the students come together as a group, and the college teacher helps the students construct theory to fit what they have discovered from experience. At other times instructors teach theory and recall incidents that illustrate them. This is an ideal teaching situation for the college instructor. One is never at a loss for topics to discuss, materials to show, or problems to solve. They are always there.

For the preservice student the field experience makes the theory that is presented meaningful and relevant. It is meaningful because the student has a wealth of experience to draw on to aid with understanding, and it is relevant because the theory can be immediately applied in the teaching situation. Students eventually develop their own theory based on their trial-and-error research in the classroom.

Visibility

One of the major obstacles to teacher growth is isolation. Teachers spend most of their time with children and not only have little opportunity to observe other teachers but also tend to hide from being observed themselves. They are sure that they are not living up to the idealistic teacher model that was presented to them in their preservice days, and they don't want anyone to know. Isolation and idealism are also factors that contribute to teacher stress (Fimian 1982).

Graduates of the Hunter College field-based program do not slip into the isolation trap. They tend to be more open to supervision and to work well in a team situation. They share with other teachers, are flexible, open, and willing to be visible. This is because they have already spent four years working in classrooms where they have grown accustomed to being on display. They are seldom alone during the preservice field experience. They constantly work with and are observed by other students, cooperating teachers, and college instructors. Like children from large families, they have no place to hide. And they not only grow used to team teaching, they become dependent on it. They want to share, to work together, to give and receive feedback.

A second reason why graduates from the Hunter College program are not likely to slip into the isolation pose is that their experience has taught them there is no reason to hide the fact that they are not perfect teachers. They know that the perfect teacher does not exist. This enables them to accept their own weaknesses and to expose them. They realize that other teachers are struggling with the same problems and that through collaboration and trust teachers can help each other. This may be one of the greatest benefits of the Hunter College program, for these attitudes prevail when they become classroom teachers.

Contextual Immersion

Another aspect of the program that leads to enhanced learning for the teacher trainer is the fact that the student is immersed in the elementary school classroom setting. This, of course, is the dimension that makes it a field experience as distinguished from a practicum or simulated teaching experience. The latter two are experiential — that is, the learner is learning from *doing* — but the extent of the learning is much more limited and therefore only partially applicable to the postgraduate teaching experience.

Participants in the TTT program have tried a variety of approaches in providing practice experiences for the preservice students. Children have been taken out of classrooms and tutored one-on-one by the college student. Groups of children have been brought to the TTT room and used for demonstration lessons by students or college instructors. The practice that most TTT instructors have settled on is assigning one to three students to a classroom and allowing the classroom teacher to plan activities for them. Although this approach relinquishes control to the classroom teacher, the advantages of this method far outweigh the disadvantages.

Since the student is immersed in the actual setting, he or she is experiencing a great deal of incidental learning that cannot be duplicated in simulated experiences. Also the teacher trainee is learning most accurately how complex and involved teaching thirty students can be. The college students learn how to talk to one child while watching twenty-nine others. They learn how to dash a note off to another teacher while supervising the lining up of children. Teaching is a very complex act that requires one person to pay attention to twenty-five or thirty individuals while performing a multitude of other tasks. Skills like these are only developed in the actual setting of the classroom.

SUMMARY

The chapter thus far has focused on the advantages of the TTT program. As with anything in life, there are disadvantages and problems that do exist in the day-to-day operation of the program.

In the first place it is more difficult and time consuming to participate in a teacher-education program that is field based than it is to work in a program that is based on campus. Students and professors spend time and money commuting back and forth between school and college. Materials must also be transported to and from the schools. This makes working in the program less appealing to faculty who have many responsibilities on campus. It also causes some students who cannot withstand the demands of the program to drop out after one or two semesters. Then, too, some participants applaud such rigor as a method for weeding out more inadequate students.

Another difficulty with the implementation of the TTT program is that since the neighborhoods where the schools are located have high crime rates, some people are fearful about participating. Even though there has been very little harassment in the fifteen years that the program has been in operation, there are some faculty and students who cannot overcome their fears. Fortunately, most faculty and students recognize that if one is going to teach in New York City, one must be willing to go into the neighborhoods where the schools are located.

Despite the difficulties mentioned, the Hunter College TTT program remains firmly established. It has been in existence since 1970. It has lived through open enrollment, reduced funding, a teacher glut, three deans, complete changeovers in staff, students, and schools, and now, a teacher shortage. In spite of all these changes and obstacles, it has survived. And it survives because the extra effort and risks are worth it. A field-based program is a most effective approach for preparing students for teaching in today's inner-city schools.

Since not every teacher-education program is situated in the center of a densely populated urban area with a multitude of schools and thousands of children available to them, the Hunter design would be difficult to duplicate in other kinds of ethnographic and environmental settings. However, field experience of some kind should be provided as an integral part of every course in a preservice education program. Field-based training is the most efficient and profitable approach to teacher education existing today.

BIBLIOGRAPHY

Farber, B. "Teacher Burnout: Assumptions, Myths, and Issues." *Teachers College Record* 86, no. 2(1984):330–31.

Fimian, M. "What Is Teachers' Stress?" *The Clearing House* 56(1982):101–2.

Joyce, B., and R. Clift. "The Phoenix Agenda: Essential Reform in Teacher Education." *Educational Researcher* 13, no. 4(1984):6.

Purnick, J. "City's Poor Districts Are Hit Hard by a Severe Teacher Shortage." *New York Times,* Feb. 29, 1984, p. 1, col. 5.

13 | Teacher Education at Berea College: Building a Rationale for Uniqueness in a Liberal Arts Setting

WALTER P. OLDENDORF

SITUATED HIGH ON A RIDGE marking the border between Kentucky's blue-grass and the Cumberland Plateau, Berea College in Berea, Kentucky, has enjoyed a history as colorful, varied, and unique as the geography it strad-dles. Founded in 1855 as an outgrowth of nineteenth century reform move-ments, Berea prepared mountain youth to be teachers, ministers, and farmers in an atmosphere committed to abolition, the dignity of labor, and coeducation. Interracial from the beginning, the college fought segregation all the way to the Supreme Court in 1904. The college's Christian commit-ment is tempered by the Finneyite notion that Christian truth is attained through free and open discussion (Brown 1978, 8, 11). The Education De-partment of Berea College has evolved its programs within the unique tra-ditions of the college; this chapter will describe those aspects of Berea teacher education that best reflect the unique nature of the college and the department.

This chapter is focused on the nature of the assumptions about learn-ing and teaching that underlie the curricula of Berea College and on the effects of these assumptions on its programs. The special nature of Berea teacher education lies in the consequences of these assumptions rather than in the sequence or content of courses, which are largely dictated by state mandates. The chapter also articulates this basic assumption because such rationale building is a critical activity in countering both attacks on teacher education as antiintellectual and irrelevant and pressures on education pro-

Walter P. Oldendorf is interim associate director of the North Carolina Center for the Advance-ment of Teaching at Cullowhee, North Carolina.

grams for conformity and uniformity. The values of uniqueness and variety in education must be well grounded in articulate rationales to withstand these forces. This essay, therefore, seeks to make explicit the rationale that undergirds teacher education at Berea through (1) an examination of the relationship between the liberal arts tradition of the college and its teacher-education curriculum; (2) a description of the assumptions about the nature of teaching and learning that guides teacher education within the goals and values of the college; (3) a demonstration of how the values, traditions, and assumptions of the college and department manifest themselves as features of the teacher-education curriculum; and (4) a description of the labor program at Berea and its relationship to teacher education.

LIBERAL ARTS AND TEACHER EDUCATION

Teacher education at Berea College takes place within the framework of the liberal arts program; all Berea education students meet the requirements for the bachelor of arts degree as well as the teaching certificate. This grounding of teacher education in the Berea liberal arts tradition means that teacher-education students share fully in the remarkable spiritual and intellectual tradition dating from Berea's founding in 1855. Both Berea and Oberlin College, from which its first president and many of its faculty came, were part of the Finneyite movement, which emphasized freedom of speech and thought in arriving at Christian truth (Brown 1978, 8, 11, 16). Other early influences that remain strong at Berea include an emphasis on multiracialism, plain living, and the value of manual labor (Brown 1978, 24). These and other values are summarized as the Great Commitments of the College (Berea College 1985, 6):

> To provide an educational opportunity primarily for students from Appalachia who have high ability but limited economic resources.
> To provide an education of high quality with a liberal arts foundation and outlook.
> To stimulate understanding of the Christian faith and to emphasize the Christian ethic and the motive of service to mankind.
> To demonstrate through the Labor Program that work, manual and mental, has dignity.
> To promote ideals of brotherhood, equality, and democracy, with particular emphasis on interracial education.
> To maintain on our campus and to encourage in our students a way of life characterized by plain living, pride in labor well done, zest for learning, high personal standards, and concern for the welfare of others.
> To serve the Southern Appalachian region primarily through education but also by other appropriate services.

As a result of its historical roots as expressed in the great commitments an atmosphere of free intellectual inquiry exists where all students work to earn credit toward the cost of their education, and where the principal requirement for admission beyond academic ability is that one's parents may not earn too much money!

All students who are admitted to Berea College must be eligible for financial aid. In practice, this means students come from families with incomes less than $25,000 (for a family of four) to $40,000 (for a family of eight). Each student is then guaranteed a cost of education grant of $6500. All students work in the college labor program, and their work is valued at $2000 toward the cost of education. The rest of the cost of education is made up of endowment income, gifts, and state and federal assistance.

A basic assumption of the teacher education program at Berea is that a liberal arts education will provide the content knowledge base essential to teachers. As students in the liberal arts curriculum, Berea teacher candidates must satisfy rigorous general education requirements well in excess of state mandates (sixty-six semester hours at Berea compared to the forty-five semester hour state mandate). In addition to fulfilling basic proficiency requirements in communication skills and mathematics, students must complete a one-semester freshman composition course and at least six additional courses emphasizing the use of effective written communication skills in a content area. All students must fulfill a requirement of twelve semester hours of a cultural area or foreign language, twelve semester hours of natural science, four semester hours of computer science, and eight semester hours of social science. (Secondary students must also complete all the usual requirements for their teaching major with a grade point average of not less than 2.5.) The core curriculum is also required of all Berea students, and it is designed to incorporate the Great Commitments of the College directly into a four-year sequence focusing on contemporary and historical issues in the arts, sciences, humanities, and religion.

The extensive background of Berea teacher candidates in subject matter preparation is reflected in their National Teacher Examination scores. All forty graduates in 1984–85 scored above the Kentucky cutoff scores for teacher certificates, and nearly two-thirds scored above the fiftieth percentile (national norms) on NTE tests of communication skills, general knowledge, and specialties (Berea College 1986, 202–4). Table 13.1 presents percentile rankings for Berea students in NTE communication skills assessment. Table 13.2 covers general knowledge, Table 13.3 covers professional knowledge, and 13.4, specialty areas.

As Lee Shulman (1986) points out, the relationship between content knowledge and teaching is ill-defined and unresearched; "the ultimate test

Table 13.1. Percentage of teacher-education graduates scoring in each quartile of the percentile ranks on the NTE test of communication skills, 1982–85

Percentiles	1982–83 N=39	1983–84 N=55	1984–85 N=40
75–99	18	24	23
50–74	46	33	40
25–49	21	27	28
1–24	15	16	10

Table 13.2. Percentage of teacher-education graduates scoring in each quartile of the percentile ranks on the NTE test of general knowledge, 1982–85

Percentiles	1982–83 N=39	1983–84 N=53	1984–85 N=39
75–99	26	19	28
50–74	26	40	36
25–49	38	26	26
1–24	10	15	10

Table 13.3. Percentage of teacher-education graduates scoring in each quartile of the percentile ranks on the NTE test of professional knowledge, 1982–85

Percentiles	1982–83 N=39	1983–84 N=54	1984–85 N=39
75–99	8	13	33
50–74	51	46	38
25–49	31	22	21
1–24	10	19	8

Table 13.4. Percentage of teacher-education graduates scoring in each quartile of the percentile ranks on the NTE specialty area tests, 1982–85

Percentiles	1982–83 N=31	1983–84 N=53	1984–85 N=40
75–99	39	42	30
50–74	16	26	33
25–49	35	23	28
1–24	10	9	10

of understanding rests on the ability to transform one's knowledge into teaching." Although we may not know much about the transformation process, a major assumption of Berea's program is that there must be some knowledge to transform.

ASSUMPTIONS ABOUT THE NATURE
OF TEACHING AND LEARNING

The Berea Education Department program is guided by the Great Commitments of the College, particularly those values that emphasize the liberal arts foundation, the labor program, and service to the southern Appalachian region through education. The department faculty also shares many assumptions about the nature of teaching and teacher education that strongly affect the content and implementation of our program.

From a historical viewpoint the thinking of our department has its roots in the traditions of James, Dewey, and Piaget, rather than Watson, Thorndike, and Skinner. This is not to say that we preclude exploration of the ways in which the behaviorist tradition does effectively explain and predict some phenomena of education; rather we encourage the notion that education is a complex enterprise that cannot be completely explained by any single point of view, and that each point of view must be judged not for its truth or falsity as a complete explanation but in terms of its comprehensiveness and power. We do entertain the notion that teaching and learning involve interactions of human minds as well as the effects of human behaviors. We do promote the concept that professionals can explain and justify their actions within the historical and philosophical traditions of their profession.

In an era when education moves in ever more mindless directions, insistence that the qualities of teaching be a direct reflection of the qualities of mind takes on growing importance. "Mindless" is an appropriate term in two senses. Mindless can refer to the assertion that all human mental phenomena can be understood as behavior that is a consequence of the physiology of the human brain (Sagan 1977, 7). The study of teaching and learning then becomes a study of behavior and physiology. Mindless also refers to the lack of adequate rationales characteristic of proposals for educational reform. The consequence of this kind of mindlessness is a stream of educational fads that come and go without noticeably improving American education (Shaver 1977).

What a teacher does in the classroom flows directly from the complex intertwining of ideas we term the "mind." It follows that the principal object of attention in teacher education ought to be development of the mind not training of behaviors. Lest the reader scoff at the suggestion of "training teacher behavior," note that several states already require their teacher candidates to exhibit specific behaviors to evaluation committees to qualify for certification (Oldendorf 1983).

The mind of the teacher must grow in many dimensions, but none will be more fundamental to good teaching than the understanding of the nature of education. Because the phenomena of education are so complex and varied, the prospective teacher cannot really be educated by teacher-preparation programs based primarily on either inchoate, unexamined classroom experience or simplistic, "scientifically" derived maxims for "effective teaching." Such training may indeed elicit specific responses to specific situations without developing the intellectual capacity to analyze situations and produce unique, ethical, and rational solutions. To truly educate, not just train prospective teachers, we must help them to understand the complex, ideological nature of education on their own terms and to develop reasoning processes through which they may make choices of educational goals and procedures that are most ethical and adequate for the particulars of their situations.

These assumptions about teacher education underscore the fact that the teaching/learning process can be understood in various ways, none of which can be proved conclusively complete or comprehensive. The ideological frameworks through which we conceptualize education consist of organized systems of assertions about the nature of knowledge and values that provide the parameters for investigating teaching. Although each ideology seems to explain education on its own terms, some frameworks can be shown to be more adequate and generalizable than others in explaining the phenomena of education.

The existence of multiple frameworks such as the subject matter–centered, the child-centered, and the Deweyan should itself be a major topic of study for students in teacher education. (See Oldendorf 1980, chap. 3.) A primary goal of the Berea curriculum is thus to help students to examine and comprehend the complex and sometimes contradictory nature of research and practice in teaching and to stimulate them to construct their own framework of understanding.

To be effective in educating prospective teachers it is necessary that we demonstrate to our students how we find a particular framework, the Deweyan framework, more adequate than other points of view. In adopting such a framework a corollary assumption is that one must consistently apply the particular philosophy and pedagogy being advocated. Being consistent with Deweyan notions about teaching means, for example, viewing learning at any age as the development of mental structures (Piaget's schemes and Kohlberg's stages of cognitive moral development), which are increasingly more adequate in helping the learner understand and deal with his or her social and physical environment. Consequently, the goal of teacher education in the broadest sense is the development of integrated mental structures for relating, analyzing, and synthesizing the phenomena of education, rather than the simple transmission of isolated knowledge or training of behavior patterns based on limited and fragmentary empirical research. The development of adequate structures enables future teachers to select, justify, and implement the methods and goals of their teaching in a variety of contexts.

FOUR FEATURES OF BEREA TEACHER EDUCATION

Four instructional features can be derived from the notion of teacher education as the development of structures: dialogue, active participation, development and reorganization, and moral reasoning. These four features occur throughout the department curriculum beginning with "Introduction to American Education" and culminating with the seminars of the student teaching experience. The scope and sequence of education department courses is in large part determined by the state mandates and NCATE guidelines, but within these parameters the manner and mode of instruction reflects our assumptions about the nature of teaching and learning. As John Dewey reminds us, the content of the lesson may well be the least important thing that is learned. "Perhaps the greatest of all education fallacies is the notion that a person learns only what he is studying at the time. Collateral learning in the way of forming enduring attitudes . . . may be and often is more important than the spelling lesson or lesson in geography or history . . . for these attitudes are fundamentally what count in the future" (1938, 48).

So also with teacher education. To *tell* teachers that teaching is *not telling* will not do. To use dialogue, direct experiences, and moral reasoning in bringing forth the content of our courses is to help our future teachers develop the structures that will in turn enable their effectiveness in their classrooms. So throughout the curriculum students are challenged to actively participate in the process, developing and teaching their own lessons, participating in dialogue, taking field trips to model school programs, visiting the state legislature, taking part in environmental education programs, traveling to professional conferences, but always in a reflective mode.

The following sections elaborate on the four features in greater detail and give examples of how they shape the nature of education department courses. Finally, examples are provided of student writing that reflect the effects of these features on their thinking.

1. *Learning occurs primarily through dialogue between student and environment rather than transmission from the environment to the student.*

What is taught is learned largely through experience and dialogue rather than passive reception, since there is no single truth to be transmitted. Course work in teacher education should thus emphasize philosophical dialogue through which students and teachers examine the nature of implications of the topic at hand. Example: "Introduction to American Education" (Akural 1986a) has as its major aim "students begin to think about the nature of education and develop their own ideas about the meaning and purposes of education." Also typical of the course is the exam question, "How did Socrates teach? Was his method consistent with his epistemological theory? Why or why not?" Example: Reading can also be thought of as a dialogue "an interaction between the language and thought of the reader and thought of the author. Only when there is a sufficient degree of common ground between the two participants does comprehension occur" (Akural 1986b). Students in the course "Reading in the Content Areas" are also asked to keep a "journal of reflections . . . to provide an account of your developing thoughts and questions on topics and ideas central to this course." Example: Operant conditioning as a theory of learning enjoys considerable popularity in teaching. In "Human Development and Learning" (Oldendorf 1986a) we question what assumptions about the nature of knowledge underlie this theory and what the further implications for human development of these assumptions might be. We also examine the ethical difficulties inherent in reliance on operant conditioning through the same dialogue process. The facts and generalizations embedded in this theory are analyzed in the context of the development of overall schemes for critically examining learning theory in general.

An example of the student building an understanding through nature was a weekend field trip to Pine Mountain Settlement School for an elementary science class. It offered the students an opportunity to understand the geological and ecological conditions that have shaped life in the Cumberland region and to share the insights of the Pine Mountain Staff not only on natural phenomena but also on the extraordinary educational program at Pine Mountain past and present. The group also visited Lilley Cornett Woods, the last area of virgin forest in Kentucky.

The objectives for this trip were both cognitive and affective. The class learned some basic facts about the natural phenomena of the region as well as comprehended the relationships between the natural environment and human life. The course insured that they had personal contact with the way the geography of the region shaped human life and the way in which humans have in turn reshaped the ecology of the region.

This field trip also served to promote certain values that ought to be attached to science education. The science programs developed in the intense curricular reforms of the sixties and seventies made advances in helping children develop the intellectual processes essential to science, but little may have been accomplished in what is an equally vital area of science, the development of a sense of awe at the intricate and complex beauty of the natural world. This kind of feeling and attitude is essential to developing a strong interest and commitment to science as a way of knowing and doing, and, more importantly, to developing an organized set of moral and esthetic values within which science can operate. These values and attitudes are essential attributes of a good science teacher. We believe that this set of values is best developed through experiences that provide direct, intense contact and interaction with people and natural phenomena as well as through the reflective processes of the classroom. The Pine Mountain trip provided such experiences.

2. *Students must actively participate in the learning process.*

The dialogue described in (1) requires that students as well as teachers think and contribute to the discussion. Class assignments are designed to involve active problem-solving processes of analysis, synthesis, and evaluation. Student investigation and solution of problematic situations are a significant aspect of every course. In the words of Sherrie White (1981, 1), an elementary education major:

> Rote memorization, drill and testing are not ways for children to learn. . . . Learning must have facts, of course, but the facts must have a purpose also. They must relate to ideas and situations which seem real and useful to children before they will learn. Children learn and grow by the interaction of their thoughts with the materials we present to them. They are not merely passive recipients of our knowledge, but are active participants in experiences which lead to growth.

Excerpts from their journals (Oldendorf 1986b) reflect education students' thoughts on active participation after the three-day field trip to Pine Mountain.

> For a child cannot learn through the eyes of others, he must use his own. He must experience to know, he must touch to recall. Yet, how can we as educators fill a child's mind when we ourselves are in the dark. *We* must first experience and use our senses before we can even begin to truly relate and transfer knowledge to a child. — Becky Gentry

> On my way to breakfast this chilly morning I saw one of the most beautiful sights I have ever seen. At first I was disappointed because I did not have my camera, but I looked long and carefully so I *do* have the picture forever, inside. It was one mountain lit up from the sunrise bright orange because of its fall leaves. But part way up it was covered with the shadow of the mountain behind me. I've seen shadows of houses, cars, telephone poles, our city water tower, and some trees early in the morning. But I've never seen a mountain's shadow against another! — Sherrie White

If anyone had asked me to write a fourteen page paper on some subjects, I would have looked on it as near impossible. But this paper has flowed out of me, and it got so long because I wanted to get each moment in, because they were all so important to me. Perhaps we should think of this when we assign a paper to our students. It is a hundred times harder to write a paper from a reference book than it is to write from personal, meaningful experience. — Kathy Coffey

3. *Structures of the mind develop and reorganize in a process of interaction with the environment.*

Classroom study and discussion is a kind of interaction that leads to growth, but it is limited in its scope. Constructing an environment (curriculum) to include a wide variety of resources outside the classroom expands both the variety and the level of experiential interaction and consequently enlarges the opportunity for mental development and reorganization. Personal contact with the way the geography of a region has shaped human life and the way in which humans have in turn reshaped the ecology of the region can develop mental schemes for coping with these experiential interactions in a way that no amount of classroom study and discussion could accomplish.

Again the Pine Mountain journals demonstrate changes in the way future teachers comprehend the interrelationship between the natural environment and human life.

I found the description of [this family's] life almost unbelievable. I had a hard time understanding how people could live under such harsh conditions. I feel this is very important to teach the children. Nowadays people take all of their conveniences for granted. You are considered poor if you don't have a color TV. These people didn't even have complete walls. Their walls were made of logs with large gaps between them. They heated their homes with one fireplace and ground flour and meal by hand. I think this is part of our history and it should be taught to everyone. Pine Mountain is a very good resource for this. — Nancy Spangler

Much of this field trip was a humbling experience for me. I had never realized before how miraculous our environment is and how important it is to our lives. How amazing to think that minerals which were at the top of Pine Mountain millions of years before I was born were torn away by water and moved down to the bottom where they are now nourishing the thick healthy grass there! How humbling to hold a 300 million year old compressed log and to think of the energy it holds when we can't make a battery that lasts more than 10 years! — Sherrie White

There's so much in Science that relates to our daily lives. Children will understand so much better if they can experience nature. Head knowledge will not help much if they cannot apply it. We are dependent on our earth and must take care of it if we want to live! We must never take it for granted. — Rosita Blank

4. *Values acquisition occurs through reasoning processes that progress through successively more adequate stages of maturity.*

Values in this context mean the discrete concepts and systems of concepts of the desirable that influence our choices between ways, means, and ends of our actions. A critical component in developing solutions to the problem of teaching moral values in public schools should be an emphasis on the *reasoning* process through which values can be derived rather than on the content of values in particular. If the main concern of the teacher is for the quality of the reasoning process, then difficulties from teaching specific values or doctrines should not arise. Example: All teacher-education classes develop a persistent theme, that the everyday actions of classroom teachers in structuring their classroom, in student governance, and in discipline procedures have as much consequence for the moral development of their students as any specific class time devoted to "values education."

More examples from the Pine Mountain journals indicate the degree to which the environmental education experience influences student thinking.

We could have learned from mother nature's battery. She built the most energy efficient battery ever. Coal has stored usable energy for ages. It took ages to put it there too. Nature didn't rush things. She took the time for the old to become new. She reused her sources over and over. She replenished what was taken and never overdrew. Where has man left her now? We won't see replenishment in our lifetimes. We may be the energy source of future generations or we may be the last generation. The choice is ours to make. — Heather Taylor

This was my first visit to a mine. It wasn't at all what I had expected. I suppose I had envisioned a deep mine rather than a strip mine. The destruction was terrible. The hill which once was probably a steep, beautiful slope, was now a high vertical wall with a ledge below. It looked like a road construction job. Unfortunately, it will never be finished. It was sad and yet inspiring to see small stands of weeds and grass attempting to reclaim the land so terribly injured.

I also wondered how a trip such as this would affect kids. Any part of this would be enough to spend the whole day on. Would they get out of the trip as much as I have? Would they see the problems and effects of strip mining? And most of all, would they see the importance of their roles in shaping the destiny of the land? Somehow, I think they would. — Linda Wilson

I have wondered why coal is so important that people would destroy the beauty of the land around them. I guess I really know the answer to that. Anything that people can make money off of then they will do anything. The mountains of Pine Mountain are so beautiful, I hate to look around and see what strip mining has done to the environment, as well as to the people. It is obvious that stripping a mountain is harmful, but I don't think that the effects on the people are quite as obvious. From the very beginning that coal was mined in the area, the people's value of the land went away. The early settlers took only from the land what they needed. Now people take everything and put nothing back in return. — Cathy Edelen

Human beings have stripped away in the name of "progress" what has taken nature thousands of years to produce. With the taking of coal, valuable top soil, land, and timber have been destroyed. Pine Mountain reminds me of the story of the *Giving Tree* where the tree gives everything to the boy, even its life. The boy kept taking until there was nothing left to take. He then realized what a mistake he had made. It is the same with Eastern Kentucky, the people take and take and never give back. I hope they realize a lot sooner than the boy did. — Donna Whitis

THE LABOR PROGRAM AT BEREA

Every Berea student holds a part-time job in some aspect of the college's operation. Satisfactory completion of a labor assignment is as much a college requirement as is academic work. The concept of work-learning is basic to the philosophy of Berea and has been a part of the program since 1859. The labor program is essential to the economics of the college and to the social and educational experiences of the students.

Through the fellowship of meaningful work experiences, an atmosphere of democratic living prevents social and economic distinctions and instills an awareness of social responsibility. As an educational tool, the labor program provides opportunities for acquiring skills, applying learning, exploring areas of knowledge, and developing creativity and personal abilities. (Berea College 1985, 12–14)

In addition to working in every academic department of the college, students also fill positions in community services, student industries, student personnel services, and all campus offices.

Students employed in a variety of tasks around campus are paid $1.20 to $2.75 per hour in addition to the $2000 contribution to the cost of education. Much of the campus clerical and maintenance work is performed by student workers, and they may progress to higher levels of pay and responsibility through a program of regular evaluation by faculty supervisors. In the education department, students perform clerical and janitorial tasks in beginning positions and may advance to office manager, curriculum librarian, or teaching associate. Students for Appalachia provide a wide range of services to the community including tutoring of potential dropouts and assistance in GED programs. The most visible student workers, of course, are those engaged in crafts and services for which the college is famous, ranging from broom-craft to the management of Boone Tavern.

The college treats the labor program on an equal basis with the academic program. Satisfactory progress in both areas is necessary for continued enrollment and graduation. Philosophically, the college is committed to the value and dignity of work shared by all in an atmosphere of democratic living and social responsibility. Employers comment positively about the effects of the labor program, and it is not unusual for Berea students to find jobs more related to their labor experience than to their academic major.

The experiences Berea students have in the labor program constitute a valuable source of the experiential part of their education. In the Education Department, the student position of teaching associate provides the opportunity to involve students in increasingly difficult tasks related to teaching and the opportunity for faculty to reflect with students in that role about the nature of their experiences. Lorie Yaste (1981), a teaching associate for three years, was particularly articulate about the role of her labor in her education.

> As an elementary education and child development student, I could easily fall into the mold of thought which would allow me to become complacent in my efforts and studies. This has not happened, in part because of the atmosphere of learning in which I am a part. "It's important to know how one knows," "it's an art to enable people to see the good in themselves," and "we need to learn how one encourages continual learning"—all of these statements reflect values to which I adhere. These values are not "shelf items" to be pulled in a few years when I'm teaching elementary school; they are a part of the self who lives and related to others while a student at Berea College.

During her three years as teaching associate Lorie became increasingly able to handle complex tasks, eventually taking substantial responsibility for the revision and implementation of a new field study component for our course in human development and learning. "I also view my labor experience as an opportunity to actively employ that which I learn in the classroom. As office manager, teaching associate and one of the student secretaries for the Education department, I've had innumerable opportunities to draw upon the knowledge gained in the classroom concerning the nature and content of education."

Millie Hughes (1986), another teaching associate in the Education Department, points out how her labor assignment differed from her student teaching experience.

> My experience as a teaching associate proved to be different from any other teaching experience I had while in college. It was not like student teaching because the students were a different age. My student-teaching experience with first graders and kindergarteners was very enjoyable because I feel extremely comfortable with children of that age, but my teaching associate experience was also worthwhile. It was good for me to have to prove what I was saying. College students are not quite as worshipful of their teachers as primary-aged children, and I found that in tutoring sessions with college students I had to clearly explain a concept and then be able to prove why this concept was important to consider. First graders would be more likely to accept something as worth studying just because the teacher said it was so. College students want to find their own reasons for learning, and the students I tutored knew I had recently taken the class, so they were curious about my reasons for learning the material and if it benefited me in student teaching. . . . I spent some time thinking about the value of assuming the roles of student and teacher simultaneously. Often teachers forget what it takes to learn. Time has passed since they were students, and they don't remember how much time it takes to learn and how important it is to relate new information to previously learned, already understood material in order to comprehend. I hope that I can remain a student while a teacher so that I can remember and be conscious of my students' need to take time to relate new material to what they already know, their need to fit new information into already formed ideas of their own.

Millie also comments on the role teaching plays in reflective thinking.

> I believe that my college teaching experiences were valuable because if I had only been given college texts and lectures about teaching and learning and not been allowed to learn through teaching, I might have accepted all I read and heard at face value. It was the teaching experience that caused me to reflect on what I had read and heard and begin to form my own ideas. Teaching is the step that causes me to question theories about learning. College gave me the chance to listen, to read, to reflect, to create, and to use the product of those activities to teach, which is by no means the final step since teaching will inevitably prompt more listening, reading, reflecting, and creating.

Finally, Lorie Yaste adds a Deweyan thought on the role of labor in making a college education not just a preparation for life.

I think there is an art involved in making the educational process a part of one's life relevant to the experience of "now." It demands a dedication of the faculty to provide experiences that have inherent value for the present life of the student. It demands that all of us see school not only as a preparation for "something in the future", but as a way of life right now.

Above all, it demands that a student absolutely refuse to let his/her experiences become stagnant or devoid of meaning because he/she can't see through the cloud of "content to be learned" to "content to be experienced, practiced, used . . . " Implicit in this refusal to be blinded is a dedication not only to future goals, but also a dedication to the worthiness and uniqueness of experiences and learning processes of the present.

IN CONCLUSION

This chapter demonstrates that the uniqueness of Berea's teacher-education program lies in the way the traditions and values of the college have combined with the philosophy of the Education Department in affecting the way the program has been implemented. The chapter clearly illustrates several explicit assumptions about the nature of teaching and learning that, taken together, constitute the rationale for the way our teacher-education curriculum is implemented. Our assumptions about the nature of learning and teaching vitally affect the manner in which we teach.

Given the guidelines provided by the state and NCATE for our programs, we still have a tremendous latitude in deciding how those guidelines will be implemented. This is a critical message that we also try to pass on to our graduating teachers: the increasing number of state mandates defining what you will teach and how long you will teach it still leave you with great flexibility. How you use this flexibility will depend on your rationale for your program and how well you are able to defend it.

This is an era that demands more than ever before that good teachers be knowledgeable about the psychological and philosophical bases of their profession, and that good teachers be able to articulate their knowledge and concerns.

An eight-year-old I know recently reported that he really liked his third-grade teacher because "she knows that some questions have more than one right answer." That third grader certainly identified a quality of mind that we, as teacher educators, would hope that our students are developing. In a period when educators are under increasing pressure to produce right answers it is difficult to resist the notion that a "science of education" will provide definitive solutions to our problem. Perhaps the greatest single challenge in teacher education today is to help develop those qualities of mind that foster an acceptance but also an examination of the necessarily tentative and changing nature of knowledge about teaching without concluding that all such knowledge is relative and of equal uselessness.

BIBLIOGRAPHY

Akural, K. *Introduction to American Education: Course Syllabus.* Berea, Ky.: Berea College Education Department, 1986a.

_____. *Reading in the Content Areas: Course Syllabus.* Berea, Ky.: Berea College Education Department, 1986b.

Berea College, Department of Education. *A Report to the National Council for Accreditation of Teacher Education,* Vol. I. Berea, Ky.: Berea College, 1986.

Berea College Catalog (1985). Series 43, no. 4. Berea, Ky.: Berea College, 1985.

Brown, D. *Spiritual and Intellectual Roots.* Berea, Ky.: Berea College, 1978.

Dewey, J. *Experience and Education.* New York: Macmillan, 1938.

Oldendorf, W. "Defining Good Teaching in the Social Studies: Implications of the Deweyan Position in an Era of Competency Assessment." Paper presented at the College and University Faculty Assembly of the National Council for the Social Studies, San Francisco, 1983.

_____. "Extended Education: A Rationale for a Young Adolescent Citizenship Education Curriculum Combining the Resources of School and Community." Doctoral diss., Northwestern University, Evanston, Ill., 1980.

_____. *Human Development and Learning Course Syllabus.* Berea, Ky.: Berea College Education Department, 1986a.

_____, ed. "The Pine Mountain Journals." Unpublished collection of essays. Berea, Ky.: Berea College, 1986b.

Sagan, C. *The Dragons of Eden.* New York: Random House, 1977.

Shaver, J. "A Critical View of the Social Studies Profession." *Social Education* 41(1977):300–307.

Shulman, L. "Those Who Understand: Knowledge Growth in Teaching." *Educational Researcher* 15(1986):4–14.

White, S. "Social Studies Thinker." Unpublished essay. Berea, Ky.: Berea College, 1981.

14 | Internationalizing an Education Department: The Wittenberg Design

DONNA J. COLE

MOST INSTITUTIONS WITH TEACHER-PREPARATION PROGRAMS recognize the need to develop an international awareness among their students. The reality that we live on a finite, precarious spaceship whose future rests on appropriate organization and ethical interactions has made it imperative that teachers assist children of the twenty-first century to understanding the "other" (the other referring to those differing from ourselves). This chapter will present a case study detailing how an education department in a liberal arts institution addressed this charge.

The charge to understand the universe can be traced to the third century B.C. when Eratosthenes of Cyrene, chief librarian of Alexandria, used the mathematical wisdom of his day to establish the circumference of the earth as 24,662 miles. Now we send astronauts around the earth and into outer space. In 2000 years scientific understanding of the solar system has propelled our thinking far beyond our local communities. The rate and volume of discovery continually increase as does the vision to understand the mysteries of the galaxies. It is a paradox that while we seek knowledge of the limits of the universe, we have been less than successful in understanding others here on earth.

As Klassen and Leavitt state in *Teacher Education and Global Perspectives,* "just as our visions transcend contemporary conditions and knowledge, so our comprehension of Earth as a global entity exceeds our ability to cope with its complexity. Though we view ourselves as members of a

Donna J. Cole is an assistant professor of education at Wright State University, Dayton, Ohio.

world community, we have yet to learn behaviors and attitudes appropriate to achieving the common goals of that communit;" (1982, 3–4).

It is wise that we emphasize the need to understand others on planet Earth, particularly recognizing our interconnectedness. Sanders stresses in *The Professional School and World Affairs* that "for better or worse, every man, every family, every people shares in the daily interaction of a world which—because it is more compact—forces all of us to be more broadly involved with our neighbors" (1967, 19). The various developed political states depend on each other to survive or at least to continue their desired life-styles. Examples of this interdependent connectedness include these statistics:

- At least one in eight American jobs depends on exports (Hansen 1982).
- U.S. trade with foreign markets has been increasing at astronomical rates. Between 1975 and 1980 the following increases occurred: Africa, increases in exports of 198 percent and imports of 388 percent; East and South Asia, up 234 percent and 291 percent; Near East, up 145 percent and 320 percent; Latin America, up 226 percent and 230 percent; Europe, up 164 percent and 58 percent (Hansen 1982).
- Nearly half of the oil consumed in the United States is imported (Mehlinger et al. 1979).
- In 1980 there were 50 international governmental organizations; today there are 250 such organizations (Mehlinger et al. 1979).

This connectedness that shrinks the globe results in the need for expanding human relations. This global reduction dictates an understanding of the international "other."

Educational mandates call for national understanding of the American subculture "others." Policies to promote knowledge of America's pluralism exist but requirements to understand the diversity in world family are limited. Whereas courses in the history, politics, and economy of the United States help to inform our citizenry about our nation, other courses should likewise develop a global understanding. According to Mehlinger et al. in *Global Studies for American Schools,* "Schools at the elementary through university level have the primary responsibility for developing this global perspective in youth" (1980, 11–12).

WITTENBERG'S MOVEMENT TOWARD GLOBAL UNDERSTANDING

Wittenberg University is committed to international education. Founded in 1845, Wittenberg is a Lutheran-related, independent, undergraduate, liberal arts school located in Springfield, a city of approximately 80,000 in southwestern Ohio. Wittenberg's 2200 full-time, residential students come from 33 states and some 13 countries and represent widely diverse cultural, ethnic, and religious backgrounds. The students are an academically select composite (their mean SAT scores are for the verbal 484 and the math 535; their mean ACT score is 22; and the mean high school grade point average is 3.3). Wittenberg offers nineteen academic departments, two interdepartmental majors (American studies and East Asian studies), and several interdisciplinary emphases including Russian studies, future studies, and urban studies. The University's faculty members are accomplished scholars committed to undergraduate teaching (*Wittenberg Registrar's Catalog, 1984–86*).

The development of international education at Wittenberg results from more than a decade of growth rather than from a single, systematic plan. It represents a long-range, flexible, and sustainable curricular orientation. This is the outcome of two processes: first, the cultivation of various constituencies in the university, and second, the development of faculty consensus on appropriate curricular foci. Other institutions may reverse the sequence of these actions, but they will undoubtedly have to accomplish both if the goal is to heighten international awareness at an institution (Chatfield 1983).

The Education Department contributed to the growth of international education at Wittenberg. The department faculty believed that public school teachers must have the opportunity to develop an international perspective. Mehlinger et al. (1979) supports the department's conviction when stating

> At the heart of education is the impact teachers can have on conceptual and value problems. Teachers as a group have particular opportunities not available to others in American society: they can influence what millions of American youngsters will think and value in a global society. In this way teachers can influence how substantive and procedural problems will be handled one day when their current students occupy positions of influence. Unless teachers help youngsters conceptualize human experience in appropriate ways, as adults the students will fail to recognize and solve the problems that will confront them in the future.

Four years ago the education faculty set about developing a departmental design for international exposure in courses and activities of the department as a whole. A Title VI grant entitled "Global Perspective in the Undergraduate Curriculum of Wittenberg University" aided the project. Now clear signs of international dimensions are visible throughout the Education Department.

The major goals of this project were (1) to increase awareness of international issues in student teaching experiences of preservice teachers and (2) to establish international student teaching experiences with close institutional collaboration and accountability. Six categories for decision and actions were found crucial to achieving the two international goals: (1) Foundations, (2) Curriculum Content, (3) Practicum, (4) Resources, (5) Faculty Participation, and (6) Administrative Commitment.

1. *Foundations*

The education faculty elected an international subcommittee that moved directly to construct a foundation and framework for specific action to accomplish the goals. After generating a statement of rationale placing the department's intent within the larger context of the university's aims, the committee identified major concerns listed in the form of questions. Articulating answers became the agenda for subsequent committee work.

The committee identified the following five questions as central issues: (1) How can we induce an awareness of global issues in all of the preservice teachers we recommend for certification? (2) What are the characteristics of a good international field experience? (3) What international sites can provide these characteristics? (4) How can we decide which students may participate in international field work? and (5) How can we determine if our goals for them are being achieved? Taken together, the questions signaled the department's intent to take seriously its responsibility for providing high-quality experiences for preservice teacher educators and for assuring as much success as possible in those experiences.

In analyzing the first issue, that related to global awareness, the department decided that only an infusion model wherein global understanding permeated all courses would be acceptable. In addition, the department endorsed specific course designs for multicultural and global education recommended as electives available to all students. Participation in international "field experiences" was limited to "student teaching." These course designs are treated more extensively later in the section on curriculum.

To address the remaining questions the department reviewed the university's international involvements and engaged experienced consultants from other universities. The basic concern was to determine the feasibility of a relatively small institution's entering directly into arrangements with international schools and to judge whether strong programs were possible in such an arrangement. Qualitative results in this area are addressed more extensively in the section of this chapter that focuses on the practicum.

2. *Curriculum*

The committee sought to strengthen the international dimension in all aspects of professional preservice teacher education. As stated earlier, the committee was also committed to a general principle of infusion. Therefore, the committee moved to develop three concurrent curriculum emphases that were used to prepare the students who were going abroad: (1) to establish two courses, International and Comparative Issues in Education and Multicultural Education: Toward a Culturally Pluralistic Perspective; (2) to assist faculty in developing global units in existing courses; and (3) to support student selection of courses outside the Education Department that developed global awareness.

As a step toward infusion, the department moved to establish the two elective courses for global understanding. One course, International and Comparative Issues, was developed to allow students to examine various societies through historical, religious, political, economic, societal, geographic, and educational perspectives. Emphasis was placed on relating those societal factors that influence change in developed and developing countries to those social forces that affect change in educational institutions.

The other course, Multicultural Education: Toward a Culturally Pluralistic Perspective, focused on (1) the rich cultural mosaic of the United States and (2) those foundations of knowledge, skills, and attitudes necessary for multicultural teaching competencies. The central goal of the course was to have students living, functioning, and teaching effectively in our pluralistic society. Topics included cultural pluralism, culture, ethnicity, race, sexism, the WASP ethic, and the U.S. mosaic. Special attention was given to developing a rationale for multicultural teaching.

These two courses were essential in establishing an international perspective but were by no means the total curriculum packet. The education faculty developed units in existing courses to emphasize knowledge, skills, and attitudes in global awareness. The faculty selected those global concepts that correlated with their course materials and developed units or lessons on them. (Example: In Reading Methods international story books and adventures were presented; in Math Methods international measures were addressed.)

The third curriculum component of the program was the requirement that education department students take course work in an area entitled "Other Cultures." These courses, offered in several departments, promote global awareness and understanding. Students may fulfill this requirement either by taking a course in cultures foreign to their own or by living experiences outside their own. Courses or experiences in minority cultures in the United States, if they require a reorientation perspective, may also be taken.

3. *Practicum*

Project planners also explored requiring a practicum on international student teaching. This became a requirement. The students would fulfill their student teaching requirements. They would also receive the same credit for the work done abroad. Student teaching overseas had been a long tradition at Wittenberg, but the department was disenchanted by the lack of direct involvement in placement and supervision. To ensure a clearer understanding of both Wittenberg's goals in preservice international education and those of international schools in the field setting, the committee designed a plan calling for site-selection research and visitation.

To establish and maintain a successful field component for international-based student teaching, the subcommittee carefully analyzed past site selections. Evidently many rich ties had lapsed, and there were now few associations in which to discuss cooperating international schools.

To help the committee to think more specifically about alternatives, two consultants were invited to campus. The first was the former director of one of the nation's largest international student teaching consortia. The other was the current director of a highly successful international program housed in a liberal arts college (similar to Wittenberg).

The first consultant explained three viable alternatives: (1) to become an active participant in a first-rate consortium already in operation, (2) to establish a small consortium that supervised the experience with other similar schools; or (3) to develop one-to-one relationships with international school sites. The department vetoed both options one and two. Option one appeared to be similar to the model with which we were dissatisfied in the past. Large consortia welcomed our students and placed them in international school sites. However, the cooperating school had no real connection with Wittenberg, and Wittenberg had limited involvement with the programs. Option two would require more time, money, and personnel than the department could provide. Option three was compatible with our desired outcome. This option would require immediate funding for establishing one-to-one relationships. The money was available to us through the Title VI grant. Our second consultant added further professional support to our decision and assisted in providing us with contact points in international settings.

After cautious exploration the Education Department chose five European and two Mexican sites. The department selected two international committee members to take information about Wittenberg to these sites. Armed with a folder of data on Wittenberg's education program, the university, and the project, the faculty members were asked to get information such as a description of the school (philosophy of school); statistics on students, teachers, and administrations; a school schedule; a description of facilities and setting; an appraisal of the student body, accreditation, admission policies, curriculum, and faculty; educational, cultural, and social opportunities for student teachers; housing/transportation/living costs for student teachers; the selected school's past and present collaboration with other universities; and provisions for supervising student teachers.

The returning committee members reported their findings along with suggested criteria for site selection to the department. These criteria included what the school should have: a supportive environment for U.S. students; cooperative personnel; cultural resources available; high academic standards; potential for student teacher supervision; available housing, and so on. The department used these criteria, ultimately choosing three European schools and one Mexican international school. The director of student teaching completed the negotiations.

4. Resources and Facilities

To make the desired international goals attainable, proper resources and facilities must be available. The preservice teacher-training faculty was able to achieve its goals through funding from the Title VI grant, the International Education Office, and other university support. (The director of international education received the Title VI grant for the university as a whole. One sector of the grant, however, had been proposed for Education Department use.) Through careful and deliberate work, the education faculty used the money to realize its goals. University support will sustain the project. The cost to each student is very reasonable. They pay the same fee as a nonparticipating student; they are housed with local families. The only additional expense is the round-trip fare to/from the site.

5. Faculty Participation

The education faculty was the major variable that made the project possible. Each member of the faculty gave attention to the international goals. The department members were responsible for putting global concepts into their course content. The Education Department faculty also attended three workshops on global awareness, multicultural education, and East Asia. Guest speakers were coordinators of the first two workshops, and the East Asia Department on Wittenberg's campus was responsible for the third. The Wittenberg University faculty at large was involved both as visiting speakers in education courses and as instructors in "global understanding" courses.

The four selected international student teaching sites provided personnel for exchange programs and visitations. Since the cooperating international schools were informed about Wittenberg's education program, they were more likely to collaborate in the development of future teachers at Wittenberg.

6. *Administration and Management*

Indispensable to the success of the Education Department's program development in global education has been the support of the university administration and the help of persons already involved in international programs, particularly the university's director of the office of international education. This statement is offered not merely to give credit and appreciation to those who have helped us but rather to affirm that we have become unequivocally convinced that such resources and support are necessary for the success of an Education Department in any small college that hopes to generate a program of such magnitude and complexity. Specifically, in times of tight budgets and shrinking programs it takes a great deal of courage for university administrators to commit such support to programs that expand rather than restrict a curriculum. Furthermore, the in-house expertise available from the director of international education frequently helped to focus and extend the committee's work. The director often sat as an adviser in our working sessions.

Of further note has been the importance of naming the director of student teaching as an integral committee member. The director was particularly helpful in the committee's consideration of the logistics of selecting and evaluating students. She also suggested procedures for obtaining direct institutional arrangements with schools overseas and provided a sense of procedures necessary to administer programs effectively once they were under way.

IN CONCLUSION

The movement toward infusing an international dimension into the Education Department's program at Wittenberg has not been always swift or without setbacks. But at this point two achievable goals are visible. A small liberal arts institution can establish student teaching experiences overseas with close, direct collaboration between the university and selected foreign schools. Our optimism has been fueled particularly by the admiration we have gained for the high quality of education provided in international schools. (One problem was minimized since these schools use English as their language of instruction.) They are private and enjoy many advantages in support and student population unavailable in the typical American public schools. After four years, of the sites originally chosen, two remain and one new site has been added. The Mexican school and one European site proved to have unresolvable complications. One country in Europe could not get governmental permission for student teaching visas. When the school in Mexico restructured its activities, it could no longer host international student teachers. The new site selected was most appropriate because the headmaster is a Wittenberg graduate who frequently returns to Springfield to visit family; thus he can continually update his knowledge of the Wittenberg Education program. The present sites include the American School of London, the International School of Berne, Switzerland, the American School of Brussels, Belgium, and Mary Mount International School, Italy.

The Education Department learned three significant lessons by developing these sites. First, it was productive to concentrate on two or three dependable and high-quality international schools. By limiting our sites we could more thoroughly guarantee an exceptional student teaching experience for our future educators. Second, to secure the finest student teacher participation it was necessary to set extremely high requirements for those participating in the project. (Students entering the program must hold a 3.0 GPA; demonstrate global and regional understanding; have an intermediate level of the country's language; have completed course work in comparative cultures, society, and politics as well as a history course on the country. Finally, the student must have approval of the Education Department and, if a secondary education student, the approval of the department in the student's major field.) Third, the department needed to provide international programs other than student teaching. A subcommittee is currently exploring possibilities with the international education director. The director has shared information about study abroad programs that offer courses in comparative education or field study in the foreign country's schools.

The second achievable goal is that global issues pertinent to education can be respectably fused into all courses. Part of our optimism proceeds from the desire of all education faculty to accomplish the international goals. Part is also due to our understanding the relationship between global and multicultural issues in education and our proven ability to increase our students' awareness and acceptance of these matters. Underwriting both, however, is a sense that overall public awareness of the interrelatedness of all the world's citizens is increasingly apparent due in no small part to the efforts of educational associations. Our students and those who employ them are not only aware of the dimensions of global issues but also more insistent that these issues be addressed in our schools. As Klassen and Leavitt poignantly suggest, "The nation's teachers and teacher educators must play an important role in incorporating the current understanding of the globe, in all of its unity and diversity, into the substance of education. They must create learning environments that encourage exploration of alternative ways of coping with global complexity" (1982, 4).

Thus, Wittenberg's program was established to develop international understanding in future instructors. This chapter has summarized our deliberate movement toward fully realizing that goal.

BIBLIOGRAPHY

AACTE Commission on Multicultural Education. *Multicultural Teacher Education: Guidelines for Implementation,* 4. Washington, D.C.: American Association of Colleges for Teacher Education, 1980. ERIC Document Reproduction Service No. ED 186 423.

Agency for International Development. *AID World Development Newsletter,* November 26, 1980, 3.

Atkinson, C., and J. Rowe. "Problems in International Lending: Are U.S. Banks Headed for Trouble?" *Washington Post,* March 14, 1982, G1.

Chatfield, C. "Internationalizing an Institution: The Wittenberg Approach." Mimeograph, International Education Department, Wittenberg University, Springfield, Ohio, 1983.

Hansen, R. *U.S. Foreign Policy and the Third World Agenda 1982.* New York: Praeger, 1982.

Klassen, F., and H. Leavitt. *Teacher Education and Global Perspectives.* Clearinghouse on Teacher Education. ERIC Document Reproduction Service No. ED 216 993, 1982.

Mehlinger, H. D., et al. *Global Studies for American Schools.* Washington, D.C.: National Education Association, 1979.

Rosengren, F., et al. *Internationalizing Your School.* New York: National Council on Foreign Language and International Studies, 1983.

Sanders, I. T., et al. *The Professional School and World Affairs.* New York: Education and World Affairs, 1967.

Wittenberg Registrar's Catalog — 1984–1986, Wittenberg University, Springfield, Ohio.

Index

231